Farm to Fork
The Margy Way

Margy Hooker

Published by:
Golden Rock, Inc.
2427 S. Hadley Rd.
Fort Wayne, IN 46804

FARM to FORK - THE MARGY WAY

About the Author

Margy Hooker has 30 years experience in the food and beverage industry including four years as owner of Margy's Cafe in Ft Wayne, Indiana. She is mother of two daughters, grandmother to 6 grandchildren, and one of six siblings. Margy obtained her Bachelors of Business Administration from The University of St. Francis, Ft. Wayne, Indiana in 1991 and was the recipient of the 2004 Women's Bureau, *Celebrate Her Spirit* Award, Ft. Wayne, Indiana.

Also by Margy Hooker

Margy's Favorite Recipes
Published April, 2001

Table of Contents

Dedication   4

Acknowledgment   4

Introduction   5

Appetizers   7

Beverages   23

Breads   35

Breakfast   51

Canning and Preserving   79

Desserts   95

Dressings   145

Entrees   153

Farm to Fork Recipes   195

Salads   211

Sandwiches   233

Sauces   243

Soups   255

Vegetables and Sides   281

Cooking Terminology   293

Family Meal   297

Fresh Fruit Equivalents   305

Helpful Hints   306

How to Use Herbs   308

Miscellaneous Food Equivalents   310

Seasonal Fruits and Vegetables   311

Substitutions   316

Healthy Recipe Makeover Substitutions   317

The Benefits of Menu Planning   320

The Farm to Fork Phenomenon   321

Weight and Measures and Common Abbreviations   325

Wine Basics   326

Index   332

Dedication

I would like to dedicate this book to:

My husband, Richard Barnes
My daughter, Candas DeHoff and husband Jeff
My daughter, Camille Cupa
My step-daughter, Myah St. John and husband Josh
My Grandchildren; Mason DeHoff, Sophie, Halle and Ian St. John, Jack and Reshma Barnes
My parents, Alice and Joe Hooker
My brothers and sister; Joe, Jim, Rob, Deb, and Rick
My husband's family; mother Mary Barnes, sisters Betty and Karen

This is the ten year anniversay of my first book, *Margy's Favorite Recipes.*
Since my first publication we have lost several friends and loved ones so I would also like to dedicate this book *in loving memory* of them:

Jack Barnes	*Ed Doyle*	*Joe Kandis*
Jerry Beam	*Tom Guin*	*Nick Kandis*
Annette Bowman	*Jimmy Hall*	*Virginia Kane*
Edie Carpenter	*Robert E. Lee Hooker*	*Gene Long*
Tom Davis	*Tommy Hooker*	*Janice Scherf*
		Wilma "Tissy" Blazer

Acknowledgments

To: Mary Barnes, Patty Beam, Mary Ann Bilcer, Camille Cupa, Candas DeHoff, Trish Fox, Aimee Fryar, Gloria Gaither, Karen Gorrell, Deb Hall, Bonnie Hecht, Alice Hooker, Joe Hooker, Tammy Hooker, Virginia Kane, Mona Kioebge, Deb Kruse, Julianne Lassus, Ramona Lee, Bun Lim, Tracy McKee, Betty Oakes, James Ross, Myah St. John, Marilyn Vandentop, Charlotte Wehr, and Bonnie Windsor. Thank you for contributing your special recipe for us to share.

Special thanks to Indiana University-Purdue University Fort Wayne (IPFW) and its Division of Continuing Studies for the cover photo which was featured on their summer 2010 continuing education catalog. (Photographer: Neal Bruns of Capture Photography).

Cover photo location courtesy of Arbor Home Building Corporation

Special thanks to The Journal Gazette, Fort Wayne, Indiana for the photo taken by photographer, Swikar Patel. Copyright 2011.

Proof Readers: Linda Barnes and Krystal Sichting

Introduction

The *Farm to Fork* phenomenon has been growing across the country. People of all walks of life are interested in knowing more about the food they eat including nutritional values, freshness, how it was grown, who grew it, and, how to prepare it. *Farm to Fork – the Margy Way*, will walk you through your local farmers' market in search of the most delicious seasonal fresh fruits and vegetables to create the ultimate family meal. It will provide you with simple, fresh flavors, all the while guiding you to shop and eat sustainably. This book also supplies you with recipes, tips, and facts that will build your skills and knowledge, at the market and in your kitchen. You will find delicious recipes, which I have collected and created over the years, using farmers' market produce for every course of the meal. You will see a lot of fresh berry recipes because of our farm and the many health benefits berries offer. The recipes are designed to be family friendly and simple enough for even the busiest home cook to prepare anytime of the week.

My love of gardening began in 1979 with the purchase of my first house which came with a huge garden, a patch of red and black raspberries, beautiful grape vines, and apple, cherry, and pear trees. The previous owner, Fred Vietmeyer, gave me gardening lessons with the sale of the house. Being pregnant with my second child, I began studying food nutrition and health as I wanted to make sure I was eating well for the baby. My findings in regard to the chemicals being sprayed on food crops and fed to the animals we eat, and the impact on human health, were shocking and very impressionable.

When we started Margy's Café in 1996, our menu items were prepared and cooked with only fresh ingredients with no MSG. It was difficult to buy very much locally grown produce back then so we began a small garden at our home and farm on Hadley Road. Over the years, this small garden grew into Tanglewood Berry Farm. Tanglewood Berry Farm is a USDA Certified Organic Farm that began in 2002 by my husband Richard Barnes. My daughter, Camille Cupa, Grower and Farm Manager, started working at Tanglewood in 2002. In 2004, Camille attended State University of New York and obtained a bachelors degree in Plant Science Horticulture in 2008. After graduation, Camille moved back home to Fort Wayne to help out at the farm. Under Camille's management, the farm has been expanded a little each year to meet our customers' needs. Expansion has included plantings of additional raspberries and blackberries as well as new fruits and vegetables such as strawberries and more than 40 varieties of vegetables and herbs. Currently, we sell our produce to country clubs, restaurants, local farmers' markets, and in 2010 we opened our farm to the public one day a week to buy our fresh picked organic produce from our farm stand. As we grow we plan to open our farm to the public more days a week and eventually offer a u-pick area. One of our goals is to create a farm experience for our customers in which they can learn how to grow healthy, chemical free fruits and vegetables, with sustainable practices.

I have included some pictures from our farm including wildflowers, farm animals, berries, and family dinners and holidays.

By requests, I have included some of the more popular recipes (120) from my first cookbook *"Margy's Favorite Recipes"*, with 368 new recipes. When we created Margy's Café, our intention, along with the good food, was to create a cheerful place that people would remember (since we have so many grey days in Fort Wayne). We made it a sunny, bright décor, with a menu of California cuisine which complimented the fresh fruit themed décor. After being closed for more than ten years, people still talk about the café and how they miss it.

Sandy Thorn Clark (the Journal Gazette Food Critic at the time) best captured our theme with her many articles:

- *"Margy's Café is a breath of fresh air. The upscale breakfast and lunch eatery is exciting - it's a refreshing change of pace for the local restaurant scene in everything: atmosphere, menu, and food."*

- *"Beyond the tropical paradise created within Margy's walls is a menu with some of Fort Wayne's most imaginative breakfasts, and interesting lunches. Margy's concentrates on homemade and light fare – a trend that, thankfully, has arrived here."*

The reason I bring up Margy's Café is that after more than 10 years since the closing of the restaurant, people still tell me how much they loved the café and miss it. I am surprised, yet flattered at how often I hear this. So for this reason I have been inspired to write *"Farm to Fork – the Margy Way"*. This book continues with my original fresh, homemade theme and is dedicated to the wonderful people we met through the café; many whom are now like family to us.

I have included a chapter called *Farm to Fork* that consists of recipes that I have literally picked from my "garden buffet" to make dinner. There are many recipes in this book from my "garden buffet" but this chapter is totally dedicated to the buffet.

My husband has become a vegan since my last cookbook so you will see quite a few vegan recipes. A vegan diet excludes animal protein, eggs, and dairy.

I enjoy cooking a favorite dish and special foods for friends and loved ones. It makes them feel special and is truly a good feeling to see them happy and to know that I've contributed to that happiness.

Appetizers

Hot
Asparagus Spears Baked in Puff Pastry
Baked Brie
Baked Crab Dip
Coconut Shrimp
Crab Cakes
Crab Stuffed Mushrooms
Cranberry Jalapeño Meatballs
Greek Spinach Pie
Ham Balls with Pineapple Sauce
Hot Bacon Cheese Dip
Hot Broccoli Cheddar Dip
Mediterranean Flat Bread Pizza
Spinach Artichoke Cheese Dip
Vegetable Tart

Cold
Black Bean Mango Salsa
Cheddar Cheese Ball
Corned Beef Cheese Ball
Crab Martini
Deviled Eggs
Guacamole
Hummus
Roasted Red Pepper Hummus
Roasted Tomato Bruschetta
Shrimp Cocktail
Shrimp Cocktail Sauce
Sun-dried Tomato Basil Cheesecake

Asparagus Spears Baked in Puff Pastry

Makes: 8-12 spears   Prep Time: 30 minutes

1	pound	asparagus spears, fresh, cut to 3 inch, blanched
1	sheet	puff pastry, cut to 2x2 inch strips
¼	pound	ham, medium sliced, cut into 1 ½ inch strips
3	ounces	herb cream cheese or 6 slices of Swiss cheese

Defrost the puff pastry sheet according to the package. Place the ham on a pastry strip, spread the cream cheese on top of the ham, place an asparagus spear on top and roll up the pastry. Place seam side down on a baking sheet. Bake in a preheated 400 degree oven for 10-12 minutes, or until pastry is lightly browned.

Baked Brie

Makes: 12 servings   Prep Time: 45 minutes

1	pound	brie, wheel
1	sheet	puff pastry
½	teaspoon	cinnamon
1	tablespoon	butter
1	tablespoon	sugar
3	ounce	almonds

Defrost the puff pastry sheet according to package directions. Melt the butter in a skillet; add the almonds, cinnamon and sugar. Put the almond mixture on top of the brie. Place the pastry over the top of the brie and covering the bottom, tuck in all open ends of the pastry. You can use a dab of water to set the pastry. Bake at 400 degrees until pastry is golden brown for approximately 25-30 minutes, let set for about 30 minutes before serving. Serve with nice crackers. You can top the brie cheese with a variety of ingredients. I like to spread raspberry or apricot jam on top of the brie then add toasted pecans or almonds. When I use raspberry jam I garnish the top center of the baked pastry with fresh mint and raspberries which is very pretty for the summer or holiday season.

Baked Crab Dip

¼	cup	green onions, diced fine
2	cloves	garlic, minced
1 ½	cups	jumbo, lump crab meat
½	teaspoon	salt
1	dash	pepper
½	teaspoon	ground mustard
1	teaspoon	hot sauce
1	teaspoon	lemon juice
1	tablespoon	Worcestershire sauce
¾	cup	mayonnaise
¼	cup	parmesan cheese
1	cup	pepper jack cheese, shredded
1	cup	bread crumbs
¼	cup	butter, melted

Pre-heat oven to 350 degrees. Combine all ingredients except bread crumbs and melted butter. Put mixture in greased casserole dish. Mix bread crumbs with melted butter and sprinkle on top of mixture. Bake 35 minutes or until bubbly hot. Serve hot with crackers or crostini.

Coconut Shrimp

25	21-25 count	fresh shrimp, cleaned, de-veined and butterflied with tail on
1	cup	coconut milk
¼	cup	milk
4	whole	eggs, beaten
1	cup	flour
1	teaspoon	salt
1	cup	plain bread crumbs
2	cups	sweetened coconut
		vegetable oil for frying

Note: Use 21-25 count shrimp for appetizer size shrimp and 16-20 count for entrée size shrimp.

Egg Wash-Mix together the coconut milk, milk and eggs.

Seasoned Flour-Mix together, 1 cup flour and 1 teaspoon salt.

Breading-Mix together in food processor, 1 cup plain bread crumbs, 2 cups sweetened coconut.

Dip shrimp in the following order: egg wash, seasoned flour, egg wash, and breading. Fry shrimp in vegetable oil heated to medium high. Fry until browned on both sides. Don't cook on too high of heat or the shrimp won't cook all the way through.

For more coconut flavor you can marinate the shrimp in the left over coconut milk for a few hours. This recipe is from my chef friend, Bun Lim. The Apricot Horseradish sauce goes perfect with this.

Crab Cakes

Makes: 12 appetizer size crab cakes   Prep Time: 30 minutes

1	pound	lump crab meat
¾	cup	bread crumbs
½	cup	parsley, chopped
1	large	egg yolk
1	teaspoon	lemon juice
1	teaspoon	Worcestershire sauce
1	teaspoon	Tabasco sauce
6	teaspoons	Dijon mustard
½	teaspoon	paprika
½	teaspoon	thyme, dried
½	teaspoon	celery seeds or flakes
¼	teaspoon	black pepper
1	dash	salt
4	tablespoons	olive or canola oil
¼	cup	onions, chopped fine
¼	cup	green peppers, chopped fine
¼	cup	red pepper, chopped fine

Mix all ingredients together in a large bowl. Form into 6 flattened balls. Melt butter in pan on medium heat; add crab cakes and fry until brown. Bake in preheated 350 degree oven 10-15 minutes or until hot throughout. These can also be made ahead in a log, then wrapped in saran wrap and frozen. When ready to use, defrost, slice and bake. This is the perfect way to also make uniform size mini crab cakes for appetizers. These are really good and full of crab.

Crab Stuffed Mushrooms

Makes: 8 servings   Prep Time: 1 hour

35	medium	white button mushrooms, stemmed and cleaned
1	pound	lump crab meat
1	teaspoon	garlic, minced
1	teaspoon	Worcestershire Sauce
1	dash	hot sauce
¾	teaspoon	cayenne pepper
½	teaspoon	salt
½	teaspoon	pepper
4	ounces	cream cheese, softened
¾	cup	parmesan cheese
¼	cup	mayonnaise
½	cup	green onions, chopped
¼	cup	parsley, fresh, chopped
1/8 – ¼	cup	bread crumbs
¼	cup	jack cheese, shredded
¼	cup	cheddar cheese, shredded
1-2	tablespoons	oil for mushrooms

In large bowl toss mushrooms in oil and season with salt and pepper.

In a separate, medium size bowl combine the crabmeat, garlic, Worcestershire sauce, hot sauce, cayenne, cream cheese, parmesan cheese, salt, pepper, mayo, green onions, parsley and bread crumbs. Mix the shredded jack and cheddar cheese together. Stuff the mushrooms with the crab meat mixture and top with the shredded cheese. Bake in a preheated 375 degree oven for 25 minutes. Serve warm. These are delicious!

Cranberry Jalapeño Meatballs

Makes: 12 servings   Prep Time: 1 hour

2	cups	cranberry sauce, jellied or regular
1	jar	jalapeño pepper jelly
2	pounds	meatballs, cooked

Combine sauces in a large saucepan. Cook over medium low heat stirring until smooth. Add the meatballs cover and cook 15 minutes until meatballs are heated through, stirring occasionally. These hold up nicely in a chaffer or crock pot.

Greek Spinach Pie

Makes: 12 servings

Prep Time: 1 hour

Filling

3	cups	spinach, fresh, finely chopped
12	ounces	cottage cheese, small curd
1	pound	feta cheese drained, crumbled
5	whole	eggs
1	medium	onion, chopped fine

Phyllo

1	package	Phyllo dough
2	sticks	butter, melted

Filling: Mix the filling ingredients together.

Assembly-Layer 12 Phyllo sheets brushing each one with butter in a 9"x13" pan. Put half the spinach filling on top of the Phyllo. Layer 6 more Phyllo sheets and brush each with butter. Put the remaining filling on top. Layer final 6 sheets of Phyllo and brush each with butter. Score top and bake at 350 degrees until golden brown; approximately 30 minutes.

Ham Balls with Pineapple Sauce

Makes: 50 small balls

Prep Time: 2 hours

Ham Balls

1	pound	ham, ground
1	pound	pork, ground
1 ½	cups	plain bread crumbs
1	whole	green pepper, diced
1	whole	egg
¼ -½	cup	milk
1	medium	onion, diced fine

Sauce

½	cup	brown sugar
2	tablespoons	dry mustard
½	cup	water
2 ½	tablespoons	vinegar
8	ounces	pineapple, crushed
1	tablespoon	molasses
⅛	cup	ketchup

Ham Balls-Mix the ingredients together adding milk at the end to moisten enough to form balls. Shape into small balls and bake in a 350 degree preheated oven for 20 minutes, drain fat and cool.

Sauce-Combine all ingredients and heat to boiling; simmer for 10 minutes. Pour over ham balls and serve. These hold up great in a crock pot. You can serve these over parsley buttered egg noodles as an entrée.

Hot Bacon Cheese Dip

Makes: 6 servings   Prep Time: 30 minutes

½	cup	mayonnaise
1	8 ounce package	cream cheese
1	cup	sharp cheddar cheese, grated
½	cup	jack cheese, grated
2	each	green onions, chopped finely
1	dash	cayenne pepper
½	cup	bacon, cooked and crumbled, (about 8 slices bacon)

Preheat oven to 350 degrees. In a medium bowl mix mayonnaise, cheese, onions and pepper. Transfer to a shallow baking dish. Bake for 15 minutes. Remove from oven; top with bacon. Serve immediately with crackers or bagel chips.

Hot Broccoli Cheddar Dip

Makes: 2 cups   Prep Time: 20 minutes

2	cups	broccoli, fresh, chopped
8	ounces	sharp cheddar cheese, shredded
4	ounces	cream cheese, cubed
2	tablespoons	milk
1	teaspoon	hot sauce
½	teaspoon	pepper
1	dash	salt

Cook broccoli in a small amount of water in sauce pan on stove or in covered dish in microwave. Make sure to drain out all the water. While still hot add the remaining ingredients. Heat another minute or two until melted. Stir until smooth. It will thicken as it cools. Low fat (not fat-free) cheeses work great in this recipe. Serve with crackers and or fresh vegetables for dipping.

Mediterranean Flat Bread Pizza

1	whole	flat bread (I use Flat-Out)
2	tablespoons	red pepper hummus (see recipe), or use store bought
1/8	cup	Kalamata olives, pitted and halved
1/2	cup	roasted red peppers, sliced thin
1/2	cup	spinach, fresh, sliced thin
1/4	cup	feta cheese, crumbled
1	dash	salt and pepper
1/4	cup	artichokes, chopped
		olive oil

Preheat oven to 350 degrees. Spray a baking sheet with olive or canola oil. Place flat bread on pan and spray with oil. This will make it crunchy. Spread hummus on top then layer the rest of the ingredients on the flat bread. Spray the fresh spinach with oil, salt and pepper. Bake for 15 minutes.

Spinach Artichoke Cheese Dip

1/2	cup	fresh spinach leaves, chopped
10	ounces	artichoke hearts, chopped
1/2	teaspoon	garlic powder
8	ounces	cream cheese, softened
1/2	cup	parmesan cheese, shredded
3/4	cup	mayonnaise
1/2	teaspoon	lemon juice
1/2	teaspoon	cayenne pepper
1/2	cup	cheddar cheese, shredded
1/2	cup	Monterey Jack cheese, shredded

Mix all ingredients except the cheddar and Jack cheeses. Put in casserole dish and top with the cheddar and Jack. Bake in 350 oven for 20 minutes or until hot and cheeses on top are melted. Serve with chips and salsa.

Note: You can add chicken to make a casserole.

Vegetable Tart

Makes: 8 servings   Prep Time: 45 minutes

1		unbaked pie crust	or 1 puff pastry sheet
2-3	tablespoons	olive oil or canola oil
2	cloves	garlic, sliced thin or 1 teaspoon minced garlic
12	halved	cherry or grape tomatoes
1	dash	salt
1	dash	pepper
8	ounces	feta cheese, crumbled
½	cup	basil, fresh, sliced
12	spears	asparagus or zucchini (or whatever is in season)

Rub asparagus with a teaspoon of the oil then season it with the salt and pepper. Roast 350 degrees for 10 minutes. Mold pie crust to fit into a tart pan. In sauté pan, heat remaining oil, add garlic, sauté 1 minute. Add salt, pepper and tomatoes, sauté until golden 3-4 minutes. Lightly brush bottom of crust with oil, top with cheese, basil and tomatoes. Arrange asparagus in a fan shape on top. Drizzle ½ the pan dripping over top. Bake 375 degrees until crust is golden brown approximately 15-20 minutes. This can also be made in mini tart pans.

Black Bean Mango Salsa

Makes: 8 serving   Prep Time: 30 minutes

2	whole	mangos, diced fine
1	cup	black beans, cooked
4	whole	green onions, chopped fine
1	whole	jalapeño, diced fine
2	teaspoons	ginger, dried
1	cup	cilantro, fresh, chopped
¼	cup	mint, fresh, chopped
3	tablespoons	lemon juice
1 ½	tablespoons	olive oil
1	tablespoon	brown sugar
1/8	teaspoon	salt
¼	teaspoon	pepper
½	whole	red pepper, diced fine

Mix well. Be careful with mangos if they are too ripe they will be mushy. Serve with tortilla chips. This salsa is also very good served on top of chicken breasts or fish. This will keep for 2-3 days.

Mango Salsa-Eliminate the black beans.

Cheddar Cheese Ball

Makes: 8 servings   Prep Time: 15 minutes

8	ounces	cream cheese, softened
1	pound	cheddar cheese, shredded
1	teaspoon	garlic powder
½	teaspoon	Worcestershire sauce

Mix all ingredients in food processor, blender or mixer. If too thin of a consistency, add more cheddar.

Corned Beef Cheese Ball

Makes: 8 servings   Prep Time: 15 minutes

4	ounces	corned beef, deli
8	ounces	cream cheese, softened
¼	cup	green onion, diced
½	teaspoon	garlic powder
½	cup	sour cream
2	tablespoons	onion, minced fine

Mix all ingredients in a food processor, mixer or blender. Serve with crackers or vegetables. To make a hot dip, add 2 tablespoons of milk and 2 tablespoons chopped green pepper and heat in the microwave.

Crab Martini

2	cups	V-8 juice or use ½ clam-tomato and ½ V-8
½	cup	red pepper, diced
½	cup	yellow pepper, diced
¼	cup	jalapeño pepper, diced
½	cup	avocado, firm, chopped
¼	cup	fresh cilantro, chopped
1	clove	garlic, minced fine
2	tablespoons	lime juice, fresh
2	tablespoons	cider vinegar
1	tablespoon	hot sauce
1 ½	teaspoons	sea salt
1	teaspoon	cumin
1	teaspoon	black pepper
1	pound	jumbo lump crabmeat
1	whole	cucumber, sliced

In large pitcher or bowl, combine all ingredients except the crab and cucumber. Cover and refrigerate until ready to serve. To serve, place chunks of crabmeat in small martini glasses. Top with tomato mixture and garnish with a cucumber slice on the side of the glass. This recipe is from Julianne Lassus. Thanks Julianne.

Deviled Eggs

8	whole	eggs, hard boiled
¼	cup	mayonnaise
2	teaspoons	sugar
2	teaspoons	sweet pickle relish
1	teaspoon	yellow mustard
		salt to taste
1	dash	cayenne pepper
		paprika for garnish

Hard Boil Eggs-Place eggs in a large saucepan and fill with cold water to cover the eggs. Bring the eggs to a boil over high heat. As soon as the water boils, turn off the heat and let the eggs stand, covered for about 15 minutes. Run cold water in the pan to stop the cooking; peel eggs and cut lengthwise. I find the eggs easier to peel if peeled while they are still warm.

Filling-Scoop out the yolks and transfer them to a mixing bowl. Mash yolks, mayonnaise, sugar, pickle juice and mustard with a fork until smooth. Add more mayonnaise if needed and season with salt and cayenne pepper. Spoon or pipe yolk mixture into the halves (the 2 extra eggs are for yolks). Chill loosely covered and sprinkle with paprika before serving.

Guacamole

Makes: 4 servings   Prep Time: 15 minutes

2	large	avocados, ripe, chopped
1	teaspoon	lemon juice, fresh
½	teaspoon	garlic powder
1	dash	salt
¼	cup	cilantro, fresh, chopped
1	whole	tomato, diced
1	tablespoon	onion, minced fine

Mix all ingredients together and serve immediately.

Hummus

Makes: 4-6 servings   Prep Time: 15 minutes

1-15	ounce can	garbanzo beans (chickpeas), drained
1	tablespoon	canola or olive oil
½	teaspoon	crushed red peppers
1	teaspoon	cumin
1	half	lemon, juiced
½	teaspoon	Kosher or course salt
1	tablespoon	crushed garlic
1 ½	tablespoons	tahini paste

Process all ingredients together in food processor or blender. Serve with warm pita. I like to stuff pitas with hummus, diced vegetables and chicken topped with feta cheese.

Roasted Red Pepper Hummus

14-18	ounce s	red peppers, roasted and chopped
2	tablespoons	lemon juice
1	clove	garlic, minced
1 ½	cups	hummus (see recipe)
1	teaspoon	red peppers, crushed
1	teaspoon	salt

Place peppers in a food processor with the lemon juice and garlic. Pulse grind the peppers then add the prepared hummus and process until smooth and evenly red in color. Transfer dip to a bowl and garnish with fresh parsley leaves and crushed red pepper flakes. Serve with toasted pitas or fresh vegetables.

Roasted Tomato Bruschetta

Makes: 4 servings

Prep Time: 60 minutes

2	pints	grape or cherry tomatoes, halved
2	tablespoons	olive oil
1	dash	salt
1	dash	pepper
12	whole	garlic cloves, peeled
1	whole	baguette

Preheat oven to 425 degrees. Wrap the garlic cloves in foil; drizzle with olive oil, cover and roast for 30-45 minutes until tender. Drizzle oil on the tomatoes; roast on baking sheet for 15-20 minutes. Arrange 12 thin baguette slices on a baking sheet; brush with oil, salt and pepper then bake at 425 for 6 minutes or until toasted. Top the bread with the tomatoes and garlic.

Shrimp Cocktail

Makes: 6-8 servings   Prep Time: 30 minutes

2	pounds	shrimp large, 25 count to a pound
¼	cup	pickling spice
¼	cup	lemon juice
1 ½	gallons	water

In large pot with water, add lemon juice, lemon rind, pickling spice. Bring to a rolling boil. Add shrimp, cook for 4-5 minutes or until shrimp are pink. Drain shrimp and cover with ice right away. Serve with cocktail sauce. (See recipe).

Shrimp Cocktail Sauce

Makes: 6 servings   Prep Time: 15 minutes

½	cup	chili sauce
½	cup	ketchup
3	tablespoons	prepared horseradish or 2 tablespoon fresh grated
1	teaspoon	lemon juice
½	teaspoon	Worcestershire sauce
¼	teaspoon	hot sauce

Mix together and let set for a few minutes in refrigerator. Serve with shrimp cocktail. (See recipe).

Sun-dried Tomato Basil Cheesecake

Makes: 6 servings   Prep Time: 2 hours

1	pound	cream cheese, softened
1	whole	egg
¼	cup	basil, fresh, chopped
½	cup	green onion, chopped
¾	teaspoon	garlic, minced
½	cup	sun-dried tomatoes, chopped

Mix cream cheese and egg in food processor until well blended. Add the remaining ingredients into the food processor with the cream cheese and process until blended. Do not over-blend, just enough to incorporate well. Put in 2 sprayed mini cheesecake pans and place on a baking tray about 3 inches apart. Bake at 250 degrees for 1 hour, or until center does not jiggle. Remove from oven and cool for 2 hours before removing from pans. Wrap and refrigerate for 2 hours before serving. Serve with nice crackers. This is very good and pretty. Garnish with fresh basil leaves and whole sun-dried tomatoes. You can use reduced fat cream cheese but not fat free; it does not bake well.

Beverages

Cranberry Punch

Daiquiri
Raspberry
Strawberry
Watermelon

Hot Apple Cider

Iced Tea
Blackberry
Raspberry
Sweetened Brewed Iced

Lemonade
Blackberry
Strawberry
Watermelon

Milkshake
Orange Dreamsicle
Summer Berry

Mulled Wine

Popsicles
Peach
Strawberry

Smoothies
Berry Blast
Bing Cherry Bash
Black and Blue
Black Belt
Blackberry
Blueberry Banana
Peanut Butter Banana
Pear Raspberry
Strawberry Orange Banana
Strawberry Swirl
Watermelon-Strawberry

Simple Syrup

Summer Sangria

Watermelon Bellini's

Cranberry Punch

Makes: 3 ½ quarts   Prep Time: 15 minutes

2	16 ounce cans	jellied cranberry sauce; chilled
1	cup	orange juice
¼	cup	lemon juice
1	liter bottle	Ginger Ale or 7-up, chilled
		Ice

Whisk cranberry sauce until smooth by hand or blender. Mix all ingredients together and add ice. This is very popular with the kids at our family Christmas gatherings. I serve this in a punch bowl or a nice pitcher. I found this recipe in a *Taste of Home Magazine*.

Raspberry Daiquiri

Makes: 6 servings   Prep Time: 10 minutes

6	ounces	raspberries, fresh
¾	cup	simple syrup (see recipe)
1	tablespoon	fresh lemon juice
3	cups	crushed ice
½	cup	rum

Combine all ingredients into a blender and puree until smooth.

Strawberry Daiquiri-Substitute strawberries for raspberries.
Watermelon Daiquiri-Substitute watermelon for raspberries.

Hot Apple Cider

Makes: 12 servings   Prep Time: 30 minutes

2	quarts	apple juice
3	cups	cranberry juice
¼	cup	brown sugar
2	whole	cinnamon sticks
½	teaspoon	whole cloves
½	teaspoon	salt

Boil together in a large pot for 3 minutes then simmer for 15-20 minutes. Serve warm. This is perfect for the holiday season.

Blackberry Iced Tea

Makes: 7 cups   Prep Time: 1 hour 30 minutes

3	cups	fresh or frozen blackberries, thawed
1 ¼	cups	sugar
4	cups	boiling water
2	family size	tea bags
2 ½	cups	cold water
		Mint for garnish

Combine blackberries and sugar in large container. Crush blackberries with potato masher or wooden spoon. Set aside. Pour 4 cups boiling water over tea bags; cover and let stand 3 minutes. Discard tea bags. Pour tea over blackberry mixture; let stand at room temperature for 1 hour. Pour tea through wire mesh strainer into a large pitcher, discarding solids. Add 2 ½ cups of cold water, stirring until sugar dissolves. Cover and chill until ready to serve. Garnish with fresh blackberries and a fresh sprig of mint.

Raspberry Iced Tea

Makes: 8 servings   Prep Time: 30 minutes

8	cups	water
¾	cup	sugar
1	cup	raspberries, fresh or frozen
5	individual	tea bags
2	tablespoons	lemon juice, fresh

In a large pot, bring water to a boil. Add sugar and remove from the heat. Stir sugar until it dissolves. Add the raspberries and the tea bags. Steep for 10 minutes then stir in the lemon juice. Strain; discard the berries and tea bags. Transfer to a large container or pitcher. Refrigerate until chilled. Serve over ice. For those who prefer unsweetened tea this is also great with out the sugar. Follow the same procedure just eliminate the sugar. This is so refreshing on a hot summer day.

Sweetened Brewed Iced Tea

Makes: 8 servings   Prep Time: 10 minutes

2	large	tea bags
4	cups	water
1 ½	cups	sugar
64	ounce	pitcher

Boil water with tea bags 5 minutes. Pour boiled tea into pitcher with sugar. Let it dissolve the sugar. Fill pitcher the rest of the way with tap water.

Blackberry Lemonade

Makes: 1 serving   Prep Time: 3 minutes

1	12 ounce	glass
6	whole	blackberries, fresh
1 ½	ounces	Stoli blackberry vodka
1	splash	simple syrup (see recipe)
1	splash	7-Up
4-5	ounces	lemonade
		ice

Put berries in the bottom of a glass and smash them with a fork. Fill glass with ice, add vodka, simple syrup, 7-Up and fill the rest of the glass with lemonade.

Non-Alcholic Blackberry Lemonade-Substitute blackberries for the strawberries in the strawberry lemonade recipe.

Strawberry Lemonade

Makes: 2 quarts   Prep Time: 15 minutes

4	cups	cold water
1	quart	strawberries, fresh, stems removed
¾	cup	sugar
¾	cup	lemon juice, fresh or bottled

Process water, strawberries and sugar in blender until smooth. Stir in lemon juice. Add additional water if too tart for your taste. Easy alternative: Add pureed strawberries to a frozen concentrated lemonade following the directions on the can.

Watermelon Lemonade

Makes: 4 quarts   Prep Time: 15 minutes

1	medium	watermelon, seedless, pureed
1	can	lemonade, concentrated, frozen or 6 cups fresh lemonade

Prepare lemonade according to directions then add the pureed watermelon and stir well. This is healthy and wonderful on a hot summer day.

Orange Dreamsicle Milk Shake

Makes: 4 servings   Prep Time: 10 minutes

1	pint	vanilla ice cream
1	cup	orange juice
1	whole	orange, zested
	segments	from 1 orange

In a blender combine ingredients and process until smooth.

Summer Berry Milk Shake

Makes: 4 servings   Prep Time: 10 minutes

1	pint	vanilla ice cream or fat free yogurt
2 ½	cups	fresh berries (strawberries, raspberries, blackberries)
½	cup	milk

In a blender combine ingredients and process until smooth.

Mulled Wine

Makes: 8 servings   Prep Time: 30 minutes

2	bottles	dry red wine
4	ounces	port or brandy
12	whole	cloves
4		cinnamon sticks
1	large	orange, zested

Combine ingredients in a large pot and bring to a simmer. Do not allow mixture to boil. Heat 20 minutes and serve in a large, heat resistant punch bowl. This is perfect for the holiday season.

Peach Popsicles

Makes: 12 popsicles   Prep Time: 4 hours 30 minutes

2	cups	peach slices, fresh
¼	cup	sugar
1 ⅓	cups	pineapple juice
1	tablespoon	lemon juice

Toss together peaches and sugar in a small bowl. Cover and chill 10 minutes.

Process all ingredients in a blender until smooth. Pour into 14 (¼ cup) plastic Popsicle molds. Insert sticks: freeze at least 4 hours.

Strawberry Popsicles

Makes: 12 popsicles   Prep Time: 4 hours 30 minutes

1	cup	water
½	cup	sugar
1	pint	strawberries
2	tablespoons	lemon juice
2	tablespoons	orange juice

Bring water and sugar to a boil in a saucepan, stirring until sugar dissolves. Remove from heat and cool. Process cooled sugar mixture, strawberries, and juices in a blender until smooth, stopping to scrape down sides. Pour into 12 (¼ cup) plastic Popsicle molds. Insert Popsicle sticks, and freeze for 4 hours until firm.

Berry Blast

Makes: 4 servings   Prep Time: 10 minutes

¾	cup	raspberry or cranberry-raspberry juice
2	tablespoons	lemon juice, fresh squeezed
½	cup	strawberries
½	cup	raspberries
½	cup	blackberries
½	cup	blueberries

In a blender, combine raspberry juice, lemon juice, and berries. Blend until smooth.

Bing Cherry Bash

Makes: 2 servings   Prep Time: 10 minutes

¼	cup	apple juice
1	whole	banana, cut into chunks
1	cup	Bing cherries, pitted
½	cup	raspberry sorbet

In a blender, combine ingredients and blend until smooth.

Black and Blue

Makes: 4 servings   Prep Time: 10 minutes

½	cup	apple juice
1	cup	blackberries
½	cup	blueberries
1	whole	banana, cut into chunks
½	cup	raspberry sorbet

In a blender, combine juices, berries, banana and sorbet. Blend until smooth.

Black Belt

Makes: 4 servings   Prep Time: 10 minutes

¾	cup	orange juice, freeze squeezed
½	cup	blackberries
¼	cup	blueberries
2	whole	bananas cut in chunks

In a blender, combine orange juice, berries and banana. Blend until smooth.

Blackberry Smoothie

Makes: 4 servings   Prep Time: 10 minutes

1	cup	milk
1	pint	vanilla yogurt, frozen fat free
1	whole	banana, cut into chunks
1	cup	fresh blackberries

Process all ingredients in a blender until smooth. Serve immediately. You can substitute strawberries, blueberries or raspberries.

Blueberry Banana

Makes: 4 servings   Prep Time: 10 minutes

2	cups	plain yogurt or frozen yogurt
2	cups	blueberries
1	whole	banana, cut into chunks

In a blender, combine yogurt, blueberries and banana. Blend until smooth.

Peanut Butter Banana

Makes: 2 servings   Prep Time: 10 minutes

½	cup	peanut butter
½	cup	fat free frozen yogurt
1	whole	banana, cut into chunks
⅛	cup	low fat milk

In a blender, combine peanut butter, frozen yogurt, banana and milk. Blend until smooth.

Pear Raspberry

Makes: 4 servings   Prep Time: 10 minutes

¼	cup	raspberry or cranberry-raspberry juice
2	tablespoons	lemon juice, fresh squeezed
2	whole	pears, quartered
1	cup	raspberries
¼	cup	frozen yogurt, vanilla flavored

In a blender, combine juices, pear, raspberries and frozen yogurt. Blend until smooth.

Strawberry Orange Banana

Makes: 4 servings Prep Time: 10 minutes

¼	cup	orange juice
¼	cup	apple juice
12	whole	strawberries
1	whole	banana, cut into chunks
½	cup	orange sherbet

In a blender, combine juices, fruit and sherbet. Blend until smooth.

Strawberry Swirl

Makes: 4 servings Prep Time: 10 minutes

½	cup	cranberry-raspberry juice
2	tablespoons	lemon juice, fresh squeezed
12	whole	strawberries
¼	cup	raspberries
2	tablespoons	yogurt, frozen, fat free

In a blender, combine juices, berries and yogurt. Blend until smooth.

Watermelon-Strawberry Splash

Makes: 4 servings Prep Time: 10 minutes

½	cup	raspberry or cranberry juice
2	tablespoons	lemon juice, fresh squeezed
1	cup	chopped watermelon
1	cup	strawberries

In a blender, combine juices, watermelon and strawberries. Blend until smooth.

Simple Syrup

Makes: 1 ½ cups

Prep Time: 45 minutes

1 ¼	cups	sugar
1	cup	water

Combine sugar and water in small saucepan; bring to a boil. Cook 1 ½ minutes or until sugar dissolves, stirring occasionally. Refrigerate until chilled. Will keep refrigerated for a month or more.

Summer Sangria

Makes: 4 servings

Prep Time: 30 minutes

1	bottle	light white wine (like a Sauvignon Blanc), chilled
¼	cup	peaches, peeled and sliced
¼	cup	blueberries or blackberries
¼	cup	raspberries or strawberries, sliced

Put the fresh assorted fruit in the bottom of a glass pitcher, mash with a fork just a little then pour the chilled wine over the fruit and refrigerate for about 30 minutes. Serve in wine glasses with fruit in the bottom of the glass. This is a very refreshing and pretty summer cocktail.

Watermelon Bellini's

Makes: 8 glasses

Prep Time: 15 minutes

3	cups	watermelon, cubed, seeded
2	tablespoons	fresh lemon juice
3	cups	chilled champagne, divided
8		champagne flute glasses

Place watermelon, lemon juice and 1 cup champagne in blender; process until smooth. Pour 1/3 cup watermelon mixture into a champagne flute. Pour the ¼ cup remaining champagne into each glass. Serve immediately. These are perfect for a summer brunch or bridal shower.

Breads

Cornbread

Fritters
Apple
Corn
Zucchini

Muffins
Blackberry
Blueberry
Lemon Sour Cream
Orange Sour Cream
Pumpkin
Raspberry Streusel

Scones
Apple
Pumpkin
Strawberry

Sweet Breads
Banana Chocolate Chip
Blackberry or Raspberry
Blackberry Buckle
Blueberry
Carrot Cake
Lemon
Monkey
Orange Cranberry
Pumpkin
Strawberry
Zucchini

Sweet Potato Rolls

Cornbread

¾	cup	flour
2	tablespoons	sugar
1	teaspoon	baking powder
1	teaspoon	salt
1 ½	cups	cornmeal
2	whole	eggs
1¼	cups	buttermilk
¼	cup	butter, melted

Sift first 4 ingredients together: add cornmeal. Combine eggs and milk in small bowl. Stir into flour mixture blending well. Mix in butter; spoon into greased 9" pan. Bake at 425 for 25-30 minutes until brown.

Note: you can get creative and add blueberries, chopped jalapeños or shredded cheddar cheese just to name a few.

Apple Fritters

Makes: 1 dozen   Prep Time: 30 minutes

1	cup	flour
1	teaspoon	baking powder
1	teaspoon	salt
2	whole	eggs
½	cup	milk
1	teaspoon	canola oil
1	whole	apple, chopped
		canola oil for frying

Blend dry ingredients in bowl. Mix eggs, milk and oil then add to dry ingredients. Add chopped apples. Heat oil to 375 degrees using a fryer or skillet. Skillet should not be more than ⅓ full of oil; oil should be 1" deep. Just enough to float the food.

Drop by tablespoons into hot fat. Fry until golden brown, drain on paper towel and roll in powdered sugar while still hot. My kids loved these when they were little and still do.

Corn Fritters-Substitute apples with 1cup fresh corn or drained canned corn.
Zucchini Fritters-Substitute apples with 1 cup shredded (water sqeezed out) zucchini.

Blackberry Muffins

Makes: 1 dozen

Prep Time: 20-35 minutes

2	cups	flour
½	cup	sugar
1	tablespoon	baking powder
½	cup	sour cream
½	cup	milk
½	cup	butter, unsalted, melted
1	whole	egg beaten
1	tablespoon	sugar
1 ½	cups	blackberries, fresh or frozen

Preheat oven to 400 degrees. Spray muffin tins or use papers. In large bowl combine flour, ½ cup sugar and baking powder. In small bowl combine sour cream, milk, butter and egg until blended. Stir into flour mixture just until moistened. Gently fold in blackberries and spoon into muffin cups. Sprinkle remaining sugar over tops. Bake 15-20 minutes for regular size muffins, 20-25 minutes for large muffins or until toothpick comes out clean.

Blueberry Muffins

Makes: 12 muffins

Prep Time: 45 minutes

1	cup	sugar
¼	cup	butter, softened
1	whole	egg
2 ½	cups	flour
4	tablespoons	baking powder
1	teaspoon	vanilla
1	cup	milk
1 ½	cups	blueberry, fresh or frozen
½	teaspoon	cinnamon
2/3	cup	flour
¼	cup	butter, cold

Cream ½ cup sugar and soft butter until fluffy; beat in egg. In separate bowl combine 2 ½ cups flour and baking powder. Add dry ingredients to sugar-egg mixture alternately with milk beginning and ending with flour mixture. Add vanilla and mix well. Gently fold in blueberries; spoon into sprayed muffin tin. In small bowl mix ½ cup sugar, cinnamon, 2/3 cup flour and cold butter until crumbly. Sprinkle over muffin batter. Bake in preheated 375 degree oven for 20-25 minutes or until golden brown.

Lemon Sour Cream Muffins

Makes: 12 muffins   Prep Time: 30 minutes

2	cups	flour
½	cup	sugar
1	tablespoon	baking powder
1	teaspoon	lemon peel
1	tablespoon	lemon juice, fresh
1	cup	pecans, chopped
½	cup	sour cream
½	cup	milk
½	cup	butter, unsalted, melted
1	whole	egg beaten
1	tablespoon	sugar
Glaze		
¼	cup	sugar
3	tablespoons	lemon juice

Preheat oven to 400 degrees. Spray muffin tins or use papers. In large bowl combine flour, ½ cup sugar, baking powder, lemon peel and pecans. In small bowl combine sour cream, milk, butter and egg until blended. Stir into flour mixture just until moistened. Add lemon juice; spoon into muffin cups. Sprinkle remaining sugar over tops. Bake 15-20 minutes for regular size muffins, 20-25 minutes for large muffins or until toothpick comes out clean.

Glaze-Mix sugar and lemon juice together. Poke holes in warm muffins with fork and drizzle glaze over muffins. Cool and enjoy.

Orange Sour Cream Muffins

Makes: 12 muffins   Prep Time: 30 minutes

2	cups	flour
½	cup	sugar
1	tablespoon	baking powder
1	teaspoon	orange peel
1	tablespoon	orange juice, fresh
½	cup	sour cream
½	cup	milk
½	cup	butter, unsalted, melted
1	whole	egg beaten
1	tablespoon	sugar

Preheat oven to 400 degrees. Spray muffin tins or use papers. In large bowl combine flour, ½ cup sugar, baking powder and orange peel. In small bowl combine sour cream, milk, butter and egg until blended. Stir into flour mixture just until moistened. Add orange juice; spoon into muffin cups. Sprinkle remaining sugar over tops. Bake 15-20 minutes for regular size muffins, 20-25 minutes for large muffins or until toothpick comes out clean.

Orange muffin turkey sandwiches-For tea parties, bridal parties or luncheons, I make these in mini muffin tins, slice them in half add turkey and cranberry relish. They are as pretty as they are delicious.

Pumpkin Muffins

Makes: 12 muffins   Prep Time: 35 minutes

1	cup	brown sugar
1	cup	canola oil
1 ½	cups	(15 ounce can) pumpkin
1	whole	egg
2	cups	flour
1	teaspoon	baking soda
1	teaspoon	cinnamon
½	teaspoon	nutmeg

Cream sugar, oil, egg and pumpkin. Mix pumpkin and flour add soda and cinnamon. Spray muffin tin and fill ¾ full. Bake at 350, 13-15 minutes for mini muffins, 20-30 minutes for regular size muffins and 25-35 minutes for large muffins. Sprinkle powdered sugar on top of cooled muffins.

Raspberry Streusel Muffins

Makes: 12 servings

Prep Time: 45 minutes

Streusel Topping

¼	cup	pecans, chopped
¼	cup	brown sugar
¼	cup	flour
2	tablespoons	butter, melted

Batter

1 ½	cups	flour
½	cup	sugar
2	teaspoons	baking powder
½	cup	milk
½	cup	butter, melted
1	whole	egg, beaten
1	cup	raspberries, fresh or frozen

Pecan Streusel Topping: Mix first four ingredients together until resembles moist crumbs.

Muffins: Pre-heat oven to 375 degrees. Grease muffin tins. In a large mixing bowl, combine flour, sugar, and baking powder. In small bowl, combine milk, butter and egg until blended. Stir into flour mixture just until moistened. Carefully fold raspberries into batter. Fill muffin tins ¾ full. Sprinkle streusel over tops of muffins. Bake 25-30 minutes or until golden and pick inserted in center comes out clean. Blueberries or blackberries can be substituted for raspberries.

Apple Scones

1 ½	cups	flour
1 ½	cups	wheat flour
⅔	cup	sugar
2 ½	teaspoons	baking powder
1	teaspoon	baking soda
1	teaspoon	salt
¾	cup	butter, softened
¾	cup	buttermilk
2	teaspoons	vanilla
1	teaspoon	almond extract
2	whole	eggs
1	whole	apple, peeled, diced
½	teaspoon	cinnamon
½	cup	walnuts, chopped (optional)

Mix the first six dry ingredients together. Add butter to dry mix. Add liquids and egg to dry ingredients until just combined. Fold in apples, walnuts and cinnamon. Divide dough in half. Pat dough into two flattened balls, two inches thick. Brush top with beaten egg. Cut into six pie shaped pieces. Place on greased baking sheet one inch apart. Bake at 400 degrees for 15-18 minutes. Don't overbake. The scones should be lightly browned.

Pumpkin Scones

2 ¼	cups	flour
¼	cup	brown sugar
2	teaspoons	baking powder
1 ½	teaspoons	pumpkin pie spice (or cinnamon and nutmeg)
¼	teaspoon	salt
¼	teaspoon	baking soda
½	cup	butter, cold
1	whole	egg
½	cup	pumpkin
⅓	cup	milk
¼	cup	pecans, chopped

In large bowl combine flour, sugar, baking powder, spice, salt and soda. Cut in butter until resembles coarse crumbs. In small bowl; whisk the egg, pumpkin and milk; add to crumb mixture just until moistened. Stir in pecans. Turn dough onto floured surface, knead 10 times. Pat into an 8" circle. Cut into 8 wedges; separate wedges and place on greased baking sheet. Bake in a preheated 400 degree oven for 12-15 minutes or until golden brown.

Strawberry Scones

Makes: 12 scones   Prep Time: 1 hour

3	cups	flour
2/3	cup	sugar
2 ½	teaspoons	baking powder
1	teaspoon	baking soda
1	teaspoon	salt
¾	cup	butter, softened
½	cup	buttermilk
2	teaspoons	vanilla
1	teaspoon	almond extract
2	whole	eggs
¾	cup	strawberries, fresh, chopped

Mix first five dry ingredients together. Add butter to dry mixture. Mix last four wet ingredients together and add liquid mixture to dry ingredients and mix until just combined. Divide dough in half. Pat dough into two flattened balls, 2 inches in diameter. Brush top of each with beaten egg and sprinkle with sugar. Cut into 6 pie shaped pieces (or roll out the dough and cut into different shapes with cookie cutters. You can put an indentation on top and fill with strawberry jelly.) Place on greased baking sheet, 12 to a sheet, or one inch apart. Bake at 400 degrees for 15-18 minutes; don't over bake. They should be very lightly browned. These are wonderful served with Strawberry Butter (see recipe) and whip cream.

Note: This recipe will make twelve large or twenty-four small scones. If making small scones, only bake 7-8 minutes.

Banana Chocolate Chip Bread

Makes: 1 loaf   Prep Time: 1 hour

2	cups	flour
1	teaspoon	soda
1	stick	butter, softened
1	cup	sugar
2	whole	eggs
1	teaspoon	vanilla
4	whole	bananas, mashed
1	cup	chocolate chips
1	cup	walnut, pieces

Mix flour and soda together. Cream the butter, sugar and eggs together. Add vanilla and dry ingredients. Stir in mashed bananas, nuts and chocolate chips. Put in greased 9"x 5" loaf pan and bake 45-50 minutes on 350 (325 for convection oven) until toothpick comes out clean.

Blackberry or Raspberry Bread

Makes: 2 loaves   Prep Time: 1 hour 15 minutes

3	whole	eggs
1	cup	canola oil
2	cups	sugar
3	cups	flour
2	teaspoons	cinnamon
½	teaspoon	baking powder
1	teaspoon	baking soda
3	teaspoons	vanilla
2	cups	raspberries or blackberries, fresh or frozen, crushed

Streusel Topping

¼	cup	butter
½	cup	sugar
½	cup	flour
½	cup	nuts, chopped

Beat eggs, oil and sugar. Add flour, cinnamon, soda, baking powder and vanilla. Add berries. Pour into 2 loaf pans that have been greased and sprinkle with topping. Bake in a 350 degree preheated oven for 1 hour and 15 minutes. Check at 1 hour. When toothpick comes out clean they are done. These can also be made in mini loaf pans or muffin tins; reduce baking time.

Streusel- Cut butter into sugar and fold; add nuts and sprinkle over batter.

Blackberry Buckle

Makes: 1 loaf   Prep Time: 1 hour

½	cup	butter
¾	cup	sugar
1	whole	egg
2	cups	flour
2 ½	teaspoons	baking powder
¼	teaspoon	salt
½	cup	milk
2	cups	blackberries, fresh, crushed
Topping		
½	cup	sugar
½	cup	flour
½	teaspoon	cinnamon
¼	cup	butter

Cream butter and sugar; add egg and beat till light and fluffy. Mix flour, baking powder and salt together then add to creamed mixture alternately with milk. Gently fold in crushed blackberries. Spread in greased bread pan.

Topping- Mix ½ cup sugar, ½ cup flour and cinnamon; cut in butter until crumbly; sprinkle over top. Bake in a 350 degree preheated oven for 45 minutes. Cut and serve warm. You can use blueberries or raspberries in place of the blackberries.

Blueberry Bread

Makes: 1 loaf   Prep Time: 1 hour 15 minutes

½	cup	butter, softened
1	cup	sugar
2	whole	eggs
½	teaspoon	vanilla
1	cup	sour cream
2	cups	flour
1	teaspoon	baking powder
1	teaspoon	baking soda
1	cup	blueberries, fresh or frozen

In a large bowl cream the butter and sugar with mixer. Beat in eggs, vanilla and sour cream. Mix in the flour, baking powder, and baking soda. Slowly fold in the blueberries. Pour the batter into a greased 5"x 9" loaf pan. Bake in a preheated 350 degree oven for 1 hour (check at 45 minutes) or until toothpick comes out clean.

Carrot Cake Bread

Makes: 2 loaves   Prep Time: 1 hour 30 minutes

Batter

3	whole	eggs
1	cup	canola oil
2	cups	brown sugar
3	cups	flour
3	teaspoons	cinnamon
½	teaspoon	nutmeg
½	teaspoon	baking powder
1	teaspoon	baking soda
3	teaspoons	vanilla
2	cups	carrot, shredded
½	cup	walnuts
½	cup	pineapple, crushed, drained well

Cream Cheese Icing

2	ounces	cream cheese
1 ½	cups	powdered sugar
6-8	teaspoons	milk

Batter-Beat eggs, oil and sugar. Add flour, cinnamon, nutmeg, soda, baking powder and vanilla. Add carrots, nuts and pineapple. Pour into 2 loaf pans that have been greased and bake in a 350 degree, preheated oven for 1 hour and 15 minutes. Check at 45 minutes if using and 8" loaf pan. Cover with foil if browning too quickly. When toothpick comes out clean they are finished. Cool. These can also be made in mini loaf pans or muffin tins; reduce baking time.

Icing-Whisk ingredients together until smooth and glaze like. Drizzle over bread right before serving.

Lemon Bread

Makes: 1 loaf   Prep Time: 1 hour 30 minutes

½	cup	canola oil
1	cup	sugar
2	large	eggs
1 ¼	cups	flour
1	teaspoon	baking powder
½	teaspoon	salt
½	cup	milk
1	tablespoon	lemon zest
½	cup	pecans
Glaze		
¼	cup	sugar
3	tablespoons	lemon juice, fresh

Pre-heat oven to 350 degrees. Grease loaf pan. In large bowl, combine canola oil and sugar and beat until blended. Add eggs one at a time, beating well after each addition. In medium bowl, mix flour, baking powder and salt. Add to the oil mixture, along with the milk and zest, and beat until blended and smooth. Stir in ½ cup pecans at this point if you desire. Spread evenly in prepared pan, bake until toothpick in center comes out clean - about 1 hour or 25 minutes for small loaves. While the bread bakes, make the glaze. Combine the ¼ cup sugar and 3 tablespoons lemon juice. Remove the finished bread from the oven and gently poke holes in several places on the top with a fork. Stir the syrup and drizzle the glaze over the bread. This bread is great sliced and topped with fresh fruit and whipped cream.

Monkey Bread

Makes: 12 servings   Prep Time: 1 hour

½	cup	sugar
3	teaspoons	cinnamon
½	stick	butter
1	cup	brown sugar
8	ounces	cream cheese, cut into 20 pieces
2	12 ounce	cans of buttermilk biscuits (or equivalent to 12 homemade biscuits)
1 ½	cups	pecans, chopped

Preheat oven to 350 degrees. Spray a bunt pan with non-stick cooking spray. Mix the cinnamon and sugar together. In a medium saucepan melt the butter and brown sugar over low heat stirring well; set aside. Press the biscuits out with your fingers and sprinkle each with ½ teaspoon of the cinnamon sugar mixture. Place a cube of the cream cheese in the center of each biscuit, wrapping the dough around the cream cheese. Sprinkle ½ the nuts in the bottom of the bunt pan. Place half of the prepared biscuits in the bunt pan. Sprinkle with cinnamon sugar, pour half the melted butter over the biscuits, and sprinkle on half the nuts. Layer the remaining biscuits on top, sprinkle with the remaining cinnamon sugar, pour the remaining butter over the biscuits, and sprinkle with the remaining nuts. Bake 30 minutes. Remove from oven and cool. Place a plate on top and invert. Serve warm or room temperature.

Orange Cranberry Bread

Makes: 1 loaf   Prep Time: 1 hour

½	cup	canola oil
1	cup	sugar
2	whole	eggs
1¼	cups	flour
1	teaspoon	baking powder
½	teaspoon	salt
½	cup	milk
1	tablespoon	orange zest, finely grated
½	cup	cranberries, dried
½	cup	pecans, chopped, (optional)

Orange Syrup

¼	cup	sugar
3	tablespoons	orange juice, fresh

Preheat oven 350 degrees. Grease or spray a bread pan or use small individual bread pans. In large bowl combine the oil and sugar and beat until blended. Add the eggs, one at a time, beating well after each addition. In a medium bowl stir and toss together the flour, baking powder, and salt. Add to the canola oil mixture, along with the milk and orange zest, and beat until blended and smooth. Stir in cranberries and pecans. Spread evenly in the pan. Bake until a wooden toothpick comes out clean in the center. The center will spring back when you touch it when it is done. Bake a large loaf about 1 hour check after 45 minutes. Bake the small individual loaves about 30 minutes. Check after 25 minutes.

While the bread is baking make the syrup by combining the sugar and orange juice in a small bowl. Set aside, stirring occasionally. Remove the bread from the oven and using a fork gently poke the top in several places on the top of the bread. Slowly drizzle the syrup over the top of the bread. Cool in the pan 15 minutes. When the bread is cooled it is pretty wrapped in a plastic bag and tied with ribbon or raffia. This bread is great in gift baskets.

Pumpkin Bread

Makes: 2 loaves   Prep Time: 1 hour

4	whole	eggs
3	cups	sugar
16	ounces	pumpkin
3 ½	cups	flour
1 ¼	teaspoons	salt
1	teaspoon	baking powder
1	teaspoon	baking soda
1	teaspoon	cinnamon
1	cup	canola oil
¾	cup	water
½	cup	raisins, golden
½	cup	walnuts, chopped

Cream eggs, sugar and pumpkin. Mix in separate bowl, flour, salt, baking powder, soda and cinnamon. Add the dry flour mixture alternately to the egg mixture with the oil and water, 1/3 at a time. Beat well after each. Stir in raisins and nuts. Pour into greased loaf pans filling ¾ full. Bake at 350 degrees for about 70 minutes. Cool.

Spring wildflowers at the farm

Rich, his mother Mary, goats Bell and Rosie and Fred the Peacock, all enjoying the spring wildflowers

Strawberry Bread

Makes: 2 loaves   Prep Time: 1 hour 30 minutes

3	cups	flour
1	teaspoon	baking soda
1	teaspoon	salt
3	teaspoons	cinnamon
2	cups	sugar
1	cup	strawberries, fresh, chopped
¼	cup	strawberry glaze
4	whole	eggs, beaten
1 ¼	cups	vegetable oil
1 ¼	cups	nuts, chopped

Mix dry ingredients together. In a large bowl, mix remaining ingredients. Stir in dry ingredients just until blended. Grease two 9"x 5" loaf pans. Pour in batter, smoothing top. Bake at 350 degrees for 1 hour. Cool in pans 10 minutes then remove from pans and cool on rack. For smaller loaves, decrease baking time to 50 minutes. Great served for tea with Strawberry Butter. (See recipe)

Zucchini Bread

Makes: 2 loaves   Prep Time: 1 hour 30 minutes

3	whole	eggs
1	cup	canola oil
2	cups	sugar
3	cups	flour
3	teaspoons	cinnamon
½	teaspoon	baking powder
1	teaspoon	baking soda
3	teaspoons	vanilla
2	cups	zucchini, shredded
½	cup	walnuts
½	cup	raisins

Beat eggs, oil and sugar. Add flour, cinnamon, soda, baking powder and vanilla. Add zucchini, nuts and raisins. Pour into 2 loaf pans that have been greased and bake in a 350 degree, preheated oven for 1 hour and 15 minutes. Check at 1 hour. When toothpick comes out clean they are finished. You can add chocolate chips instead of raisins. These can also be made in mini loaf pans or muffin tins; reduce baking time.

Sweet Potato Rolls

Makes: 3 dozen

1 ½	cups	milk, warm
½	cup	sugar
1	teaspoon	cinnamon
½	cup	Crisco, butter flavored
1	teaspoon	salt
2	large	eggs
8	cups	flour
2	cups	sweet potatoes, cooked/mashed
2	packages	yeast, rapid rise
¼	cup	warm water

Dissolve yeast in warm water. Stir in remaining ingredients. Let dough rise until doubled in proofer or warm place. Shape and put in greased muffin tins. Let rise again. Bake at 350 degrees for 10-15 minutes until lightly brown. Serve with Orange Honey Butter on the side (see recipe). This dough can be frozen. Let set out at room temperature to defrost before baking. This dough can be mixed in a food processor if you don't have a mixer. This is also the dough used to make the cinnamon rolls.

Breakfast

Baked Cheese Grits

Baked Oatmeal

Benedicts
Cafe Benedict
Cheesesteak with Smoked Cheddar
  Hollandaise
Crab Cake Benedict
Eggs Benedict with Hollandaise
Egg, Tomato and Bacon with Basil
  Hollandaise
Florentine Benedict

Breakfast Casseroles
Breakfast Casserole
Ham and Broccoli Strata
John Wayne Casserole
Sausage Cheese Casserole

Breakfast Sandwich

Coffee Cake
Cinnamon Streusel
Peach Coffee Cake

Cinnamon Rolls

Corned Beef Hash

Compotes and Syrups
Blackberry Syrup
Blueberry Compote
Cinnamon Syrup
Mixed Berry Compote
Peach Compote

Crepes
Chicken Crepes
Ham and Egg with Mushroom Sauce

French Toast
Apple, Pecan French Toast Casserole
Berry Baked French Toast
French Toast

Fruitarian

Granola

Pancakes-Buttermilk
Apple
Banana
Blueberry
Carrot Cake
Chocolate Chip
Granola
Strawberry
Zucchini

Pancakes-Multigrain
Carrot Cake
Pumpkin

Poached Eggs

Quiche
Apple, Ham and Cheddar
Basic Quiche Recipe
Sausage and Cheddar
Southwestern Chicken
Spinach, Feta Sun-dried Tomato
Three Cheese

Baked Cheese Grits

Makes: 8 servings   Prep Time: 1 hour

4	cups	boiling water
1 ½	teaspoons	salt, added to boiling water
1	cup	uncooked grits
2	whole	eggs, beaten
1	stick	butter
1 ½	cups	cheddar and jack cheese, combined, shredded
½	cup	green onions, chopped
½	cup	bacon, cooked and crumbled
1 ½	teaspoons	seasoned salt
1	teaspoon	cayenne pepper
1	pound	fresh medium size shrimp, uncooked
2	teaspoons	blackened seasoning (see recipe) or hot sauce
1	tablespoon	butter

Slowly add the of grits to the boiling water. Stir constantly for 1 minute. Cover and simmer, stirring occassionally, until grits are thick and creamy. Temper (see cooking terminology) eggs with a small amount of the hot grits, then add back to the remaining grits. Combine remaining ingredients with grits and pour into a greased 2 quart casserole dish. Bake for 45 minutes or until center is firm. Top with additional cheese if desired. Melt the butter, add either the blackened seasoning or the hot sauce to the butter. NOT both. Add the shrimp and sauté until the shrimp is pink/done. It is best to have your kitchen fan on for ventialtion while doing this or grill them outside. Serve the shrimp on top of the grits.

This was a popular Sunday special at the restaurant. Variations: you can use ham instead of bacon or eliminate the meat all together; add different cheeses or vegetables.

Baked Oatmeal

Makes: 6-8 servings   Prep Time: 60 minutes

3	cups	quick or old fashioned oats
¾	cup	brown sugar
2	teaspoons	cinnamon
2	teaspoons	baking powder
1	teaspoon	salt
1	cup	milk
2	whole	eggs, beaten
½	cup	butter, melted
2	teaspoons	vanilla
¾	cup	dried fruit or fresh fruit
¼	cup	walnuts (optional)

Preheat oven to 350 degrees. Mix the oats, brown sugar, cinnamon, baking powder and salt together. Add the remaining ingredients. Bake in a sprayed 9"x13" pan for 35-40 minutes until firm. Serve warm with milk and or warm maple syrup.

Cafe Benedict

Makes: 1 serving   Prep Time: 15 minutes

2	poached	eggs
1	whole	english muffin, halved
2	ounces	ham (2 slices)
2	slices	tomato
2	ounces	Monterey Jack cheese (2 slices)
2	teaspoons	sour cream
½	teaspoon	chives, fresh, chopped

Poach eggs to easy. Toast muffin lightly. Warm the ham. Place a slice of ham on each muffin half then top each half with tomato, poached egg, Monterey Jack cheese (pop in oven for a few seconds so the cheese will melt) sour cream and chopped chives.

Cheesesteak Benedicts with Smoked Cheddar Hollandaise

Makes: 4 serving   Prep Time: 30 minutes

1	pound	flat iron steak, sliced thin against the grain
1	whole	red pepper, julienne sliced
1	whole	onion, julienne sliced
2	tablespoons	butter
1	dash	salt and pepper to taste
2	cloves	garlic, fresh, minced
2	whole	wheat hoagie buns, split and toasted
4	whole	eggs, poached
1	recipe	smoked cheddar hollandaise sauce (see recipe)

Heat 1 tablespoon of butter in large skillet. Sauté onions and peppers on medium-high heat until they begin to soften. Add garlic and continue cooking until vegetables are lightly brown. Remove from pan and set aside. Add remaining tablespoon of butter to the hot pan and add the sliced steak. Sauté the steak and allow it to brown; add the vegetables back in and season with salt and pepper. Serve meat and vegetables open faced on top of toasted hoagie buns, top with a poached egg and a tablespoon of cheddar hollandaise over the top.

Smoked Cheddar Hollandaise Sauce

Makes: 4 servings   Prep Time: 15 minutes

¼	pound	butter
2	each	egg yolks
½	teaspoon	lemon juice
1/8	teaspoon	cayenne pepper
¼	cup	smoked cheddar cheese, shredded

Add egg yolks, lemon juice, smoked cheddar and cayenne pepper to a large metal mixing bowl and place over a sauce pan of boiling water; stir mixture until the cheddar begins to melt. Slowly drizzle in the hot butter while whisking vigorously. If butter is too hot, the sauce will break. Serve over cheesesteak benedicts.

Crab Cake Benedict

Makes: 6 servings   Prep Time: 1 hour

12	each	crab cakes, cooked (see recipe)
6	each	english muffins, Sara Lee/ Wolferman's-frozen
½	cup	spinach, fresh leaves
1	whole	tomato, fresh, 12 thin slices
12	each	poached eggs, hot
1	cup	hollandaise Sauce, with Dijon mustard (see Hollandaise recipe)

Poach eggs to easy. Toast english muffins lightly. Use a thick fluffy english muffin if you can't find Sara Lee. Cook crab cakes. Put spinach, a slice of tomato, crab cake and a poached egg on top of each muffin. Top each Benedict with 1 tablespoon of Dijon Hollandaise Sauce (see recipe). Sprinkle tops with fresh chopped parsley. Serve immediately.

Eggs Benedict

Makes: 1 serving   Prep Time: 15 minutes

2	each	eggs, poached
1	whole	english muffin
2	slices	canadian bacon
2	tablespoons	hollandaise sauce (see recipe)
1	teaspoon	parsley, fresh, chopped

Poach eggs to easy. Toast english muffin lightly. Heat the Canadian bacon. Put a slice of Canadian bacon on each muffin half, top with the poached egg and hollandaise sauce. Sprinkle with fresh chopped parsley for garnish.

Hollandaise Sauce

Makes: 4 servings   Prep Time: 10 minutes

¼	pound	butter
2	each	egg yolks
½	teaspoon	lemon juice
⅛	teaspoon	cayenne pepper

Melt butter in microwave. Put egg yolks in to a food processor. Blend for about 15 seconds then slowly add warm butter. If butter is too hot, the sauce will break. With processor still on, add lemon juice and cayenne. Do not heat this sauce, it will break. Serve at room temperature or lighlty warmed.

Dijon Hollandaise Sauce-To make dijon hollandaise sauce for crab cake benedicts, add 1 teaspoon of dijon mustard when adding lemon juice and cayenne.

Egg, Tomato and Bacon Benedict with Basil Hollandaise

Makes: 1 serving   Prep Time: 30 minutes

½	cup	onion, chopped
1	cup	potatoes, peeled, grated,
½	cup	zucchini, grated, water squeezed out and dried on paper towels
½	teaspoon	salt
¼	teaspoon	pepper
2	tablespoons	canola oil
2	slices	bacon, cooked and crumbled
4	large	eggs, poached
4	¼ inch	tomatoes, sliced
1	cup	Basil Hollandaise Sauce (see recipe)

In a bowl, combine onion, potatoes, zucchini, salt, pepper and bacon. For each pancake, spread ½ cup of mixture on a heated and oiled skillet, keeping pancakes 2 inches apart. Cook over moderately low heat, undisturbed, for 20 minutes. Increase heat to moderate, and cook 5 or 10 minutes more until underside is browned. Turn pancakes and cook 10 more minutes. (keep warm in 250 degree oven while poaching eggs.) Arrange pancakes on plates, top each pancake with a tomato slice, top each tomato slice with a hot poached egg. Spoon Hollandaise over eggs, garnish with fresh basil.

Basil Hollandaise Sauce

Makes: 1 cup   Prep Time: 15 minutes

1	cup	basil leaves, fresh, chopped
1	stick	butter
2	large	egg yolks
2	teaspoons	lemon juice, fresh
2	teaspoons	Dijon mustard
1/8	teaspoon	cayenne pepper
	to taste	salt

Melt butter over moderate heat. In a blender or food processor, blend egg yolks, lemon juice, mustard, cayenne pepper and basil leaves for 5 seconds. With motor running, add hot melted butter in a slow stream until mixed. Season with salt. If butter is too hot, the sauce will break.

Florentine Benedict

Makes: 1 serving   Prep Time: 15 minutes

2	each	eggs, poached
4	large	spinach leaves, fresh
2	slices	tomato
1	each	english muffin
¼	cup	mushrooms, fresh, sliced
2	tablespoons	Hollandaise Sauce (see recipe)
1	teaspoon	parsley, fresh, chopped

Poach eggs to easy. Lightly toast English muffin. Place two spinach leaves on each muffin half. Top with tomato, mushrooms, egg, Hollandaise sauce and parsley.

Breakfast Casserole

1	pound	herb roasted potatoes, cooked (see recipe)
½	cup	cheddar cheese, shredded
½	cup	Monterey Jack cheese, shredded
½	cup	breakfast sausage, cooked and crumbled

Place potatoes in baking dish, top with sausage and cheeses. Bake at 350 degrees for 20-30 minutes or until hot throughout.

Ham and Broccoli Strata

12	slices	bread, cubed
16	ounces (4 cups)	cheddar, mozzarella or swiss, shredded
4	cups	milk,
8	whole	eggs, beaten
1	teaspoon	dry mustard
2	tablespoons	onion, minced
2	cups	broccoli, chopped
2	cups	ham, cubed
1	dash	cayenne pepper
1	dash	salt
½	cup	butter, melted

Toss bread cubes with butter. Place ½ in a greased 13"x 9" sprayed baking dish. Top with half the cheese and broccoli; sprinkle with ham. Top with remaining bread, broccoli and cheese. In a large bowl, whisk the eggs, milk and pepper. Pour over casserole. Make sure cubes of bread are covered with egg. You may need to push them down into egg mixture. Bake uncovered, at 350 degrees for 35-40 minutes or until a knife inserted in the center comes out clean. Let stand for 5 minutes before cutting. This makes a great brunch dish and can be made a day ahead. Keep in the refrigerator the night before and bake in the morning.

John Wayne Breakfast Casserole

Makes: 6-8 servings   Prep Time: 1 hour 30 minutes

1	large	onion, chopped
½	cup	red pepper, chopped
1	whole	banana pepper, diced
1	whole	jalepeno pepper, minced
1	clove	garlic, minced
1 ½	tablespoons	butter
1	tablespoon	pepper
6	whole	eggs (whites and yolks divided)
¼	cup	milk
½	cup (minus 2 tbsp)	flour
1 ½	cups	jack cheese, shredded
1 ½	cups	cheddar cheese, shredded
16	ounces	sour cream
½	cup	corn tortilla chips
1	teaspoon	dry mustard
		salsa

Sauté the onions, banana pepper and red pepper in the butter in a large skillet until tender. Add the garlic and jalepeno, and sauté a few more minutes. Remove from heat and set aside. In a large mixing bowl put in 6 egg yolks, milk, flour and pepper, then add the sour cream, cheeses, tortilla chips and the now cooled vegetables and mix all together. Beat the egg whites until stiff; fold into the mixture. Pour the mixture into a 9"x13" greased baking dish and place in a preheated 350 degree oven for approximately 1 hour. The dish is done when the top is a little crusty and starts to crack. Serve with sour cream and salsa on the side.

Sausage Cheese Casserole

Makes: 12 servings   Prep Time: 1 hour

1	pound	sausage, browned and drained
2 ¼	cups	milk
10	whole	eggs, beaten
1 ½	teaspoons	dry mustard
½	cup	banana peppers, chopped
½	cup	onions, chopped
½	teaspoon	salt
1 ½	cups	cheddar cheese, shredded
½	cup	jack cheese, shredded
½	cup	provolone, shredded or sliced
4	slices	bread, torn into pieces

Preheat oven to 350 degrees. In large bowl, combine milk, eggs, dry mustard and salt. Beat one minute. Stir in 1 ¼ cups of the cheddar cheese, peppers, onions, bread and sausage. Pour into greased 13"x 9"pan. Top with remaining cheese and bake in a preheated 350 degree oven for 30-40 minutes or until inserted knife comes out clean.

Tip: To make ahead, prepare, cover and refrigerate overnight. Do not top with remaining cheese until right before going in the oven. Bake at 350 degrees for 40-50 minutes. It is always best to let set at room temperature for 15 minutes or so before baking after being refrigerated. You can add vegetables and different meats and cheeses.

Breakfast Sandwich

Makes: 4 sandwiches   Prep Time: 30 minutes

1	package	puff pastry sheets (frozen food section)
4	slices	ham
4	whole	eggs, scrambled soft
4	ounces	cheddar cheese, shredded
1	dash	salt and pepper to taste

Thaw pastry according to directions. Cut each pastry sheet into 4 squares (there are 2 per package). Put 1 slice of ham in center of each square. Top ham with eggs and cheese. Lay a pastry square on top of of ham, egg and cheese and crimp sides together. Put on sprayed baking sheet. Bake in a 400 degree preheated oven for 15 minutes or until golden brown.

Cinnamon Streusel Coffee Cake

Makes: 12 servings   Prep Time: 1 hour

Coffee Cake batter

3	cups	flour
1	cup	sugar
1	tablespoon	baking powder
1	teaspoon	cinnamon
1	teaspoon	salt
1	cup	butter, cold
2	whole	eggs
1	cup	milk
1	teaspoon	vanilla

Streusel filling

1	cup	brown sugar
2/3	cup	flour
1/2	cup	butter, cold, sliced
1 1/2	tablespoons	cinnamon
1/4	teaspoon	salt

Topping

1/4	cup	butter
1/2	cup	sugar
1/2	cup	flour
1/2	cup	nuts, chopped

Batter- Mix 3 cups flour, 1 cup sugar, baking powder, cinnamon and salt in a bowl. Cut in 1 cup cold butter until resembles fine crumbs (you can use a pastry blender by hand or pulse in food processor). In another bowl combine eggs, milk and vanilla. Add to flour mixture until blended. Spread half of the batter into a sprayed bunt pan.

Streusel Filling-Pulse together in food processor until crumbs form. Spread over cake batter. Spread remaining coffee cake batter over streusel.

Topping- Cut the butter into sugar and flour. Add chopped nuts-pecans or walnuts and sprinkle over batter.
Bake at 350 degrees for 45-50 minutes or until toothpick comes out clean.

Note: You can make the batter, streusel and topping a few days ahead just keep refrigerated in separate containers and put together when ready to bake.

Peach Coffee Cake

3	cups	peach compote (see recipe)
3	cups	flour
1	cup	sugar
1	tablespoon	baking powder
1	teaspoon	cinnamon
½	teaspoon	nutmeg
1	teaspoon	salt
1	cup	butter
2	whole	eggs, beaten
1	cup	milk
1	teaspoon	vanilla, pure
½	cup	sugar
¼	cup	butter
½	cup	flour
½	cup	pecans, chopped

Mix 3 cups flour and 1 cup of sugar, baking powder, cinnamon, nutmeg and salt in a bowl. Cut in 1 cup of butter until mixture resembles fine crumbs. In another bowl combine eggs, milk and vanilla. Add to flour mixture until blended. Spread half of the batter into a 9"x 13" greased baking dish. Spread 1 ½ cups cooled compote over batter, make sure you cover to the edges. Spread remaining batter in small mounds over fruit and spread out. Cut ¼ cup butter into ½ cup of sugar and ½ cup flour. Add ½ cup of chopped pecans and sprinkle over batter. Bake at 350 degrees for 45-50 minutes or until tooth pick comes out clean. Cool slightly, cut, and serve remaining warm peach compote on top of coffee cake. You can also use the Berry Compote or Blueberry Compote for this recipe. (See recipes in this section.) The batter and topping can be made 2 days ahead and kept in refrigerator. The batter can also be frozen up to one month. This coffee cake was very popular at the restaurant and for caterings.

Cinnamon Rolls

Makes: 20 servings

Prep Time: 3 hours

1	recipe	sweet potato rolls (see recipe)
2	cups	apples, fresh, chopped
1	cup	pecans, chopped
¾	cup	brown sugar (mix with cinnamon)
2	teaspoons	cinnamon
1	cup	Caramel Sauce (see recipe)

Make Sweet Potato Roll recipe and let rise. Roll out dough and top with chopped apples, cinnamon, brown sugar, and pecans. Roll up like a jelly roll and slice about 2" thick and let rise until double in size. Bake at 350 degrees for 10-15 minutes on a greased baking sheet. Serve warm with Caramel Sauce drizzled on the top and Orange Honey Butter on the side (see recipes).

Corned Beef Hash

Makes: 12 servings

Prep Time: 30 minutes

¼	pound (1 stick)	butter
2	pounds	corned beef brisket, cooked
½	cup	green onions, chopped
2	teaspoons	fresh thyme, chopped
½	teaspoon	salt
½	teaspoon	pepper
1½	cups	onion, diced
2	cups	potatoes, cooked cubed and cooled
2	tablespoons	parsley, fresh, chopped

Put butter, both onions, thyme and parsley in a bowl. Heat in microwave until butter is melted. Stir. Cut corned beef into chunks and put in food processor until shredded. Do not over shred. You can use left over baked or roasted potatoes. If not, boil potatoes as if making potato salad. Let potatoes cool and dice or put in processor; you don't want mush. Put everything in a large bowl and mix well. Add more salt and pepper if needed. Melt small amount of butter in skillet or griddle, add hash, cook until crispy and hot. This was a popular breakfast item at Margy's. It is an easy recipe and definetly worth the time to make it.

Blackberry Syrup

8	cups	blackberries, fresh, ripe
1½	cups	water
		sugar
1	tablespoon	lemon juice

Pick over, rinse and drain berries. Place them in a large heavy pot, and mash with a potato masher. Add the water. Bring the mixture to a boil over medium heat. Reduce the heat to low and simmer the berries for about 10 minutes; stirring occasionally.

Strain the berry mixture through a large sieve extracting as much juice as possible. Measure the juice into a clean, heavy pan. Add 1 cup of sugar for each cup of juice. Heat the mixture over medium heat stirring until sugar has dissolved. Increase heat to medium- high, and boil the mixture for 2-3 minutes. Remove the syrup from the heat and stir in lemon juice. If the syrup will be used within a few months, pour into clean, dry bottles or jars and store in the refrigerator. If it is to be kept longer, pour the boiling syrup into sterilized pint jars and process in a water bath for 15 minutes.

Blueberry Compote

2	teaspoons	butter, unsalted
1	cup	sugar
4	tablespoons	orange juice, fresh squeezed
3 ½	pints	blueberries, fresh or frozen

In sauce pan over medium heat, melt butter. Add sugar and orange juice, cook until sugar dissolves (3-5 minutes). Add blueberries and cook 5-6 minutes until blueberries are soft. Great served over blueberry pancakes. See Buttermilk Pancake recipe. Also good over ice cream. This compote can be used instead of the peach compote with the Coffee Cake recipe.

Cinnamon Syrup

Makes: 8 servings

Prep Time: 15 minutes

1 ½	cups	corn syrup, light
2	teaspoons	cinnamon
2	teaspoons	lemon juice

Place corn syrup in sauce pan and cook over low heat until thoroughly heated. Add remaining ingredients; stir well. Serve warm. Great on banana, carrot, pumpkin and zucchini pancakes. See pancake recipes in this chapter.

Mixed Berry Compote

Makes: 12 servings

Prep Time: 30 minutes

2	teaspoons	butter, unsalted
1	cup	sugar
4	tablespoons	orange juice, fresh squeezed
1	pint	blueberries, fresh or frozen
1	pint	raspberries, fresh or frozen
1	pint	strawberries, fresh or frozen

Slice strawberries. In sauce pan over medium heat, melt butter. Add sugar and orange juice and cook 3-5 minutes until sugar dissolves. Add blueberries and cook about 2 minutes, then add raspberries and strawberries. Cook until soft, about 3-4 minutes. Can make 2-3 days ahead if kept refrigerated. Let cool and then put in refrigerator. Great on pancakes, french toast or ice cream.

Peach Compote

Makes: 12 servings

Prep Time: 30 minutes

4	cups	peaches, fresh or frozen, sliced
1	cup	butter
½	cup	vanilla, pure
¾	cup	brown sugar

Melt butter in sauce pan and add peaches, vanilla and sugar. Stir. Simmer over low heat for about 10 minutes or until peaches are soft, not mushy. This sauce is used for Peach French Toast, and Peach Coffee Cake. This recipe is also great on pancakes.

Chicken Crepes

Filling

1	tablespoon	butter
¼	cup	onion, minced
2 ½	cups	chicken, diced, cooked
1 ½	cups	spinach, fresh, chopped
¾	cup	parmesan cheese
½	teaspoon	salt

Sauce

6	tablespoons	butter
6	tablespoons	flour
3	cups	milk, steaming
1	cup	parmesan
1	cup	cheddar cheese, shredded
12	whole	crepes, prepared

Filling-Sauté onion in butter for 4 minutes. Add chicken, spinach, parmesan and salt. Mix well. Put crepes in greased muffin tins. Place 1 large tablespoon of mixture in each tin.

Sauce-Melt butter in large saucepan. Stir in flour and cook, stirring constantly for 2 minutes. Add milk and wisk over medium high heat until thickened and bubbly. Add cheeses and stir over low heat until cheese is melted and sauce is smooth.

Assembly-Pour sauce over filled crepes and bake in preheated 300 degree oven for 30 minutes or until heated through.

Note: You can assemble the night before (waiting to add the sauce until ready to bake), just make sure to wrap with plastic wrap and refrigerate. These can be rolled like a regular crepe. This is perfect to serve at a high tea, bridal luncheon or brunch.

Ham and Egg Crepes with Mushroom Sauce

Makes: 12 Crepes   Prep Time: 1 hour

Filling

2	tablespoons	butter
1 ¼	cups	ham, chopped
8	whole	eggs
½	cup	milk
¼	cup	water
½	teaspoon	pepper

Sauce

3	tablespoons	butter
8	ounces	mushrooms, sliced
2	tablespoons	onion, chopped
1	tablespoon	flour
¼ - ½	cup	milk
1	teaspoon	mustard
½	teaspoon	salt
½	teaspoon	pepper
1	cup	sour cream
2	tablespoons	parsley, chopped
12	whole	crepes, prepared

Filling-Sauté ham in butter 5 minutes until lightly browned. Combine eggs, milk, water and pepper; beat well. Add egg mixture to ham; cook stirring occassionally until eggs are firm but still moist. Line large (greased) muffin tins with crepe shells. Spoon ¼ cup of egg mixture in each crepe cup. Place 1 large tablespoon of mixture in each tin.

Sauce-Melt butter in large skillet; sauté mushrooms and onions in butter 3-5 minutes or until onion is tender. Add flour stirring until vegetables are coated. Cook 1 minute stirring constantly, until thickened and bubbly. Stir in mustard, salt and pepper; add sour cream and parsley. Cook stirring constantly, until sauce is thoroughly heated. When ready to bake, pour mushroom sauce over crepes. Cover and bake in a preheated 350 degree oven for 10-15 minutes until heated through out.

Note: You can assemble the night before, just make sure to wrap with plastic wrap and refrigerate. Don't add sauce until ready to bake. These can also be rolled like a regular crepe.

Apple, Pecan French Toast Casserole

Makes: 8 servings   Prep Time: 8 hours

8		left over cinnamon rolls
8	large	eggs
2	cups	half and half
1	cup	milk
2	tablespoons	sugar
1	teaspoon	vanilla
¼	teaspoon	cinnamon
1	dash	salt
1	cup	apples, fresh, chopped
Pecan topping		
2	sticks	butter, melted
1	cup	brown sugar
1	cup	pecans, chopped
2	tablespoons	light corn syrup
½	teaspoon	cinnamon

Arrange cinnamon rolls in a greased 9" x 13" baking dish. In a large bowl, combine eggs, half and half, milk, sugar, vanilla, cinnamon and salt. Whisk until blended well. Pour mixture over the cinnamon rolls, making sure all rolls are covered evenly with the egg mixture. Cover with Pam sprayed foil and refrigerate overnight.

The next day preheat oven to 350 degrees. Spread chopped apples over the top and push down into the egg covered rolls. Combine the pecan topping ingredients. Spread topping evenly over the rolls and bake 40 minutes until lightly browned. Serve warm with maple syrup.

Berry Baked French Toast

Makes: 8 servings   Prep Time: 10 hours

1	loaf	french bread, cubed
1	8 ounce	cream cheese, cubed
1	cup	berries, fresh assorted
8	whole	eggs
¼	cup	maple syrup
1	cup	milk

Line bottom of sprayed, deep baking dish with half of the cubed bread. Put the cubed cream cheese on top of the bread. Place berries on top of the cream cheese and top with the remaining cubed bread. Beat the eggs with the maple syrup and milk. Pour over the bread mixture. Cover with Pam sprayed foil and refrigerate overnight. Bake in a 350 degree preheated oven, covered for 30 minutes. Uncover and bake another 30 minutes until center is firm and toothpick comes out clean. Let set a few minutes then cut into squares and serve with warm Mixed Berry Compote or Blackberry Sauce (see recipes).

French Toast

Makes: 6 servings   Prep Time: 15 minutes

5	whole	eggs, beaten
1/8	cup	sugar
3/4	cup	half and half, or heavy cream
3/4	cup	milk (or 1/4 c Grand Marnier and 1/2 c milk)
1	teaspoon	orange zest
1/2	teaspoon	cinnamon
1	teaspoon	vanilla, pure
1	loaf	french bread (1 inch slices)

Mix eggs, sugar, half and half and milk. Use french bread (not regular bread slices) cut into 1 inch slices. Dip bread into batter and put on sprayed hot griddle. Brown on both sides. Great served with Peach Compote and topped with pecans. (See recipe this section.) You can also use a nice, thick cut regular or cinnamon bread and cut the bread into sticks. These are perfect for dipping into syrup.

Fruitarian

Makes: 1 serving   Prep Time: 10 minutes

1/2	cup	mixed fruit, fresh, chopped
1/4	cup	yogurt, plain
1/4	cup	granola (see recipe)
1	dash	cinnamon

Mix cinnamon and yogurt. Place fresh fruit on the bottom of a plate or large bowl. Top with the cinnamon yogurt then the granola.

Granola

Makes: 40 ½ cup servings   Prep Time: 1 hour 30 minutes

2	cups	brown sugar, packed
½	cup	molasses, unsulfured
1 ½	cups	honey
1	cup	cold water
¾	cup	canola oil (plus 1 tablespoon)
5	tablespoons	cinnamon
12	cups	oats, old fashioned
2	cups	walnut pieces
2	cups	pecan pieces
2	cups	almonds, sliced
2	cups	coconut, shredded
2	cups	All-Bran cereal
1	cup	banana chips
1	cup	raisins, seedless
1	cup	apricots, dried, chopped

Combine first 6 ingredients in heavy sauce pan. Bring to a boil over low heat, stirring constantly. Pre-heat oven to 325 degrees. Combine next 6 ingredients. Drizzle syrup over top and stir thoroughly. Place on sprayed cookie sheets and bake 40 minutes. Do not pile up granola on baking sheets. It should be no more than ½ inch. Stir with rubber spatula every 10 minutes for the first 20 minutes then every 5 minutes. Keep granola away from sides of pan, it tends to burn if to close to the sides. Cool granola in pans. When cooled thoroughly, place in large bowl and add dried fruits (you can use any dried fruit you like). Store in an air tight plastic container. Will keep if stored properly up to a month, maybe more. This granola is good as dry cereal with milk, as a snack instead of chips, as a parfait layered with ice cream and fresh fruit, on top of oatmeal, etc. The aroma of this while baking is fabulous. Makes 40 ½ cup servings. For a heart healthy, lower fat version eliminate the coconut.

Buttermilk Pancake Mix

Makes: 10 servings   Prep Time: 30 minutes

5	whole	eggs
2 ¼	cups	buttermilk
¾	cup	butter, melted
2 ½	cups	flour
¼	cup	sugar
2 ½	teaspoons	baking soda
¼	teaspoon	salt
2 ½	teaspoons	vanilla, pure

Beat eggs well. Dissolve soda in buttermilk. Mix flour, salt, and sugar. Add melted butter, eggs and buttermilk with soda. Add vanilla last. The key is to mix by hand. **Do not use a mixer** or you will break down the soda and have flat pancakes. Keep batter in refrigerator until ready to use. Can make a day ahead if kept cold. Use pure vanilla for best results. Batter will be thick. For best results put the pancake batter on a hot skillet or griddle. Makes thick, fluffy pancakes. Use the Mixed Berry Compote (see recipe) for a delicious alternative to syrup.

Apple Pancakes- To make apple pancakes, put the batter on a hot skillet or griddle, lay slices of apple on top. Do not flip until pancake bubbles all over. Plate the pancakes fruit side up.

Banana Pancakes- Do the same except use thin slices of fresh bananas. Plate the pancake fruit side up. Use the Cinnamon Syrup (see recipe) instead of regular as a wonderful alternative.

Blueberry Pancakes- Do the same as banana except put fresh or drained frozen blueberries on top. Plate the pancake fruit side up. Use the Blueberry Compote (see recipe) instead of syrup.

Carrot Cake Pancakes-To the above Buttermilk pancake recipe add 1½ cups finely grated carrot, ½ cup pecan pieces, 2 teaspoons cinnamon, 1 dash nutmeg, 1 dash ground cloves, 1 dash ground ginger and use brown sugar instead of regular sugar. Top with cinnamon honey butter or Maple Cream Cheese Drizzle. (See recipes).

Chocolate Chip Pancakes- Do the same as blueberry except put mini chocolate chips on top. Plate chocolate chip side up.

Granola Pancakes- Do the same except sprinkle granola on top. Plate the pancake granola side up. Cinnamon syrup is also great with the granola pancakes.

Strawberry Pancakes- Do the same as banana except put sliced fresh strawberries on top. Plate the pancakes fruit side up and top with Mixed Berry Compote.

Zucchini Pancakes- Do the same except put freshly grated (water squeezed out) zucchini on top. Sprinkle with cinnamon and add chopped nuts. Mini chocolate chips are also great added to these.

Multi Grain Pancakes

Makes: 5 medium pancakes

Prep Time: 15 minutes

⅓	cup	flour
⅓	cup + 2 tablespoons	wheat flour
⅓	cup	yellow cornmeal
2	teaspoons	baking soda
1	teaspoon	salt
2	tablespoons	sugar
1	cup	buttermilk
1	large	egg
3	tablespoons	butter, unsalted, melted

Combine dry ingredients. Combine wet ingredients. Combine wet ingredients to dry by slowly adding and stir just until combined. Put the batter on to a hot skillet or griddle. Do not flip until pancake bubbles all over.

Note: I don't use enough buttermilk to keep it on hand so it spoils. Since buttermilk is what makes the pancakes so fluffy I keep the powdered on hand and it works great.

Make dry mix ahead-You can mix a large batch of the dry ingredients to have on hand. Keep it in a airtight container in your pantry or freezer. When ready to make pancakes measure out 2 cups of the dry ingredients to the above wet ingredients; 2 tablespoons butter, 1 egg and 1 cup buttermilk.

Carrot Cake Pancakes

Makes: 5 medium pancakes

Prep Time: 15 minutes

⅓	cup	flour
⅓	cup + 2 tablespoons	wheat flour
⅓	cup	yellow cornmeal
2	teaspoons	baking soda
1	teaspoon	salt
2	tablespoons	brown sugar
1	cup	buttermilk
1	whole	egg
3	tablespoons	butter, unsalted, melted
½	cup	carrots, finely shredded
1	teaspoon	cinnamon
1	dash	cloves
1	dash	nutmeg
¼	cup	walnuts or pecans, chopped

Cream Cheese Drizzle

4	ounces	cream cheese, room temperature
2-3	tablespoons	maple syrup

Combine dry ingredients together. Combine wet ingredients together. Combine wet ingredients to dry by slowly adding and stir just until combined. Add carrots and nuts. Spoon the batter on to a hot skillet or griddle. Do not flip until pancake bubbles all over.

Drizzle-Mix until creamy; add 1 tablespoon powdered sugar if you like it sweeter or more maple syrup to thin it down to desired consistency.

Pumpkin Pancakes

Makes: 5 medium pancakes   Prep Time: 15 minutes

1	whole	egg
1	teaspoon	soda
1	cup	buttermilk
1/3	cup	white flour
1/3	cup	wheat flour + 2 tablespoons
1/3	cup	corn meal
1	dash	salt
2	tablespoons	sugar
1/2	teaspoon	cinnamon, ground
3	tablespoons	butter, melted
1/3	cup	pumpkin
1/2	cup	walnuts or pecan pieces

Beat egg. Dissolve soda in buttermilk. Mix flours, cornmeal, salt, cinnamon and sugar together. Mix melted butter, egg, pumpkin and buttermilk with soda. Add the egg mixture with the flour mixture and stir by hand. Do not use a mixer or you will break down the soda and have flat pancakes. Put pancake mix on hot griddle and then add nuts on the top side of the pancakes. Wait until the pancake bubbles in the middle before turning. Keep batter in refrigerator until ready to use. You can make this batter a day ahead if kept cold. Batter will be thick and makes thick, fluffy pancakes. I like these pancakes with the homemade cinnamon syrup warmed (see recipe) or with warm maple syrup.

Poached Eggs

Makes: 1 serving   Prep Time: 15 minutes

4	cups	water
1	tablespoon	white wine vinegar
1	whole	egg

The easiest way to poach an egg is with an egg poacher, but if you don't have one, this is the next best way. Bring water and vinegar to a simmer in a medium size saucepan. Break an egg into a cup and then slip it into the water. It is best to do one egg at a time so they don't stick together. If you need to poach more than one at a time, use a bigger pan and fill it with water. Cook for 3-4 minutes. Remove the egg with a slotted spoon. If you need to make a large amount, immediately put them, as they are finished, in a bowl of very cold ice water. This will keep them fresh. Dip them in a pan of very warm water just to heat when ready to serve.

Apple, Ham and Cheddar Quiche

Makes: 8 servings   Prep Time: 1 hour

1	cup	mayonnaise
4	tablespoons	flour
4	whole	eggs, beaten
1	cup	half and half, milk or heavy cream
1	cup	apples, fresh, sliced
1	cup	ham, chopped
2	cups	cheddar cheese, shredded
1	9-inch	pie crust, unbaked

Mix mayonnaise, flour, eggs and milk with whisk or beaters. Line the bottom of the pie crust with ½ cup of the shredded cheese. Then top the cheese with the ham and fan out slices of apples on top of the ham. Pour the egg mixture over the apples and top with the remaining cheddar cheese. Bake in a preheated 350 degree oven for 45-60 minutes until toothpick comes out clean. This sounds unusual but it is very good and one of our most popular quiches at the restaurant. My friend Charlotte came up with this combination of ingredients.

Basic Quiche Recipe

Makes: 6 servings   Prep Time: 1 hour

Filling

1	cup	mayonnaise
4	tablespoons	flour
4	whole	eggs, beaten
1	cup	milk, half and half or heavy cream
1	9-inch	pie crust, unbaked
1	dash	salt and pepper
8	ounces	cheddar cheese, shredded
1	cup	ham, diced or shredded
½	cup	green onions, chopped

Crust

1	cup	flour
1	tablespoon	powdered sugar
1	dash	salt
1	stick	butter, unsalted, cold, cubed
4	ounces	cream cheese, cubed

Filling-Combine mayonnaise, flour, eggs and milk with a whisk or beaters. Line the bottom of a 9" unbaked pie crust (or the quiche crust recipe below) with a handful of the cheese, then top with the ham and onion and a little more cheese. Pour the egg mixture over the ingredients. Top with remaining cheese. Bake in a preheated 350 degree oven for 35-60 minutes (baking time depends on how much and what ingredients you use) or until toothpick in center comes out clean. You can use a variety of meats, cheeses and vegetables. If you want to bake a 9"x 13" quiche that serves 12, you can buy puff pastry sheets in your groceries freezer. Spray the pan and put pastry on the bottom only, add the ingredients then pour in the quiche mixture and bake. It will take 35-45 minutes to bake. You can make mini quiches in muffin tins. They turn out great and make perfect appetizers.

Crust- Combine flour, powdered sugar and salt in food processor, add butter and cream cheese, then blend until dough forms around the blade. Remove from processor, wrap in plastic and chill 30 minutes. Dough can be made 1 day ahead. Roll dough out on a lightly floured surface and transfer to a 9" pie plate. Crimp the edges. Freeze the dough until firm.

Sausage and Cheddar Quiche

Makes: 8 servings   Prep Time: 1 hour

1	cup	mayonnaise
4	tablespoons	flour
4	whole	eggs, beaten
1	cup	milk, half and half or heavy cream
1	cup	sausage, cooked and crumbled
1 ½	cups	cheddar cheese, shredded
1	9-inch	pie crust, unbaked

Mix mayonnaise, flour, eggs and milk with whisk or beaters. Put ½ cup of cheese on the bottom of the crust. Layer sausage on top of cheddar. Pour quiche mixture over the sausage top with remaining cheese. Bake in a preheated 350 degree oven for 35-45 minutes or until toothpick comes out clean.

Southwestern Chicken Quiche

Makes: 6 servings   Prep Time: 1 hour

1	cup	mayonnaise
1	cup	milk
4	whole	eggs
4	tablespoons	flour
15	ounces	chili beans, canned, drained
¼	cup	green chilies, canned, chopped
¼	cup	salsa
1	9-inch	pie crust, unbaked
12	ounces	cheddar cheese, shredded
1	cup	chicken, white meat, cooked, diced
½	cup	tortilla chips, crushed
½	cup	sour cream

Mix mayonnaise, milk, eggs and flour together with wire whip or mixer until smooth. Cover the bottom of the pie crust with ½ cup of the cheddar cheese. Put diced chicken on top of cheese, then layer beans, chilies and salsa over chicken. Pour egg mixture on top of the ingredients. Put another layer of cheese, then a layer of crushed tortilla chips; top with the remaining cheese. Bake at 350 degrees for 45-60 minutes until center is firm and knife comes out clean. Serve warm with a dollop of sour cream on top and a side of salsa. This was a very popular quiche at Margy's. My friend Charlotte came up with this combination of ingredients which makes a delicious luncheon quiche.

Spinach, Feta, Sun-dried Tomato Quiche

Makes: 6 servings   Prep Time: 1 hour

1	cup	mayonnaise
4	tablespoons	flour
4	whole	eggs, beaten
1	cup	milk, half and half or heavy cream
1	9-inch	pie crust, unbaked
1	cup	spinach, fresh, chopped
½	cup	feta cheese, crumbled
½	cup	sun-dried tomatoes, julienned, not in oil

Mix all ingredients and pour into pie shell. Bake at 350 degrees for 35-45 minutes or until toothpick comes out clean. This was always our most popular quiche at Margy's.

Three Cheese Quiche

Makes: 6 servings

1	cup	mayonnaise
4	tablespoons	flour
4	whole	eggs, beaten
1	cup	half and half, milk or heavy cream
¼	cup	Monterey jack cheese, shredded
½	cup	cheddar cheese, shredded
¼	cup	swiss cheese, shredded
¼	cup	red pepper, chopped
1	9-inch	pie crust, unbaked

Mix mayonnaise, flour, eggs, and milk with whisk or beaters. Put ¼ cup of cheddar cheese on the bottom of the pie crust, top with red peppers and cheeses, (reserving about ½ cup of cheddar) and pour quiche mixture over the cheese and peppers. Put the remaining cheese on top and bake in a preheated 350 degrees for 35-45 minutes or until toothpick comes out clean.

Canning and Preserving

The Basics of Canning

Preserving by Freezing

Apple Butter

Applesauce
Apple Pear Blackberry
Blackberry
Raspberry

Blackberry Syrup

Jams and Jelly's
Blackberry Jam
Red Raspberry Jam
Strawberry Jam
Jalapeño Pepper Jelly

Pickles
Bread and Butter
Dill
Zucchini

Garden Vegetable Spaghetti Sauce

Lemon or Orange Curd
Lemon Curd Tarts

Relish
Philadelphia Pepper Relish
Zucchini Relish

Pickled Beets
Pickled Eggs

Salsa

Tomato Bisque Soup

Tomato Vegetable Juice

The Basics of Canning

There are basically two types of canning. Water bath canner is used for processing fruits, tomatoes and pickles. Pressure canner is used for processing vegetables and meats. The recipes in this chapter are all for water bath canning which is very simple and very rewarding. Following are the basics you will need to know for this chapter.

For water bath canning you will need the following:

- A water bath canner with rack

- Clean jars, lids and rings.

- A canning funnel

- Tongues and jar lifter

- Clean dry towels

- Clean wet cloth

- Hot pads

- Ladle

1. Sterilize your jars and rings. I sterilize my jars and rings by running them through the dishwasher right before I start my canning.

2. Fill the water bath canner a little more than half way with water and turn the burner to medium.

3. Prepare the food you wish to can by following your recipe.

4. Make sure the water is very hot at this point but not quite boiling.

5. Before filling jars using tongues or a jar lifter submerge the sterilized jars in the water. You want to make sure you put the ready to can foods into a hot jar, not room temperature or the jars could break. This also makes sure the jars are sterilized before filling.

6. Fill each jar with the prepared food. A canning funnel is helpful here to avoid getting the jar rims messy.

7. Fill the jars within one $\frac{1}{8}$-$\frac{1}{2}$ inch of the top. Per recipe instructions.

Margy's Local. Organic. Fresh. Continuing Education Course at IPFW; Canning and Preserving Summer 2010

The garden before the expansion; friends Charlotte and her daughter Teresa

8. Dip the lids into hot, boiling water just before placing them on the jars.

9. Make sure that the top of each jar is clean so that it will seal. (Wipe with a clean wet cloth.)

10. At this point the water needs to be at a low rolling boil.

11. Add a ring and the lid to each of the jars. You want to twist the lids on, but not too tight. You can reuse the rings but never reuse the lids as you risk the jars not sealing properly.

12. Process-Place the jars into the boiling water bath with the tongues or jar lifter. Make sure they are covered by 1-2 inches of water. Depending on your recipe. The boiling time starts once the water has returned to boiling. Once the water returns to a boil put the lid on the canner and start the clock.

13. Process (boil) as directed in each recipe, keeping water at a low rolling boil.

14. When the boiling time is reached, turn the stove off or down to low and remove the hot jars from the canner with the canning grippers.

15. Cool- Place the jars onto clean towels and as they continue cooling they will seal. You will hear a popping sound as each jar seals. There will be a dip in the lid showing that the jar has sealed.

16. If you have a jar that has not sealed you will need place that jar (once it has cooled) in the refrigerator and go ahead and eat that.

17. Label and date the jars.

18. Store sealed jars in a cool, dry place for up to one year.

If you are a beginner canner I recommend buying the Ball Blue Canning Book. This book will tell you how to can specific items. Also, there are very detailed canning instructions.

Preserving by Freezing

Freezing will help to maintain the nutrients found in your fruits and vegetables (whereas, canning does not, with the exception of tomatoes). When you are freezing produce, the quicker it freezes, the better.

How to Freeze Berries

1. Wash your berries, and drain them well. Dry on paper towels.

2. Place the berries onto a wax paper lined cookie sheet (or directly on the cookie sheet if you don't have wax paper) so the berries are not touching each other. Put in the freezer until frozen; about 30 minutes.

3. Once the berries are frozen, transfer them to plastic bags and remove the air.

4. Frozen berries are great to use in baking and smoothies throughout the year.

By freezing the berries individually it keeps them from sticking together in a big clump. This way you can grab a handful at a time and measure them for making dressings, baking, smoothies etc. It is called IQF freezing; individually, quick frozen.

How to Freeze Peaches and Nectarines
Peaches and nectarines will turn brown when frozen unless you add an acid to them to prevent discoloration. I toss them in a small amount of lemon juice or make peach syrup for them before freezing to help prevent the discoloration.

How to Freeze Zucchini and Squash
You can shred or cut up zucchini or squash and then freeze it in plastic freezer bags. I bag up the shredded in 2 cup servings to make zucchini bread or use in soups year round. When you are ready to make zucchini bread, just take the shredded out of the freezer, let it thaw then drain the excess moisture, and make your bread. I cut up and freeze quart size baggies of zucchini to use in soups. For the chopped zucchini I use for soup, I drop the frozen zucchini into the soup when the soup is almost done and very hot or boiling. The zucchini does not take long to cook. Do not peel the zucchini.

How to Freeze Pumpkin
To freeze pumpkin, I cook the pumpkin and then puree it. I then let it cool on the counter and in the refrigerator. Once it has cooled, I take the pumpkin puree, and freeze it in containers in the amounts needed for my recipes.

How to Freeze Green Beans, Corn, Sugar Snaps, Asparagus, Peas
Before freezing these vegetables, they can be blanched, and then quickly cooled in an ice bath. (See terminology).

Most of the vegetables listed above are blanched for two minutes. You want the vegetable color to look brighter, but you still want the vegetable to be crisp. Here are the exceptions: Corn on the cob will be blanched for 6 minutes, and corn off the cob for 4 minutes. Sugar snaps and snow peas are delicate and only need to be blanched for 1 minute.

To blanch your vegetables, place them in boiling water (or a steamer basket for more retained nutrients) for the amount of time listed above. Have an ice water bath ready, and immediately place them into the ice water bath. Make sure that they are thoroughly cooled before freezing them. Drain and dry them well, and then transfer to freezer bags. Note: I have frozen green beans and corn both without blanching and they are fine.

How to Freeze Tomatoes
Tomatoes freeze great for soups and casseroles. I peel them and freeze them whole. You can freeze them with or without the peels. I prefer without the peels. You can also cut them into chunks. I freeze them in quart size freezer bags (which is perfect for a pot of soup and about the same amount of a can of tomatoes.) They make a great soup base for any vegetable or chili soup.

How to Peel Tomatoes
Pour boiling water over the tomatoes and count to 10 (or when the skins start to peel away from the tomato) and drain them. Finish peeling them. It is very easy this way just make sure the water is boiling.

How to Freeze Peppers and Onions
Wash peppers, dry well and dice. Freeze on single layers on baking sheets and put in freezer. When frozen transfer them to freezer bags. I also freeze banana peppers and jalapeño peppers whole and drop them into soups and chilies or use them to flavor fajita meat. For onions I do the same as peppers. For soups I put them directly into small pint size freezer bags.

Drying your Seeds
Save your clean seeds, dry them out and save them for next year's garden.

Freezing Herbs
All herbs freeze. Wash and dry the herbs on a paper towel. Chop up the herbs and lay out on a wax paper lined baking sheet. Freeze for 15 minutes. Put into freezer bags or glass jars. Herbs will keep for 1 year or more.

Drying Herbs
Wash and dry your herbs. Lay on paper towels until completely dry.
You can either hang them to dry or lay flat on a baking sheet. Grind when dried and store in air tight containers.

Apple Butter

Makes: 4 pints   Prep Time: 5 hours

3	pounds	apples, cored –not peeled
2 ½	cups	sugar
4	teaspoons	cinnamon
½	teaspoon	ground cloves
½	teaspoon	ground allspice

Layer in slow cooker and cook 4 hours on high. Press through strainer, juice and all. Fill prepared jars and process in hot water bath for 10 minutes.

Applesauce

Makes: 6 pints   Prep Time: 1 hour 15 minutes

5	pounds	apples, peeled, cored and cut into chunks.
½	cup	water
¼ -½	cup	granulated or brown sugar (amount of sugar depends on how sweet the apples are)
1	teaspoon	cinnamon

In large heavy saucepan, bring apples, water and sugar to a boil over medium heat, stirring occasionally. Reduce heat; simmer uncovered 5 to 10 minutes until tender. Stir occasionally to break up the apples. Stir in cinnamon; simmer on medium heat for 10-15 minutes until apples are soft. Remove from heat; cool for 10 minutes and puree in the food processor or blender to desired consistency. Can in a hot water bath for 15 minutes or store covered in refrigerator.

Apple Pear Blackberry Applesauce- Divide the 5 pounds of apples with pears; 1 pound of pears to 4 pounds of apples or 2 ½ pounds of each depending on what you have available. Follow the applesauce instructions adding 1 pint of blackberries (fresh or frozen) with the cinnamon. This is my grandkids favorite of all the applesauce's I make for them.
Blackberry Applesauce- Follow the applesauce instructions adding 1 pint of blackberries (fresh or frozen) with the cinnamon.
Raspberry Applesauce- Follow the applesauce instructions adding 1 pint of raspberries (fresh or frozen) with the cinnamon.

Blackberry Syrup

8	cups	blackberries, fresh, ripe
1½	cups	water
		sugar
1	tablespoon	lemon juice

Pick over, rinse and drain berries. Place them in a large heavy pot, and mash with a potato masher. Add the water. Bring the mixture to a boil over medium heat. Reduce the heat to low and simmer the berries for about 10 minutes; stirring occasionally.

Strain the berry mixture through a large sieve extracting as much juice as possible. Measure the juice into a clean, heavy pan. Add 1 cup of sugar for each cup of juice. Heat the mixture over medium heat stirring until sugar has dissolved. Increase heat to medium- high, and boil the mixture for 2-3 minutes. Remove the syrup from the heat and stir in lemon juice. If the syrup will be used within a few months, pour into clean, dry bottles or jars and store in the refrigerator. If it is to be kept longer, pour the boiling syrup into sterilized pint jars and process in a water bath for 15 minutes.

Red Raspberry Jam

4 pints berries to make 4 cups crushed berries (see instructions to prepare berries below)

4	cups	berries, crushed
6 ½	cups	sugar
1	pouch	Certo

Prepare berries- Crush berries with potato masher, 1 pint at a time. Sieve half of the pulp to remove some of the seeds, if desired.

Raspberry Jam recipe-Prepare jars and lids. Prepare fruit as requested above. Measure exact amount of prepared fruit into a 6-8 qt sauce pot; stir in the exact amount of sugar. Stir in ½ teaspoon butter to reduce foaming. Bring mixture to full rolling boil (a boil that does not stop bubbling when stirred) on high heat stirring constantly. Quickly stir in pectin. Return to a full boil and boil exactly 1 minute, stirring constantly. Remove from heat. Skim off foam with metal spoon. Ladle into prepared jars. Wipe jars and put on prepared lids. Put jars into water bath canner; cover, bring water to a gentle boil. Process jams 10 minutes. Let stand for 24 hours.

Blackberry Jam recipe-Use the same instructions for red raspberry jam except use 2 quarts of blackberries (to make 4 cups of crushed berries) and 7 cups of sugar. This will yield 8 cups or 5-6 pints.

Strawberry Jam recipe-use the same instructions for blackberry jam, except discard stems before crushing,

The secret to a perfect jam is in the fruit. You should always pick the fruit when it is perfectly ripe (neither under ripe nor over ripe).

Jalapeño Pepper Jelly

Makes: 7 pints   Prep Time: 2 hours

36	large	*jalapeños, seeded and chopped*
¾	cup	*apple juice*
¾	cup	*cider vinegar*
6	cups	*sugar*
2	pouches	*pectin, liquid (I like Certo)*
½	teaspoon	*butter*

Puree half the peppers with half the apple juice and half the vinegar. Repeat, strain and put through sieve; measure 3 ½ cups juice. If you don't get enough juice run apple juice or water over jalapeños and strain. Once you have made the juice put it into a large heavy saucepan. Stir in sugar. Add ½ teaspoon butter (to reduce foaming if desired). Bring mixture to full rolling boil on high heat, stirring constantly. Stir in pectin quickly. Return to full rolling boil and boil for 1 minute, stirring constantly. Remove from heat; skim off foam with metal spoon. Ladle quickly into prepared jars, filling to within $1/8$ inch of tops. Wipe jars and threads. Cover with lids and screw bands on tightly. Place jars in canner; cover and bring water to gentle boil, process for 5 minutes. Remove and let stand at room temperature for 24 hours.

This makes a great sauce for meatballs, chicken wings, and a wonderful glaze for salmon or roasted corned Beef Brisket.

Bread and Butter Pickles

Makes: 4 pints   Prep Time: 3 hours 30 minutes

12	medium	cucumbers
5	medium	onions
¼	cup	salt
1	cup	sugar
1 ½	teaspoons	mustard seed
1 ½	teaspoons	celery seed
½	teaspoon	ground cloves
1	cup	vinegar
½	cup	water

Wash cucumbers, slice to ¼ -½ inch thick. Peel onions and cut into ¼ inch rings. Arrange in layers. Sprinkle salt on each layer. Let stand 2-3 hours. Rinse and drain. Combine remaining ingredients and heat to boiling. Add cucumbers and onions and simmer 10 minutes. Pack in hot sterilized jars and seal; process in hot water bath for 10 minutes.

Dill Pickles

Makes: 6 pints   Prep Time: 1 hour

3	pounds	cucumbers, small pickling
4	cups	water
4	cups	white vinegar
½	cup	sugar
⅓	cup	pickling salt
6	tablespoons	dill seeds
1	cup	onions, sliced

Rinse cucumbers and cut off the ends. Slice into ¼-½ inch slices. In large heavy pot combine water, vinegar, sugar and pickling salt. Bring to a boil. Prepare jars. Pack cucumbers and onions loosely into the hot, pint jars, leaving ½ inch head space. Add 1 tablespoon dill seeds to each jar. Pour hot vinegar mixture into jars, leaving ½ inch head space. Wipe jars; top with lids. Process in water bath for 10 minutes (start time from when water returns to boiling). Remove jars; cool on racks. Let stand 1 week.

Zucchini Pickles

Makes: 2 quarts   Prep Time: 1 hour

Zucchini pickles are as delicious as cucumber pickles. You can follow your own favorite pickle recipe or the one below.

4	cups	zucchini, sliced
1	cup	onion, sliced thin
3	whole	garlic cloves
1	cup	white vinegar
½	cup	sugar
1	teaspoon	red pepper, crushed
¾	teaspoon	kosher salt

Combine the zucchini, onions and garlic together in canning jars. Bring the vinegar, sugar, red pepper and salt to a boil and pour over the zucchini mixture. Process these in a hot water bath like regular pickles or cover and chill 24 hours.

Garden Vegetable Spaghetti Sauce

Makes: 4-5 quarts or 13 pints   Prep Time: 4 hours

12	pounds	or about 25 ripe tomatoes, peeled
3	tablespoons	brown sugar
4	teaspoons	salt
1	teaspoon	pepper
2	cups	basil, fresh, chopped
1	cup	assorted herbs, fresh chopped (I suggest all or some of the following: parsley, oregano, marjoram, thyme). You can use ⅓ cup assorted dried if you don't have fresh.
6	cloves	minced fresh garlic
1	teaspoon	lemon juice
1-2	cups	zucchini, fresh, chopped
1	cup	onion, diced
1	cup	green pepper, diced

Cut peeled tomatoes into chunks. Put them through a hand-cranked strainer to get the seeds out. Put all the ingredients into a large heavy pot cooking on medium high uncovered until it reaches a steady boil. Continue to simmer on medium high at a steady low boil for about 2-3 hours until desired consistency, (you want it to be somewhat thick), stirring occasionally. Remove from heat and let cool for about 10 minutes. Process the sauce in a food processor or blender until desired consistency. I like to make mine smooth so the kids don't know that healthy vegetables are in it.

Ladle hot sauce into sterilized canning jars leaving ½ inch head space. Wipe jar rims; put on lids. Process filled jars in a boiling –water bath canner for 35 minutes for pint jars and 45 minutes for quart size jars. Start timing when water returns to boil. Remove jars and cool. Let set at room temperature for 24 hours.

Lemon Curd

Makes: 3 half pints   Prep Time: 30 minutes

4	teaspoons	lemon rind, grated
2/3	cup	lemon juice, bottled or fresh
5	whole	eggs
1	cup	sugar
½	cup	butter, melted

Prepare three ½ pint canning jars as directed for jam. Combine lemon peel, lemon juice, eggs and sugar in a blender. Whirl until well blended. With blender on lowest speed, gradually add butter in a thin stream. Transfer mixture to a small, heavy pan. Cook over low heat, approximately 6-8 minutes, stirring constantly, until mixture is thick enough to mound slightly when dropped from a spoon. Fill the prepared hot jars with lemon curd to within 1/8 inch of top rim. Wipe rims clean, top with hot lids, then firmly screw on rings. Process jars of lemon curd in a hot water bath for 15 minutes. Let cool on a towel, away from drafts. Store in a cool dry place for up to one year.

Orange Curd-Substitute orange for the lemon throughout the recipe.

Lemon Curd Tarts

Makes: 8 servings

Prep Time: 30 minutes

1	recipe	Lemon Curd (see recipe)
8	mini	tarts
½	pint	raspberries, fresh
8	sprigs	mint, fresh

Put curd in tarts and top with fresh raspberries. Put a sprig of mint on each for a garnish. Keep in the refrigerator until ready to serve.

Philadelphia Pepper Relish

Makes: 1 ½ quarts

Prep Time: 8-10 hours

1	cup	green pepper, minced
½	cup	red pepper, minced
3	cups	cabbage, minced
1	cup	celery, minced
2	tablespoons	salt
2	tablespoons	mustard seed
2	tablespoons	brown sugar
1½	cups	vinegar

Combine minced vegetables and salt and let stand overnight. Rinse and drain thoroughly. Add mustard seed and brown sugar to vinegar and heat to boiling. Pour over drained vegetables in jar. Cool. Serve within 3 days.

This recipe is for my Philly Friends; Sharon Jeffers and Barbara Taylor.

Zucchini Relish

10	cups	zucchini, ground or shredded, seeded, skin on
4	cups	onion, ground or shredded
5	tablespoons	salt
2-3	whole	red or green peppers
2 ¼	cups	apple cider vinegar
2 ½	cups	sugar
1	teaspoon	turmeric
1	teaspoon	dry mustard
1	teaspoon	cornstarch
2	teaspoons	celery seed
¼	teaspoon	black pepper

Shred or grind the zucchini, and onions; add salt. Let them set overnight in refrigerator. Drain and rinse the next morning. Grind or shred 2-3 bell peppers (I use 2 green and 1 red). Put all ingredients into a large heavy pot and bring to a boil. Fill prepared jars and process 15 minutes in a water bath for ½ pints and pints and 25-30 minutes for quarts. This recipe is from my mother-in-law, Mary Barnes. Once you try this you will never use another relish.

Pickled Beets

2	cups	sugar
2	cups	vinegar
2	cups	water
1	whole	lemon, sliced thin
1	tablespoon	cinnamon
1	teaspoon	cloves
1	teaspoon	allspice
6	pounds	raw beets

Boil the above ingredients (except beets) together for 15 minutes. See the following note on how to prepare the beets.

To prepare the beets: Wash the beets, and remove stems but don't cut off the ends or the beets will bleed. Boil in salted water (1 teaspoon salt to 1 pint of water) until tender; about 1 ½ hours. When knife goes through beets easily they are done. Cool, peel then slice. Pack into sterilized canning jars and ladle the spice vinegar over the beets leaving a ½ inch of head space. Wipe the rims clean with a damp cloth and put the lids on tight; process in a hot water bath for 15 minutes. Carefully remove the jars and set them in a cool dark place for up to 1 year. Refrigerate any jars that do not seal promptly and use them within a month.

Pickled Eggs- Put hard boiled eggs in a jar pour the pickled beet juice over the eggs and refrigerate overnight.

Salsa

Makes: 4 quarts   Prep Time: 3 hours

5	quarts (20 cups)	tomatoes, peeled, cut up
3	each	green peppers, diced
3	each	banana peppers diced, seeded (or jalapeños if you want spicy salsa)
3	each	onions, diced
½	teaspoon	hot pepper flakes (add extra if you like your salsa hot)
1	tablespoon	garlic, diced
1 ½	teaspoons	salt
½	cup	oil
½	cup	sugar
½	cup	vinegar (white or apple cider)
⅛	cup	cornstarch

Put peppers, onions, and garlic into a blender or food processor. Then put all ingredients but the cornstarch into a large heavy pot and simmer for 1 hour. (You can add a teaspoon of hot sauce if you like your salsa spicy.) Remove from heat and add the cornstarch. The cornstarch will thicken the salsa if you have watery tomatoes. If your sauce is thick enough with out it you can eliminate it. Fill jars and process pint jars for 35 minutes and 45 for quart jars.

Note: I add salsa to my chili. I also use it to make Shrimp Creole.

Tomato Bisque Soup

Makes: 4-5 half pints

Prep Time: 1 hour

4	cups	tomatoes fresh, peeled, seeded, cut into chunks
½	cup	basil, fresh, chopped
½	cup	sweet onion, diced
2	tablespoons	chicken base (to be added later)
1 ½	cups	half and half (to be added later)

Puree the tomatoes, basil and onion together in a blender or food processor. Cook on medium-high heat for 30 minutes; then simmer 15 minutes. Fill jars and process pint jars for 35 minutes and 45 minutes for quart jars. When you are ready to serve the soup, add the chicken base, half and half and heat it on the stove. Then sprinkle with Parmesan cheese or serve with croutons on top. This makes a wonderful fresh tasting soup.

Note: This recipe is easy to double, or triple which I would suggest you do.

Tomato Vegetable Juice

Makes: 7-8 quarts

Prep Time: 2 hours 30 minutes

10	pounds	tomatoes, peeled, chopped.
3	cloves	garlic, minced
2	large	onions, chopped
2	each	carrots, cut into slices
2	cups	chopped celery
¼	cup	green pepper, chopped
¼	cup	sugar
1	tablespoon	salt (optional)
1	teaspoon	Worcestershire sauce
½	teaspoon	pepper

Place all ingredients but sugar, salt, Worcestershire sauce and pepper into a large Dutch oven or soup pot and bring to a boil. Reduce heat and simmer 20 minutes or until vegetables are soft. Cool. Press through a food mill or fine sieve. Return to Dutch oven; add sugar, salt, Worcestershire sauce and pepper. Bring to a boil. Ladle hot juice into hot, sterilized quart jars, leaving ¼ inch head space. Make sure to put lids on tightly then process for 40 minutes in hot water bath. This is great to use as a soup base for vegetable soups and chili.

Desserts

Cakes
Blackberry Spice
Butter Pecan
Chocolate Mousse
Ginger Bread
Hershey's Double Chocolate
Hershey's Chocolate Frosting
Italian Cream
Orange Pecan Pound
Raisin Spice
Raspberry
Red Velvet
Strawberry

Cheesecakes
Caramel Apple
Cheesecake, Plain
Chocolate Chip
Lemon Raspberry
New York Style
Oreo
Pumpkin
Reeces Peanut Butter
Turtle

Cookies, Bars & Brownies
Baklava
Cherry Pinwheel Cookies
Chocolate Chip Crunch
Double Chocolate Chip
Espresso Brownies
Fudge Brownies
Gingerbread Cookies
Oatmeal Carmelitas
Oatmeal Cookies
No Bake Chocolate
Peanut Butter Cookies
Peanut Butter Rice Krispies
Pumpkin Bars
Quick Cookies
Raspberry Bars
Rhubarb Crunch
Sugar Cookies
The Ultimate Brownie
White Chocolate Cherry
Zucchini Brownies

Ice Cream and Sorbets
Blackberry or Rasberry Sorbet
Black Raspberry Sorbet
Lemon or Lime Sorbet
Mango Sorbet
Strawberry Ice Cream
Vanilla Ice Cream

Miscellaneous
Buckeyes
Chocolate Bread Pudding
Chocolate Dip Strawberries
Chocolate Sundae Brownie Trifle
Easy Chocolate Fudge
Frozen Cranberry Salad
Strawberry Shortcake Cups
White Chocolate Bread Pudding

Pies, Crisps and Cobblers
Apple Dumplings
Apple Pie
Blackberry Cobbler
Blackberry or Raspberry Pie
Berry Crisp
Chocolate Chip Pecan Pie
Coconut Cream Pie
Frosty Key Lime Pie
Frosty Orange Pie
Fruit Fillings:
  Blueberry
  Cherry
  Raspberry
Lemon Meringue Pie
Mini Blackberry Turnovers
Mixed Berry Cobbler
Peach Crisp
Peach Dumplings
Pumpkin Pie
Strawberry Pizza

Blackberry Spice Cake
Grandma Poyle's

Makes: 10-12 servings

Dry Ingredients

2	cups	sugar
3	cups	flour
1	teaspoon	baking powder
2	teaspoons	baking soda
2	teaspoons	cinnamon
2	teaspoons	nutmeg
1	teaspoon	cloves
1	teaspoon	all spice

Wet Ingredients

6	tablespoons	cream
5		egg yolks
1	cup	butter, softened
2	cups	blackberries, crushed
½	cup	milk
5	eggs	whites separated

Quick Butter Icing

3	cups	confectioners sugar
1	cup	butter, room temperature
1	teaspoon	vanilla
1-2	tablespoons	whipping cream

Batter-Mix the dry ingredients together. Mix wet ingredients together, except egg whites, and combine with the dry ingredients. Beat 5 egg whites and fold into mixture. Preheat oven to 350 degrees. Bake in a greased 9"x 13" pan for 30 minutes or until toothpick comes out clean or (2) 10" spring form pans and bake 40-50 minutes. When cool, frost with butter icing.

Icing-Mix together in a mixer, the sugar and butter. Mix on low speed until well blended and then increase speed to medium and beat for 3 more minutes. Add vanilla and cream and continue to beat on medium speed for 1 minute more; adding more cream for spreading consistency as needed.

Note: Keep in mind if you use frozen berries there will be more moisture so you may need to add a little more flour. This was my great grandmother's recipe. It is a beautiful color and very good.

TANGLEWOOD

Berry Farm

LOCALLY GROWN AT
2427 S. Hadley Road - Fort Wayne, IN 46804

USDA
ORGANIC

Certified Organic by OEFFA

Camille trellising the berries at the farm

Grandkids playing in the Berry Patch

Butter Pecan Cake

Makes: 12 servings

Prep Time: 1 hour

Batter

1	cup	butter, softened
2 2/3	cups	pecan pieces, toasted
2	cups	sugar
4	whole	eggs
2	teaspoons	vanilla
3	cups	flour
2	teaspoons	baking powder
½	teaspoon	salt
1	cup	milk

Frosting

11	ounces	cream cheese, softened
2/3	cup	butter, softened
6 ½	cups	powdered sugar
1	teaspoon	vanilla
2	tablespoons	milk

Place pecans on cookie sheet and bake in a preheated 350 degree oven for approximately 10 minutes until lightly toasted. Cool.

Batter-In a large mixing bowl, cream butter and sugar until light and fluffy. Add eggs one at a time, beating well after each addition. Beat in vanilla. Combine flour, baking powder and salt; add to creamed mixture alternately with milk. Beat just until combined. Fold in 2 cups of the toasted pecans. Pour batter into 3 greased 9" cake pans. Bake in a 350 degree preheated oven for 25-30 minutes or until toothpick inserted comes out clean. Cool for 10 minutes before removing from pans.

Frosting-In large bowl beat the cream cheese, butter, powdered sugar and vanilla. Beat in enough milk to achieve spreading consistency. Spread frosting between layers, sides and top of cake. Sprinkle top of cake with the remaining pecans. Refrigerate cake.

This is as impressive looking as it is delicious. I made this for mom's birthday and she loved it (but she loves Butter Pecan anything).

Chocolate Mousse Cake

Makes: 4 cups   Prep Time: 3 hours

1	pound	semi-sweet chocolate
2	cups	heavy whipping cream
¼	cup	confectioners sugar
2	whole	eggs
4	whole	egg yolks
4	whole	egg whites
1		chocolate cake

To make the mousse: 1) Melt the chocolate and cool to room temperature. 2) Whip the heavy cream with the confectioners sugar, set aside 3) Beat 2 whole eggs and the 4 egg yolks into the chocolate 4) Whip the egg whites until peaks 5) Add egg whites to the chocolate until smooth 6) Add the cream mixture to the chocolate. Let the mousse set up in the refrigerator until it thickens; about 1-2 hours.

Put the mousse in between layers of your favorite chocolate cake or see recipe for *Hershey's chocolate cake and Chocolate frosting*. I like to put fresh raspberries on top of the mousse in between layers. This mousse is also great served in chocolate cups with fresh berries and a sprig of mint on top.

Gingerbread Cake

Makes: 12 servings   Prep Time: 45 minutes

⅓	cup	butter, cut into small pieces
⅔	cup	hot water
1	cup	light or dark molasses
1	large	egg
2 ¾	cups	flour
1 ½	teaspoons	soda
1 ½	teaspoons	ground ginger
1	teaspoon	cinnamon
½	teaspoon	salt
¼	teaspoon	cloves
		cooking spray
1 ½	cups	powdered sugar
		whipped cream

Preheat oven to 350 degrees. Combine butter and hot water in large bowl, stirring until the butter melts. Add molasses and egg, and stir until blended. Combine flour, soda, ginger, cinnamon, salt and cloves. Add flour mixture to the molasses mixture stirring just until moist. Spoon batter into a 9" cake pan coated with spray. Bake at 350 degrees for 30 minutes until toothpick comes out clean. Serve warm or room temperature with whipped cream and a sprinkle of cinnamon.

Hershey's Double Chocolate Cake

Makes: Two 9" cakes   Prep Time: 45 minutes

2	cups	sugar
1¾	cups	flour
¾	cup	Hershey's Cocoa, unsweetened
1 ½	teaspoons	baking powder
1 ½	teaspoons	baking soda
1	teaspoon	salt
2	large	eggs
1	cup	milk
½	cup	canola or vegetable oil
2	teaspoons	vanilla
1	cup	boiling water
6	ounces	semi-sweet chocolate chips

Preheat the oven to 350 degrees. Grease and flour two-9" round cake pans. Combine dry ingredients in large bowl. Add eggs, milk, oil and vanilla; beat on medium speed for 2 minutes. Stir in boiling water (batter will be thin). Stir in chocolate chips. Pour into pans. Bake 30-35 minutes until toothpick comes out clean. Cool completely then frost with Hershey's Chocolate Frosting (see recipe).

This is a very good and easy chocolate cake. I like to decorate it with strawberries or raspberries on top. I made this for my Brother Rick's 40th birthday with fresh raspberries on top and it was a big hit!

Hershey's Chocolate Frosting

Makes: 2 cups   Prep Time: 15 minutes

½	cup	butter
⅔	cup	Hershey's Cocoa
3	cups	powdered sugar
⅓	cup	milk
1	teaspoon	vanilla

Melt butter, stir in cocoa. Alternately add powdered sugar and milk, beating on medium speed to spreading consistency. Add more milk if needed. Stir in vanilla.
Garnish-You can add chocolate covered strawberries on top or you can sprinkle chocolate shavings or chocolate chips on top.

Italian Cream Cake

Makes: Two 9" cakes   Prep Time: 45 minutes

Cake Batter

1	cup	buttermilk
1	teaspoon	baking soda
5	whole	eggs, separated
2	cups	sugar
¼	pound	butter, softened
½	cup	canola oil
2	cups	flour
1	teaspoon	vanilla
1	cup	pecans, chopped
3 ½	ounces	coconut, canned

Frosting

8	ounces	cream cheese, softened
¼	pound	butter, room temperature
1	pound box	confectioners sugar
1	teaspoon	vanilla

Batter- Preheat the oven to 325 degrees. Combine soda and buttermilk; let stand a few minutes. Beat egg whites until stiff. Cream the sugar, butter and canola oil. Add egg yolks one at a time, beating well after each addition. Add buttermilk alternately with flour to creamed mixture. Stir in vanilla. Fold in egg whites gently. Stir in pecans and coconut. Bake in two-9" greased and floured cake pans. Bake 20-30 minutes or until cake tests done.

Frosting-Mix cream cheese and butter well and add vanilla. Beat in sugar a little at a time, until of spreading consistency. Optional: toast coconut and pecans for sprinkles.

Orange Pecan Pound Cake

Makes: 12-16 servings   Prep Time: 2 hours

Batter

1½	cups	butter, softened
8	ounces	cream cheese, softened
3	cups	sugar
6	large	eggs
3	cups	flour
¼	cup	orange juice
2	teaspoons	orange zest
1 ½	teaspoons	vanilla
1 ½	cups	pecans, chopped

Glaze

¼	cup	powdered sugar
3	tablespoons	orange juice
½	teaspoon	vanilla

Beat the butter and cream cheese at medium speed with an electric mixer about 2 minutes or until creamy. Gradually add sugar, beating 5 minutes. Add eggs, 1 at a time, beating until yellow disappears. Add flour to butter mixture alternately with orange juice, beginning and ending with flour. Beat at low speed just until blended after each addition. Stir in vanilla, zest and pecans. Pour batter into a sprayed 10 inch bunt pan. Bake in a preheated 325 degrees oven for 1 hour and 30 minutes or until tooth pick comes out clean. Cool in pan 15 minutes. Remove from pan and cool completely. When cake is cooled you can glaze with the following glaze recipe if desired. Mix glaze ingredients until smooth.

Raisin Spice Cake
Sometimes called Depression Cake

Makes: 6-8 servings

Prep Time: 1 hour 15 minutes

Batter

1	cup	raisins
1	cup	brown sugar
1	cup	water
½	cup	butter
1	teaspoon	cinnamon
1	teaspoon	nutmeg
1	teaspoon	cloves
1½	cups	flour
1	teaspoon	soda
½	teaspoon	salt
½	cup	walnuts, chopped, if desired

Glaze

¼	cup	powdered sugar
3	tablespoons	milk
½	teaspoon	vanilla

Batter-Combine raisins, sugar, water, butter, and spices; bring to a boil for 2 minutes then cool. Mix the remaining dry ingredients in a separate bowl then add to raisin mixture. Pour into a 9" tube or square pan then bake in a preheated 300 degree oven 50-60 minutes or until cake tests done. For a nice presentation (like for a birthday) I make a double recipe and bake in a bunt pan. It bakes the same amount of time. Then I drizzle with glaze.

Glaze-mix the ingredients until smooth. Drizzle with glaze when cake is half way cooled.

This recipe tastes like the old A&P Raisin cake from years ago. This is my Dad's favorite cake which I make for his birthday every year.

Raspberry Cake

Batter

1	package	white cake mix
1	10 ounce package	package frozen red raspberries or fresh raspberries, divided
3	tablespoons	flour
1	small package	raspberry gelatin (not sugar free)
½	cup	cold water
1	cup	vegetable oil
4	large	eggs

Icing

1	stick	butter
1	pound	powdered sugar
½	remaining package	red raspberries, thawed

Batter-Preheat the oven to 350 degrees. Grease two 9" cake pans. In a large bowl mix the dry ingredients. Add alternately oil, water and eggs one at a time (do not over beat). Break up ½ package of frozen raspberries (saving other ½ for icing) and stir into batter. Bake at 350 degrees for 30 to 35 minutes or until golden and the center springs back when touched.

Icing- Mix together all ingredients in a bowl and whip with mixer until well blended and spread-able consistency. Be sure cake is cool or even refrigerate until cold before icing between layers, top and sides of cake. Keep cool so icing will set.

This recipe is from my sister-in-law, Betty Oakes' friend Marilyn Vandentop who found the recipe in a book by Gloria Gaither. Gloria's mother, Dorothy Sickal passed this recipe down to Gloria. This recipe has been the number one cake recipe in their family for years and is enjoyed now by grandchildren and great grandchildren. Gloria's daughter Suzanne loved it so much she chose this recipe for her wedding cake. We love raspberries (of course since we have a raspberry farm) so whenever I find a good raspberry recipe I ask the owner to share. Marilyn was kind enough to do so. Thanks Marilyn and thanks to Gloria for sharing this recipe in your book for us to enjoy!

Red Velvet Cake

Makes: 12 Servings

Prep Time: 1 hour

Batter

½	cup	Crisco
1½	cups	sugar
2	large	eggs
1	cup	buttermilk
1	bottle	red food coloring
1	teaspoon	vanilla
3	tablespoons	Cocoa
2	cups	flour
1	teaspoon	soda
1	tablespoon	vinegar

Frosting

¼	cup	flour
1	cup	whole milk
1	cup	sugar
¾	cup	Crisco
½	teaspoon	salt
2	teaspoons	vanilla

Spray two-9" cake pans and bake at 350 degrees for 30 minutes.

Batter-Cream the Crisco and sugar. Mix in remaining ingredients.

Frosting-Heat the milk on low heat and add whisk in the flour. Whisk constantly until thickens then allow to cool. Cream the sugar, Crisco, salt and vanilla with mixer or food processor. Add cooled flour and milk mixture.

Allow cake and frosting to cool. Cut the two-9" cakes in half with a cake knife or dental floss to make 4 layers. Frost each layer and stack. You can decorate the cake with fresh strawberries, raspberries or edible flowers. This is a beautiful and delicious cake and perfect for Valentine's Day or a bridal shower cake made into a tiered cake. I like to use the White Chocolate Cream Cheese Frosting recipe as an alternative to the above.

My sister-in-law, Karen Gorrell, makes this recipe the best and it is my husband's favorite cake. Karen invited us to dinner one Friday in September when we first started dating. Rich told Karen it was my birthday and I loved Red Cake. So Karen made a Red Cake. I was confused when they started singing Happy Birthday to me since my birthday is in July. We still laugh about him tricking her into making this Red Cake.

White Chocolate Cream Cheese Frosting

Makes: 2 cups frosting   Prep Time: 15 minutes

1½	pounds	cream cheese, softened
1½	cups	butter, softened
18	ounces	white chocolate, melted and cooled

Whip cream cheese and butter until fluffy. Add white chocolate, whip until smooth. This goes great on red cake.

Strawberry Cake

Makes: 12 servings   Prep Time: 45 minutes

Batter

1 ½	cups	fresh sliced strawberries
2 ¼	cups	flour
2 ¼	teaspoons	baking powder
⅛	teaspoon	salt
1½	cups	sugar
½	cup	butter, softened
2	large	eggs
1	cup	buttermilk

Frosting

3	ounces	cream cheese, softened at room temperature
⅓	cup	butter, softened
2	tablespoons	orange juice
3	cups	powdered sugar
12	whole	strawberries

Batter-Preheat oven to 350 degrees. Mix softened butter with sugar and salt. Add eggs and beat. Stir in flour and baking powder. Add buttermilk and mix well. Puree or mash well, strawberries and add to cake mixture; mix until strawberries are blended into batter. Pour cake batter into (2) sprayed 8" cake pans or a 9"x 13" pan. Bake 25-30 minutes or until toothpick comes out clean. Cool and frost. Note: You can bake in a 9" spring form pan for 50-55 minutes.

Frosting-Place cream cheese, butter and orange juice in medium bowl; beat with mixer until blended. Gradually add powdered sugar, and beat just until blended. Garnish frosted cake with berries.

Cheesecakes

The house made cheesecakes were the most popular dessert at Margy's Café. We always had a variety on hand made with fresh, seasonal fruits, chocolates, candies and nuts. The cheesecake base begins with the regular cheesecake recipe and builds from there. I have included some of the most popular recipes from Margy's Café, but get creative and come up with your own using your favorite ingredients.

You will notice varying baking times with the cheesecake recipes. It is for a few reasons; 1) whether you use a 9" or 10" spring form pan 2) ovens bake differently 3) the amount of ingredients you use. Bottom line is you want to make sure the cheesecake does not jiggle in the center when you move the pan. If the cheesecake cracks it is done (try not to let it get to that point.) To keep the cheesecake from cracking I place a pan of water in the lower rack of the oven while it bakes in the center of the oven.

Caramel Apple Cheesecake

Makes: 12-16 servings   Prep Time: 8 hours

Crust

2	cups	vanilla wafer cookie crumbs (put vanilla wafers in the food processor)
6	tablespoons	butter, melted

Filling

1	pound	caramel candies
¾	cup	evaporated milk
1 ¼	cups	pecans, coarsely chopped
3	pounds	cream cheese at room temperature
3	whole	eggs
2	cups	sugar
1	teaspoon	vanilla

Topping

4	cups	apples, thin sliced
1/3	cup	sugar
½	teaspoons	cinnamon
½	cup	pecans, chopped

Crust- Preheat oven to 350 degrees. Combine butter and wafer crumbs and pat into bottom and 1 inch up the sides of a 9" or 10" spring form pan. Bake for 5 minutes. Remove pan and set aside. Turn oven temperature down to 325 degrees.

Filling-Place caramel candies and evaporated milk in a heavy saucepan and cook over medium-high heat stirring occasionally, until caramels are melted. Pour melted caramels over wafer crust. Sprinkle pecans over caramel. Set aside. Mix 3 pounds of room temperature cream cheese with 3 eggs, 2 cups of sugar and 1 teaspoon of vanilla in the food processor until smooth and well blended. Pour cream cheese mixture over caramel mixture.

Topping-Toss apple slices with sugar and cinnamon. Place coated apple slices neatly over filling (I make a fan shaped pattern to make it pretty) and then sprinkle with pecans. Bake at 325 degrees for 2 ½ to 3 ½ hours (depends on the size of pan you use and your oven) until the center does not jiggle. If it needs to bake longer check it at 15 minute intervals. Cool at room temperature for 2 hours and then refrigerate for 4-6 hours or overnight. This recipe was high on the list of popularity and my daughter, Candas' favorite.

Cheesecake

Makes: 12-16 servings   Prep Time: 4 hours

3	pounds	cream cheese, softened
2	cups	sugar
3	whole	eggs
2	cups	graham cracker or cookie crumbs, like chocolate or vanilla wafer
½	cup	butter, melted

Filling-Put cream cheese in food processor, add eggs and sugar. Blend until smooth. Add whatever flavoring you like; vanilla, almond, etc.

Crust-Combine butter and crumbs. Press over bottom and sides of a 9" spring form pan. Refrigerate.

Bake-Pour the filling into the crust and bake at 275 degrees for 2 ½ -3 hours or until the top does not jiggle or it starts to crack. Let cool at room temperature for at least 2 hours before refrigerating. Refrigerate for about 8 hours before serving.

Chocolate Chip Cheesecake

Makes: 12-16 servings   Prep Time: 8 hours

3	pounds	cream cheese, softened
1 ½	cups	sugar
3	whole	eggs
12	ounces (2 cups)	chocolate chips
1	box	brownie mix
¼	pound	butter

Melt butter and add to dry brownie mix. Spray a 9" or 10" spring form pan. Pat the brownie mixture in the bottom and as far up the sides of the pan as you can. Bake the crust for 15 minutes in a preheated 350 degree oven. Let cool. Put cream cheese, eggs and sugar into food processor and mix until smooth. Stir in the chocolate chips by hand into the cream cheese mixture. Bake at 275 degrees for 3 hours. If the center jiggles when you shake the pan, it is not done. Put back into the oven for 15 minute intervals until done. You can use low fat cream cheese for this recipe but not fat free.

This cheesecake was also very popular at the restaurant. Larry Kreigh used to make a special trip in from Ossian, Indiana, to get this cheesecake, so I finally gave him the recipe so he did not have to drive so much. Enjoy!

Lemon Raspberry Cheesecake

Makes: 12-16 servings   Prep Time: 12 hours

Crust

¾	stick	butter, melted
8	ounces	lemon cookie crumbs

Filling

3	pounds	cream cheese, room temperature
2	cups	sugar
3	whole	eggs
2	whole	lemons, juiced
2	half pints	raspberries, fresh or frozen

Crust - Mix together the butter and cookies. Put the crust mixture in a sprayed 10" spring form pan. Bake 350 for 10 minutes.

Filling-Put all of the filling ingredients together in a food processor (except the raspberries) and mix until creamy. Add the raspberries and mix by hand just until the berries are incorporated.

Bake-Pour the filling into the crust and bake at 225 degrees for 3 hours or until the top does not jiggle or it starts to crack. Let cool at room temperature for at least 2 hours before refrigerating. Refrigerate for about 8 hours before serving.

New York Style Cheesecake

Makes: 12 servings   Prep Time: 2 hours

32	ounces	cream cheese, softened to room temperature
2	cups	graham cracker crumbs
½	cup	butter, melted
1 ½	cups	sugar
3	tablespoons	flour
2	tablespoons	lemon juice
2	tablespoons	orange zest
6	whole	eggs
1	cup	sour cream

Combine butter and graham cracker crumbs. Press over bottom and side of 9" spring form pan. Refrigerate. Pre-heat oven to 400 degrees. In a large bowl, mix cream cheese on medium speed until smooth. Beat in sugar, ¼ cup at a time. Beat in flour, lemon juice and zest. Beat until mixture is high and fluffy. Add eggs, one at a time, beat until fluffy. Beat in sour cream just until combined. Pour into crust. Bake at 400 degrees for 10 minutes then at 300 degrees for 1 hour and 15 minutes. Turn oven off and leave cake in oven for 30 minutes. Refrigerate. Carefully loosen crust around edge. Release spring form and remove sides. Top with the cherry or blueberry pie filling (see recipe).

This fabulous recipe is from Grandma Virginia and is my favorite! The New York cheesecake is more dense than the regular cheesecake. You certainly can add chocolate chips or a variety of your favorite ingredients but this one I prefer topped with the cherry filling.

Pumpkin Cheesecake

Makes: 12-16 servings

Prep Time: 8 hours

Crust

32		gingersnap cookies, crushed in food processor
3	tablespoons	brown sugar
6	tablespoons	butter, melted
¾	cup	toasted pecans, chopped, if desired (grind with gingersnap cookies)

Filling

3	pounds	cream cheese, softened at room temperature
2	cups	sugar
3	whole	eggs
1 to 1 ½	cups	canned pure pumpkin (not pumpkin pie filling)
1 ¾	teaspoons	pumpkin pie spices or
1	teaspoon	cinnamon
¼	teaspoon	ground ginger
¼	teaspoon	nutmeg
¼	teaspoon	cloves

Pecan Topping

6	tablespoons	butter, softened
1	cup	brown sugar, packed
1	cup	pecans, chopped

Crust-Mix all the crust ingredients together and press into the bottom and 1 inch up the sides of a 10" sprayed, spring form pan. Set aside.

Filling-Put cream cheese in food processor or mixer; add eggs and sugar. Blend until smooth. Add pumpkin and spices; blend into cheese mixture. Pour filling into crust and bake at 225 degrees for 2 hours and 275 degrees for 1 hour. If the center jiggles when you shake the pan it is not done. Put back into the oven for 15 minute intervals until done. You can use low fat cream cheese for this recipe but not fat free. Place a pan filled with 1 inch of water on bottom shelf of oven while baking to keep the cheesecake from cracking.

Topping-In small bowl combine the butter and the brown sugar. Stir in nuts. Sprinkle over hot cheesecake the last 30 minutes of baking time.

When the cheesecake is done the center will not jiggle. Cool cheesecake for 2-3 hours at room temperature and then refrigerate overnight before cutting.

My brother Jim was a Thanksgiving baby so he gets this as his birthday cake from me every year.

Note: You can make a half recipe extra of the ginger crust and add to the top of the cheesecake before baking instead of the pecan topping. It makes a pretty presentation and a delicious topping. As an alternative you can make a sour cream topping by mixing 2 cups sour cream with 3 tablespoons of sugar and 1 teaspoon of vanilla. Add to cheesecake the last 15 minutes of baking. When cooled sprinkle with toasted pecans.

Reese's Peanut Butter Cheesecake

Makes: 12-16 servings   Prep Time: 8 hours

3	pounds	cream cheese, softened
1 ½	cups	sugar
3	whole	eggs
2	cups	Reese's peanut butter cups, chopped
1	box	brownie mix
¼	pound	butter

Melt butter and add to dry brownie mix. Spray a 9" or 10" spring form pan. Pat the brownie mixture in the bottom and as far up the sides of the pan as you can. Bake the crust for 15 minutes in a preheated 350 degree oven. Let cool. Put cream cheese, eggs and sugar into food processor and mix until smooth. Stir in the Reese's peanut butter cups by hand into the cream cheese mixture. Bake at 275 degrees for 3 hours. If the center jiggles when you shake the pan it is not done. Put back into the oven for 15 minute intervals until done. You can use low fat cream cheese for this recipe but not fat free.

This is my daughter Camille's birthday request every year.

Oreo Cheesecake-substitute the Reese cups with crushed Oreo cookies.

Turtle Cheesecake

2	cups	chocolate or vanilla wafer crumbs
6	tablespoons	butter, melted
14	ounce bag	caramel candies
5 1/3	ounces	can evaporated milk
1½	cup	pecans, chopped, toasted
3	pounds	cream cheese, softened
1½	cups	sugar
3		eggs
1	cup	chocolate chips, melted

Add crumbs to butter. Spray a 9" or 10" spring form pan. Pat the crumb mixture in the bottom and as far up the sides of the pan as you can. Bake the crust for 10 minutes in a preheated 350 degree oven. Melt caramels in milk in heavy saucepan over low heat, stirring frequently until smooth. Pour over crust. Top with 1 cup of pecans. Combine cream cheese, sugar and eggs until smooth. Blend in melted chocolate and pour cream cheese mixture over pecans. Bake at 275 degrees for 3 hours for a 9" pan. Check at 2 ½ hours for a 10" pan. If the center jiggles when you shake the pan it is not done. Put back into the oven for 15 minute intervals until done. You can use low fat cream cheese for this recipe but not fat free. Garnish with remaining pecans.

This is *Ginger Girl's* favorite cheesecake. Ginger is my longtime friend and was the front desk manager/bookkeeper at the Café.

Baklava

12	ounces	walnuts, finely chopped
4	ounces	pecans, finely chopped
½	cup	sugar
1	teaspoon	cinnamon
16	ounces	Phyllo dough, thawed according to package
1	cup	butter, melted
16	ounces	honey
1	teaspoon	lemon juice

1) In large bowl, mix nuts, sugar and cinnamon and set aside.

2) Cut Phyllo into 9"x 13" rectangles. In greased 9"x 13" baking dish, place 1 Phyllo sheet; brush with melted butter. Repeat with Phyllo and butter to make 5 more layers.

3) Sprinkle 1 cup nut mixture over Phyllo in baking dish.

4) Repeat steps 2 and 3 to make 3 more layers (4 layers total). Place remaining Phyllo on top of last walnut layer; brush with butter.

5) With sharp knife, cut just half way through layers in triangle pattern to make 24 large servings or 60 small servings.

6) Bake in 300 degree oven (preheated) for 1 hour and 25 minutes or until top is golden brown. Since oven temperatures vary, check at 45 minutes. Look for top to be golden brown.

7) In small sauce pan or microwave, heat honey and lemon juice until hot, not boiling. Evenly spoon hot honey over Baklava.

8) Cool Baklava in dish at least 1 hour. Cover with foil and let stand at room temperature until ready to serve.

9) Finish cutting all the way through.

Note: Phyllo dries out quickly when the air hits it so I keep the phyllo covered with wet paper towels while working with it. Pull a sheet from under the wet towels one at a time. The longer this sets the better it gets. This will keep at room temperature for more than a week. It also makes great Christmas gifts. I buy cute boxes, line them with wax paper and fill with Baklava. They are always well received and are my mother's favorite.

We used to have a wonderful bakery/restaurant called Zoli's which was around for years. We bought our Baklava, specialty cakes (my parents 25th wedding anniversary cake) and baked goods from Zoli's. When Zoli passed away I had to learn to make my own Baklava. His daughter was kind enough to give me some tips for this recipe. It is still not quite as good as Zoli's but I do get rave reviews and lots of requests for seconds.

Cherry Pinwheel Cookies

Makes: 2 dozen cookies

Prep Time: 5 hours

2 ½	cups	flour
½	teaspoon	salt
½	teaspoon	baking powder
1	cup	butter, unsalted, softened
1	cup	sugar
1	whole	egg
½	teaspoon	vanilla
1	teaspoon	cherry extract (can use peppermint if prefer)
1	teaspoon	red food coloring
		Powdered sugar to roll out dough
24		lollipop sticks

Sift together, flour, salt and baking powder and set aside. Cream the butter and sugar together in large bowl. Add egg and beat in. Add vanilla and cherry extract. Gradually add the dry mixture, beating until combined. Remove half the mixture from the bowl. Add food coloring, beat until fully combined. In waxed paper, roll out dough to form a large rectangle about ¼ inch thick. Repeat this step with the other half of uncolored dough. Refrigerate for 2 hours.

Tear out 1 sheet of waxed paper. Sprinkle with powdered sugar to prevent sticking. Carefully slide the red dough on top of the white dough. Trim edges if uneven. Roll dough into a log, creating a swirl effect. Place the dough back in the refrigerator and chill 2 hours.

Preheat the oven to 375 degrees. Slice the dough into ½ inch slices and place on a parchment lined baking sheet about 1 inch apart. Place lollipop stick about 1 inch through the flat side of the dough. Bake 8-10 minutes. Remove from oven and let cool.
These are easier then what they sound and are really cute.

For Christmas dinner I wrap the lollipop part of the cookie in a clear plastic goodie bag and tie a ribbon around it with a name tag and use them as the kids place card at the table.

Chocolate Chip Crunch Bars

Makes: 12 bars

½	cup	sugar
½	cup	brown sugar
1	cup	butter, softened
2	large	eggs
¼	cup	canola or vegetable oil
1	teaspoon	vanilla
1¼	cups	flour
1½	cups	oats
1	teaspoon	soda
12	ounces	chocolate chips

Cream the butter with sugars. Add eggs one at a time mixing well after each egg. Add oil and vanilla. In a separate bowl mix the dry ingredients and then add to the wet sugar mixture. Add chocolate chips. Bake in a greased 9" x 13" pan in a 350 degree preheated oven for 25-30 minutes.

Double Chocolate Chip Cookies

Makes: 36 cookies

Prep Time: 25 minutes

3 ¼	cups	flour
1	teaspoon	baking soda
1	cup	butter, softened
¾	cup	sugar
¾	cup	brown sugar
2	teaspoons	vanilla (pure)
2	large	eggs
12	ounces	semi-sweet chocolate chips
8	ounces	chocolate, cut into large pieces
¾	cup	pecans, chopped

Cream the butter and sugars. Add eggs and vanilla. Combine dry ingredients and add to butter mixture. Stir in chocolates and nuts; bake at 350 degrees for 9-12 minutes or until lightly browned.

Espresso Brownies

Makes: 9-12 brownies

Prep Time: 1 hour

4	ounces	dark chocolate, unsweetened, chopped
½	cup (1 stick)	butter, unsalted, cubed
2	tablespoon	cocoa powder
1	tablespoon	instant espresso or coffee granules
1 ½	cups	sugar
1	teaspoon	vanilla
¼	teaspoon	salt
3	large	eggs
1	cup	flour
¾	cup	walnut or pecan pieces

Melt chocolate, butter, cocoa and coffee together. Stir in sugar, vanilla, eggs and salt. Fold in flour and nuts. Preheat oven to 350 and coat an 8" pan with nonstick spray. Melt chocolate, butter, cocoa powder, and coffee in a bowl in a microwave, stirring every 30 seconds (or in a heavy saucepan over low heat). Remove when chocolate is nearly melted and stir until totally smooth. Stir in sugar, vanilla and salt. Add eggs one at a time, blending well after each. Fold in flour and nuts. Spread batter evenly in prepared pan and bake 30-40 minutes. Cool completely before cutting.

Baking tips: Test the brownies after the minimum amount of time is up. If the toothpick comes out wet and gooey, continue baking, checking every 5 minutes. When it comes out with moist crumbs attached their done.

Fudge Brownies

Makes: 12-15 brownies

Prep Time: 45 minutes

Batter

½	cup	butter
1	cup	sugar
4	large	eggs
1	cup	Hershey's Chocolate Syrup
1	cup	flour
1 ½	cups	walnuts, chopped
½	teaspoon	vanilla or almond extract.

Frosting

1	cup	sugar
¼	cup	milk
2	tablespoons	butter
1	cup	chocolate chips
½	teaspoon	vanilla or almond extract

Batter- Mix the butter, sugar, eggs, chocolate syrup, extract, flour and walnuts. Pour into a sprayed 9" x 13" pan. Bake at 350 for 30-35 minutes. Cool.

Frosting-Boil the sugar and milk. Remove from heat and add butter, extract and chocolate chips. Stir until chocolate is melted and frosting is creamy. Frost when brownies and frosting are both cooled. This is the brownie recipe I grew up with which is very easy. I believe it came from Hershey's.

Gingerbread Cookies

Makes: 60 large cookies   Prep Time: 30 minutes

4	cups	flour
1	tablespoon	ginger
2	teaspoons	cinnamon
½	teaspoon	nutmeg
½	teaspoon	cloves
½	teaspoon	baking soda
½	pound	butter
⅔	cup	brown sugar
2	large	eggs
⅔	cup	molasses

Add the dry ingredients (except sugar) in a mixing bowl and stir to combine. Beat the sugar and butter with mixer and add eggs one at a time. Add molasses. Beat in flour. Chill the dough for at least 30 minutes. Roll the dough and cut out cookies. Bake at 350 degrees for about 10 minutes until firm when pressed with fingertip. Decorate when cooled.

These cookies are awesome; the dough is very easy to work with and freezes great.
I make decorated miniature gingerbread boys and girls for the kids every year. I also make large ones with holes in the top and ribbon run through them to use as Christmas tree ornaments. I find that kids really like them if you put their names on them. I then wrap them in a clear goodie bag with a ribbon or raffia tied around it which makes a nice gift especially included in a gift basket.

Oatmeal Carmelita's

Crust

2	cups	flour
2	cups	quick cooking oats
1 ½	cups	brown sugar, packed
1	teaspoon	baking soda
½	teaspoon	salt
1¼	cups	butter, softened

Filling

1	cup (12.5 ounce jar)	caramel ice cream topping
3	tablespoons	flour
1	cup	chocolate chips, semi-sweet
½	cup	nuts, chopped

Heat oven to 350 degrees and grease a 9" x 13" pan. In large bowl, blend all crust ingredients at low speed until crumbly. Press ½ the mixture in bottom of greased pan; reserve the rest for the topping. Bake for 10 minutes at 350. Meanwhile in small bowl, combine caramel topping and 3 tablespoons flour. Remove partially baked crust from oven; sprinkle with chocolate chips and nuts. Drizzle evenly with caramel mixture; sprinkle with reserved crumb mixture. Bake at 350 for an additional 18-22 minutes or until golden brown. Cool completely. Refrigerate 1-2 hours until filling is set.

These were very popular at the restaurant and would sell out as soon as they came out of the oven.

The Best Oatmeal Cookies Ever!
Grandma Virginia's Recipe

1	cup	butter, softened
1	cup	brown sugar
2	large	eggs, beaten
2	cups	flour
1	teaspoon	soda
1	teaspoon	baking powder
1	teaspoon	vanilla
1	cup	coconut
½	cup	walnuts or pecans, chopped
3	cups	oats
½	cup	raisins or cranberries

Preheat oven to 375. Cream the butter and sugar; add eggs. Mix dry ingredients together; add to sugar/egg mixture. Add vanilla, raisins, coconuts and oats. Drop by tablespoon onto a greased cookie sheet. Bake at 375 degrees for 8-10 minutes or until golden brown. Larger cookies will take about 2-3 minutes longer.

No Bake Chocolate Cookies

2	cups	sugar
4	tablespoons	cocoa
½	cup	butter
1	teaspoon	vanilla
½	cup	milk
1	cup	peanut butter
3	cups	oats

Boil sugar, cocoa, butter, vanilla and milk for 1 minute. Add peanut butter and oats. Mix and drop by tablespoons on wax paper and refrigerate until sets up.

These are a great summer time cookie because you don't have to heat up the kitchen to bake them. My mom made these for us a lot in the summer for this reason.

Peanut Butter Cookies

Makes: 2-3 dozen

Prep Time: 20 minutes

1	cup	butter, unsalted, softened
1	cup	sugar
1	cup	brown sugar
2	large	eggs
1	teaspoon	vanilla
1	cup	peanut butter
3	cups	flour
2	teaspoons	baking soda
1	cup	peanuts, dry roasted, unsalted

Cream the butter, sugar, eggs and vanilla. Add peanut butter. Add dry ingredients and peanuts. Bake 2 inches apart on sprayed cookie sheet for 8-10 minutes in preheated 350 degree oven.

Note: I make a large batch and roll the dough into a log on a sprayed piece of plastic wrap and freeze it until I am ready to use it. Wrapped well it will keep in the freezer for 2 months. To defrost set out at room temperature for about an hour. Then slice and bake.

Peanut Butter Rice Krispie Treats

Makes: 12-15 pieces

Prep Time: 20 minutes

6	tablespoons	butter
2	10 ounce pkgs	marshmallows (or 80 large marshmallows)
2	cups	peanut butter
12	cups	Rice Krispies
6	ounces	chocolate chips

This makes a large batch because I like my Krispie treats to be thick. This recipe will fill a 9" x 13" pan to the top. You can halve this recipe if you like but most likely you will have to make it in 2 batches if you go for the full recipe. I always spray my spoon with Pam which is easier to mix these sticky ingredients. Melt butter with marshmallows. Stir in peanut butter, mix in Rice Krispies. Put in bottom of sprayed 9" x 13" pan. Drizzle 6 ounces of melted chocolate on top. If desired, you can add sprinkles on top while chocolate are still wet. These are a favorite at our family Sunday Dinners in the summer time. Refrigerate until set.

Pumpkin Bars

Makes: 12-15 bars   Prep Time: 45 minutes

Batter

1	cup	brown sugar
1	cup	canola oil
1 ½	cups	pumpkin (15 ounce can)
1	large	egg
2	cups	flour (can use white or wheat flour)
		wheat flour will make it a heavier bar
1	teaspoon	baking soda
1	teaspoon	cinnamon
1	teaspoon	nutmeg (optional)

Frosting

3	tablespoons	butter
4	teaspoons	milk
½	cup	brown sugar
1	cup	confectioners sugar
¾	teaspoon	vanilla

Batter-Cream the sugar, oil, egg and pumpkin. Mix pumpkin and flour together. Add soda and cinnamon. Spray a 9" x 13" pan. Pour in mixture and bake at 350 for 25-30 minutes.

Frosting-Combine in saucepan, butter, milk and brown sugar. Stir on medium heat until the sugar is dissolved. Let cool for 5 minutes and stir in confectioners sugar and vanilla. Stir until smooth and frost warm pumpkin bars.

Variations-You can use all white flour or all wheat flour or half and half. You can add raisins and walnuts and or butterscotch or chocolate chips to the mixture. This recipe works for muffins, bars or cookies. Bake 20-30 minutes for regular size muffins and 25-35 for large muffins. I sprinkle powdered sugar on top of the muffins instead of frosting.

This recipe came from Tracy McGee, who was a chef for us at both restaurants. Thanks Tracy for sharing this with us. As you know, Candas and Camille both love this recipe as did many of our customers.

Quick Cookies

Makes: 2 dozen cookies

Prep Time: 25 minutes

1	box	cake mix, any flavor
2	large	eggs
1/3	cup	oil

Mix all ingredients. You can add chocolate chips, nuts, chopped cherries, etc. Spray baking sheet. Bake in a preheated 350 degree oven for 12-15 minutes. Applesauce can be substituted for oil. My mother-in-law, Mary Barnes, found this recipe in a newspaper; these are great in emergency situations.

Raspberry Bars

Makes: 12-15 bars

Prep Time: 1 hour

Raspberry Filling

1	cup	sugar
½	cup	water
½	cup	cornstarch
4	cups	raspberries

Crust and topping

2	cups	flour
1	pound	butter, softened
3	cups	oats
½	cup	pecans or walnuts, chopped, optional
2	cups	brown sugar

Filling-Cook filling ingredients in saucepan on medium heat until thickened.

Crust/topping- Mix ingredients together. Layer a sprayed 9" x 13" pan with ½ the crust/topping mixture and bake for 10 minutes in a 350 preheated oven. Spread raspberry filling over the crust and top with the remaining crust/topping. Bake for 30-40 minutes at 350. Cool and cut.

Blackberry Bars-Substitute raspberries with blackberries
Cherry Bars-Use the cherry filling recipe
Blueberry Bars-Use the blueberry filling recipe

This recipe took me awhile to come up with. I wanted a really good raspberry bar to help promote our berries and to sell at the Farmer's Markets. I think this is a winner. I hope you do to.

Rhubarb Crunch

Makes: 12 bars

Prep Time: 1 hour 15 minutes

Crust and Topping

¾	cup	oats
1	cup	flour
1	cup	brown sugar
¼	pound	butter
1	teaspoon	cinnamon

Filling

3	cups	rhubarb, sliced
1	cup	sugar
1	cup	water or juice
2	tablespoons	cornstarch
1	teaspoon	vanilla

Blend crust/topping ingredients and put ½ of the mixture into a greased 9" x 13" pan.

Put all the filling ingredients together (except the vanilla) in a saucepan and cook until thickened. Add vanilla and pour over crust. Top with the saved crust/topping. Bake in a 350 degree preheated oven for 1 hour.

Sugar Cookies

Makes: 5 dozen

Prep Time: 45 minutes

1	cup	butter, softened
2	cups	sugar
2	large	eggs
1	cup	buttermilk
½	teaspoon	vanilla
½	teaspoon	almond extract
6	cups	flour
¼	teaspoon	salt
3	teaspoons	baking powder
1	teaspoon	baking soda
1	teaspoon	lemon juice

Mix butter, sugar, eggs and salt. Add soda to buttermilk. Add baking powder to flour. Alternate buttermilk and flour mixture to sugar mixture and mix. Add lemon juice, vanilla and almond. Chill dough, covered in refrigerator for 2 hours. Roll on floured or powdered sugar surface. Cut out. Place on greased cookie sheets. Bake 350 degrees for 10-12 minutes, 7-9 minutes for smaller cookies. Do not brown. Frost and decorate.To make snicker doodles, roll a ball of chilled dough in a mixture of cinnamon and sugar and flatten on cookie sheets.

These sugar cookies frosted are my grandkids (and kids) favorite cookies so I make them for every holiday get together. I have mini cookie cutters in every shape; cats, bats, trucks, apples, pumpkins, snowmen, christmas trees etc. I make small cookies for them because they fit their little hands better and so they don't eat as much (well that was the plan anyway). This dough freezes very well. I make 1 recipe (which is a large batch), and I freeze the dough in quart size freezer bags. They defrost quickly and can be ready in a jiffy for a Grandma, emergency baby sitting situation.

The Ultimate Brownie

Makes: 12-15 brownies   Prep Time: 45 minutes

12	ounces (2 cups)	chocolate chips, semi-sweet
1	stick	butter, cut into pieces
3	whole	eggs, beaten
1¼	cups	flour
1	cup	sugar
¼	teaspoon	soda
1	teaspoon	vanilla
12	ounces (2 cups)	butterscotch morsels
3	tablespoons	canola or vegetable oil
1	package	mini marshmallows

Mix flour, sugar and soda in separate bowl. Melt 1 ½ cups chocolate chips and butter in microwave checking every 20-30 seconds so it does not burn. Put into mixing bowl and stir in beaten eggs. Stir well and add the flour mixture. Add vanilla. Stir in the remaining (½ cup) chocolate chips. Bake in 9" x 13"pan at 350 degrees for 18-22 minutes.

Top the brownie with enough mini marshmallows to cover nicely and return to oven 3 minutes or until soft. Melt 12 ounces of butterscotch morsels with 3 tablespoons canola or vegetable oil in the microwave on low-medium checking every 20-30 seconds so it does not burn. Frost the marshmallow topped brownie with the melted butterscotch.

White Chocolate Cherry Cookies

Makes: 5 dozen   Prep Time: 30 minutes

4 ½	cups	flour
2	teaspoons	salt
2	teaspoons	baking soda
1	pound	butter, softened
1	pound	brown sugar
1 1/3	cups	sugar
4	whole	eggs
2	teaspoons	vanilla
1	pound	white chocolate, chopped
1	pound	dried cherries, reconstituted

Beat together butter and sugars until fluffy. Add eggs. Sift together dry ingredients and add to the butter, sugar. Stir in chocolate and cherries. Bake at 350 degrees for 12-13 minutes or until golden.

Zucchini Brownies

Makes: 32 brownies   Prep Time: 45 minutes

3	cups	flour
¼	cup	cocoa
1	teaspoon	baking soda
½	teaspoon	salt
2	teaspoons	cinnamon
2	cups	zucchini, grated, water squeezed out
½	cup	butter, melted
1¾	cups	sugar
1	cup	canola oil
2	large	eggs, beaten
1	teaspoon	vanilla
2	cups (12oz)	chocolate chips
½	cup	walnuts, chopped

Combine first 5 ingredients in a bowl, stir well. Combine zucchini and butter; add to flour mixture, stirring well. Combine sugar and next 3 ingredients; add to zucchini mixture, stirring 2 minutes. Fold in chocolate chips and nuts. Pour into greased 15" x 10" jelly roll pan. Bake in preheated 350 degree oven for 30 minutes. Let cool then frost with the following frosting recipe. Cut into bars.

These are great baked in mini muffin tins, topped with whipped cream and a raspberry or blackberry. I do this a lot for special bridal showers or teas.

Chocolate Frosting

Makes: 2 cups

Prep Time: 10 minutes

1	stick	butter
2/3	cup	chocolate cocoa
3	cups	powdered sugar
1/3	cup	milk
1	teaspoon	vanilla

Melt butter. Stir in cocoa. Alternately add powdered sugar and milk, beating on medium speed to spreading consisting. Add more milk if needed. Stir in vanilla.

Sorbet

I like to make fresh sorbet and serve it in small chocolate cups with a sprig of fresh mint. It makes a beautiful presentation and is especially nice to serve for a summer wedding along with the wedding cake or bridal shower. An assortment of the following sorbets is delicious and the colors are beautiful together:

Black Raspberry Sorbet

Makes: 12 servings

Prep Time: 6 hours

2	pounds (6 ½ pints)	black raspberries
2	tablespoons	light corn syrup
2/3	cup	water
1	cup	sugar

In small heavy saucepan over low heat, combine sugar, water and corn syrup. Stir until sugar dissolves, about 3 minutes. Increase heat to high and bring to a boil. Remove from heat and set syrup aside.

In a food processor or blender, put berries and their juices. Puree until smooth. Strain the puree through a course sieve set over a bowl to remove the seeds. Return berry puree to the processor. Add the syrup and mix well. Transfer to a bowl and refrigerate until cold, about 1 hour. Transfer the sorbet mixture to an ice cream maker and process until freezes. Transfer to a container and freeze at least 4 hours.

Blackberry or Raspberry Sorbet- Substitute with blackberries or raspberries.

Lemon or Lime Sorbet

Makes: 8 servings   Prep Time: 4 hours

2	cups	sugar
2	cups	water
1 ½	cups	fresh lemon juice (juice of about 6 lemons)
1	tablespoon	lemon zest, grated

In medium heavy saucepan combine sugar and water and bring to a boil over medium-high heat. Reduce heat to low and simmer until sugar dissolves, about 3-4 minutes. Cool completely. When cool add lemon juice and zest; stir to combine. Pour into ice cream maker and mix until thickens about 25-30 minutes. Transfer to an airtight container and place in freezer until firm, about 2 hours. You can substitute lime juice and zest to make lime sorbet which is also delicious!

Mango Sorbet

Makes: 10 servings   Prep Time: 3 hours

4	large	mangos
12	tablespoons	sugar
½	cup	light corn syrup

Mix all ingredients in a food processor and transfer to ice cream maker. Process until thickens; approximately 20-30 minutes. Transfer to freezer container and freeze at least 2 hours until firm. This is a delicious sorbet that goes great with Mexican dishes.

Vanilla Ice Cream

Makes: 5 cups

Prep Time: 4 hours

2	whole	eggs
2	each	egg yolks
1 1/3	cups	sugar
1 1/3	cups	heavy cream
1 1/3	cups	whole milk
2	teaspoons	vanilla, pure extract

Whisk eggs and yolks until light and fluffy, about 1 minute. Whisk in sugar a little at a time. Continue whisking until completely blended, about 1 minute more. Add cream and milk, stir in vanilla. Chill 2 hours or overnight. Freeze in ice cream maker as directed by manufacturer until it reaches the soft serve stage. Transfer to an airtight container and freeze for a day or 2.

Strawberry Ice Cream-Make the vanilla ice cream recipe. Mash 2 cups fresh, ripe strawberries and chill for 2 hours. Add chilled berries to vanilla ice cream then freeze in ice cream maker. Follow remaining instructions.

Buckeyes

Makes: 24 Buckeyes

Prep Time: 45 minutes

2	cups	confectioners sugar
1	cup	creamy peanut butter
1/4	pound	butter, softened
1/4	cake	paraffin wax
6	ounces	chocolate

Mix the confectioners sugar, peanut butter and softened butter together. Roll into balls and refrigerate for 15 minutes. Melt wax and chocolate in double boiler. Dip peanut butter balls with a toothpick into the melted chocolate. Put on wax paper lined baking sheet and refrigerate until firm.

This recipe is from my sister Debbie. My kids wait for Aunt Debbie to arrive at Thanksgiving and Christmas with her Buckeyes. They say she makes the best!

Mom and Mary's Birthday Tea Party with daughters and granddaughters

A variety of family event photos, including Mom and Dad's 50th Anniversary Party

White Chocolate Bread Pudding

Makes: 12 servings   Prep Time: 1 hour 30 minutes

4	cups	cinnamon rolls, cubed
3	cups	half and half
2	tablespoons	butter
3	whole	eggs
½	cup	sugar
½	teaspoon	salt
¾	cup	white chocolate, grated

Put half and half and butter together in microwave. Heat until butter is melted. Beat eggs, sugar and salt together. Add half and half and butter to egg mixture and mix. Add cinnamon rolls and white chocolate. Pour into a greased 9" x 13" pan. Bake at 350 degrees 40-50 minutes. Serve warm with Caramel Sauce. (See recipe.) For a really nice presentation, I bake them individually in large muffin tins. Spray the tins and bake as usual (check them at 25 minutes baking time). Cool and remove from tin turning them upside down. Then, pour on the caramel sauce, put a piece of mint on top and garnish with a few fresh berries or grated white chocolate. This was very popular at Margy's; is delicious and very easy to make.

Chocolate Bread Pudding-Substitute cinnamon rolls with slices of Texas toast, and white chocolate with 2 cups (12 oz) semi sweet chocolate chips. Serve with a chocolate sauce instead of caramel sauce.

Chocolate Dipped Strawberries

Makes: 12 servings   Prep Time: 1 hour

½	quart	strawberries, washed, air dried
1	cup	chocolate chips
1	teaspoon	vegetable oil or canola oil
		wax paper

Melt chocolate chips with oil in double boiler. Dip bottom half of berry in chocolate and lay on wax paper until chocolate sets. Can also use white chocolate. It looks the prettiest if you use long stemmed large strawberries. People ask me why I put oil in my chocolate, it makes it glisten and also thins out the chocolate a little so it does not get all goopy. You can leave it out if you prefer. If you are making a lot of chocolate covered strawberries I suggest using a small crock pot to keep the chocolate in and work out of the crock pot.

Chocolate Sundae Brownie Trifle

Makes: 12 servings   Prep Time: 15 minutes

1	recipe	brownies, baked
2	pints	vanilla ice cream
2	whole	bananas
1	cup	strawberries, fresh, sliced
		(1 left whole for garnish on top)
1	small	cool whip frozen topping
1	cup	pecans, chopped
		hot chocolate fudge topping

Layer in trifle bowl: brownies, ice cream, bananas, strawberries, cool whip, nuts and hot fudge. Layer until trifle bowl is filled. Top with a whole strawberry and serve right away; but take a picture first because it is very pretty. This is a popular spring or summer birthday treat for our family Sunday dinners.

Easy Chocolate Fudge

Makes: 16 pieces   Prep Time: 1 hour 30 minutes

12	ounces	chocolate chips, semi-sweet
14	ounces	sweetened condensed milk
1	cup	walnut or pecan pieces
1	teaspoon	vanilla

Melt chocolate with milk in saucepan on stove or in the microwave until smooth; stirring every minute. Stir in nuts and vanilla. Pour into 8" foil lined pan. Refrigerate until firm; about 2 hours. This recipe can be doubled, put into a 9" x 13" pan.

Frozen Cranberry Salad

Makes: 12 servings   Prep Time: 3 hours

6	ounces	cream cheese, softened
2	cups	cranberry sauce
1/8	cup	sugar
1/2	cup	pineapple, crushed, drained
1/2	cup	pecans, chopped
1 1/2	cups	Cool Whip

Mix cream cheese and cranberry sauce together with mixer. Add sugar, pineapple and nuts to cream cheese mixture. Mix in Cool Whip and put into 9" x 13" pan and freeze. Great for Thanksgiving and Christmas as a light dessert.

This is from my mother-in-law, Mary Barnes.

Strawberry Shortcake Cups

Makes: 18 mini or 12 regular   Prep Time: 20 minutes

1	quart	strawberries
4	tablespoons	sugar
1½	cups	flour
1	teaspoon	baking powder
½	teaspoon	salt
¼	cup	cold butter
1	whole	egg
½	cup	milk
		Whipped cream

Mash and slice strawberries with 2 tablespoons sugar. Set aside. In separate bowl combine flour, baking powder, salt and remaining sugar; cut in butter until crumbly. In small bowl beat egg and milk add to flour mixture.

Fill 12 greased regular sized muffin tins ⅔ full. Sprinkle with sugar and bake at 425 for 12 minutes or until golden. You can use the mini muffin pans by dropping the baking time down to 8-10 minutes. You can also bake in a round 8" or 9" cake pan which would prolong the baking time by a few minutes. Just before serving cut in half spoon berries and whipped cream between layers.

Apple Dumplings

Makes: 4 servings   Prep Time: 1 hour 30 minutes

4	whole	Granny Smith apples, peeled, cored
1	cup	sugar
2	cups	water
3	tablespoons	butter
¼	teaspoon	cinnamon
2	8"	pastry dough, rolled, cut into 7 inch squares
⅓	cup	sugar
1	teaspoon	cinnamon
1	tablespoon	butter

Pre-heat oven to 425 degrees. Peel and core one apple for each dumpling. Boil next four ingredients together for three minutes. Place apple on each square of pastry. Fill cavities of apples with mixture of cinnamon and sugar. Dot each with butter. Bring opposite points of pastry up over the apple and overlap. Moisten and seal. Lift carefully and place a little apart in baking dish. Pour hot syrup around dumplings. Bake immediately for 40-45 minutes or until crust is nicely browned and apples are cooked through. Serve warm with the syrup and ice cream. For presentation, sprinkle powder sugar on plate and a sprig of fresh mint.

Peach Dumplings- Make recipe above except use 4 pitted and pared peaches and smaller pastry squares. For pastry dough you can use Pepperidge Farms puff pastry sheets found in the freezer section at the grocery or premade pie crusts.

Apple Pie

Makes: One 9" pie   Prep Time: 1 hour 45 minutes

Crust

2 ½	cups	flour
¼	cup	sugar
½	teaspoon	salt
2	sticks	butter, unsalted, cubed
¼ - ⅓	ice	water

Filling

4	whole	Granny Smith apples, peeled, cored, sliced ½ inch thick.
4	whole	Braeburn apples, peeled, cored, sliced ½ inch thick.
½	teaspoon	lemon juice
½	cup	sugar
½	cup	brown sugar (or use all white sugar)
½	cup	flour
1	teaspoon	cinnamon, ground
1	pinch	nutmeg, optional
2	tablespoons	cold butter

Crust-Combine the flour, sugar and salt in a large bowl. Blend in butter with a pastry blender or two knives until pea size. Stir in water, just enough to keep it together but not sticky so add a little water at a time. Portion dough into two portions-1 for top crust (⅔) top crust will take more to cover the apples and 1-for bottom crust (⅓) , wrap in plastic wrap and chill 30 minutes. (Can be made a day ahead). Preheat oven to 450.

Filling-Toss all filling ingredients (except the butter) together in a large bowl and set aside.

Assemble-Roll out bottom crust on floured surface to about 12" across and ¼" thick and transfer to glass pie pan. Fill crust with pie filling, mounding mostly in the center. Dot with remaining butter cut in small slices. It will be mounded but the apples will shrink during baking. Roll out top crust to about 14" across. Transfer to pie, crimp edges, and cut steam vents on top. Brush top of crust with half and half or beaten egg white. Sprinkle with sugar. Put pie on baking sheet to catch drips and bake on shelf in lower third of the oven. Bake at 450 for 25 minutes then reduce temperature to 350 and bake about 40 more minutes or until crust is brown on bottom and juices are thick. If crust starts to get to brown, put a tin foil tent over it. Let the pie cool before cutting to give the filling time to thicken. Store pie at room temperature the day it is baked. Refrigerate day 2.

Note: You can use different apples; this recipe is a blend of sweet and tart apples.

Blackberry Cobbler

Makes: 6-8 servings   Prep Time: 1 hour

Filling

8	cups	blackberries, fresh or frozen
1	cup	sugar
¼	cup	flour or corn starch
1	pinch	salt

Topping

1	cup	flour
1	cup	coconut, sweetened, shredded
¾	cup	sugar
½	cup	pecans, chopped
½	teaspoon	baking powder
1	dash	salt
1	stick	butter, unsalted, cold, cut into cubes
1		egg

Filling-Combine all the filling ingredients in a bowl. Spoon into a sprayed 2 quart baking dish. Preheat oven to 375 degrees.

Topping-Combine the flour, coconut, sugar, pecans, baking powder and salt together in a second bowl; then knead in the butter with your fingers until incorporated. Mixture should look coarse and crumbly. Blend in 1 egg then arrange topping over the berries in clumps, covering them evenly. Bake the cobbler for 45-50 minutes, or until topping is golden and crisp, and filling is thick and bubbly. Cool for at least 1 hour as it will thicken as it sets up.

Blackberry Pie

Makes: 6 servings   Prep Time: 1 hour 15 minutes

1		pie crust

Filling

7-8	cups	blackberries
1	cup	sugar
6	tablespoons	flour
½	teaspoon	cinnamon
6	tablespoons	butter

Preheat oven to 400 degrees. Place berries in a large mixing bowl. Combine remaining ingredients, except the butter, pour over the berries, and fold gently. Put bottom crust in pie pan. Place the filling on top of bottom crust and dot with butter. Put the top pie crust on and brush with a beaten egg. Sprinkle with sugar and bake 400 degrees for 45 minutes then turn the oven temperature to 350 degrees and bake 15 more minutes or until the filling is bubbling and the crust is browned. Check at 30 minutes and if the crust is getting too brown cover with foil. Make sure to vent the top crust by making a few slits. I use a small berry shaped cookie cutter and make three cut outs so I can see the filling bubbling. I brush the cut outs with egg and attach them to the top of the crust and sprinkle with sugar. It looks as good as it tastes. Let set before cutting so it can thicken.

Raspberry Pie-Substitute raspberries for the blackberries or mix the berries.

Berry Crisp

Makes: 6 servings   Prep Time: 45 minutes

Filling

6	cups	berries, assorted fresh or frozen
1 ½	cups	sugar
2	tablespoons	flour
2	tablespoons	butter, cut into pieces

Topping

1	cup	flour
3	tablespoons	sugar
¼	teaspoon	cinnamon
¾	cup	walnuts, pecans or almonds, sliced
6	tablespoons	butter, unsalted, melted

Preheat oven to 400 degrees. Grease deep dish pie pan or 9" x 13" baking dish

Filling-Place berries, sugar and flour in a saucepan and heat to boil. Reduce heat and simmer stirring until thickens. Remove from heat and pour into greased pan. Dot fruit mixture with butter.

Topping-Combine flour, sugar and cinnamon in mixing bowl; stir to combine and add nuts. Stir in butter evenly. Set aside for 5 minutes then using fingertips break mixture into crumbs. Add topping to berry mixture. Bake at 400 degrees for 30 minutes or until topping is lightly browned.

Chocolate Chip Pecan Pie

Makes: 6-8 servings   Prep Time: 1 hour

¼	cup	butter
1	cup	brown sugar
¾	cup	light corn syrup
3	whole	eggs, beaten
1	teaspoon	vanilla
2 ½	cups	pecan pieces
6	ounces	mini chocolate chips
1		pie crust, unbaked

Melt butter, mix in remaining filling ingredients. Pour into pie shell. Bake in preheated 350 degree oven for 30-40 minutes or until custard is firm and pie is golden brown.

Coconut Cream Pie

Makes: 6-8 servings   Prep Time: 30 minutes

Crust

½	box	vanilla wafers; crushed
¼	cup	sugar
¼	pound	butter, melted

Butter the bottom of a 9" or 10" pie plate. Mix ingredients with fork until blended. Press crust into pie plate. Bake 10 minutes in preheated 350 degree oven. Remove from oven and cool to room temperature. While crust is cooling make custard mix.

Custard

2	cups	whole milk
¾	cup	sugar
¾	cup	flour
1	cup	coconut flakes
12	each	egg yolks

Bring milk to a boil in saucepan. Add flour and whisk over medium heat until thickens. Put egg yolks in large bowl and whisk hot milk in slowly. Put back on medium heat; add sugar and coconut, cook until eggs are cooked. Take off heat and pour into crust. Chill in refrigerator.

Topping

½	cup	coconut, toasted
1	cup	whipping cream
¼	cup	sugar
1	teaspoon	vanilla

Toast coconut on baking sheet in 350 degree oven until lightly brown for just a short time. Watch so that it does not burn. Cool. Whip cream until fluffy. Add vanilla and sugar gradually until blended. Spread onto custard and top with toasted coconut. This is a fabulous coconut cream pie. I love it because it is not too sweet and is a very thick consistency.

Frosty Key Lime Pie

Makes: 6 servings   Prep Time: 3 hours

1		ready-made Keebler shortbread cookie crust
1	8 ounce	package cream cheese, softened
1	4 ounce	milk, sweetened, condensed
1	6 ounce can	lime-aid juice concentrate, thawed
1	8 ounce	Cool Whip

Beat cream cheese and milk. Beat in juice. Fold in Cool Whip. Spoon into crust, cover and freeze for about 2-3 hours. This makes a very refreshing summer time dessert especially when it is too hot to bake.

Frosty Orange Pie-Substitute the lime with orange.

Lemon Meringue Pie

Makes: one 10" pie   Prep Time: 45 minutes

1	10 inch	pie crust, baked
Filling		
4	teaspoons	lemon peel, grated
⅔	cup	lemon juice
5	whole	eggs
1	cup	sugar
½	cup	butter, melted

Meringue

5	each	egg whites (set eggs out at room temp for 30 mins)
½	teaspoon	cream of tartar
⅔	cup	sugar
½	teaspoon	vanilla

Filling-Combine lemon peel, lemon juice, eggs and sugar in blender or food processor. Whirl until blended. With blender on lowest speed gradually add butter in a thin stream. Transfer mixture to a small heavy saucepan. Cook over low heat, approximately 8-10 minutes stirring constantly until mixture is thickened enough to mound slightly when dropped from spoon. Pour hot filling into pie crust.

Meringue-Beat egg whites and cream of tartar for the meringue to soft peaks with electric mixer on high. Gradually add the sugar and beat to stiff, glossy peaks and add the vanilla. Top the hot pie with the meringue, then bake at 450 degrees just until meringue is brown, about 4 minutes. Cool completely. This recipe is much easier than what you may think.

Note: for making a great meringue.
- Make sure the bowl and beaters are clean.
- Make sure the egg whites are free of yellows
- Make sure egg whites are kept at room temp for about 30 minutes before

Mini Blackberry Turnovers

Makes: 12 mini turnovers   Prep Time: 30 minutes

2		rolled out pie crusts
Filling		
2	cups	blackberries
2	tablespoons	flour or cornstarch
3	tablespoons	sugar
	pinch	salt
Glaze		
¼	cup	powdered sugar
3	tablespoons	milk
½	teaspoon	vanilla

Using a 4" round cookie cutter or ravioli cutter; cut out 3-4 rounds from each dough round. You should end up with a total of 12.

Filling-In a bowl toss together the blackberries, flour, sugar and salt.

Assemble-Lay the dough rounds on a sprayed baking sheet. Divide the berries evenly among the dough rounds. Using a pastry brush, dampen the edge of each round with cold water. Gently fold the dough over the berries to make a half moon shape, dampen the edges with the water. With the tines of a fork, press the outer edge of the dough half rounds together. Refrigerate the pockets on the baking sheet until the dough is firm, 15-20 minutes. Meanwhile, preheat the oven to 375 degrees. Bake the turnovers until golden brown, 15-20 minutes. Let set for a minute then glaze.

Glaze- Mix ingredients until smooth; drizzle over the turnovers and serve warm or at room temperature.

Note: These mini blackberry pies will disappear so fast you won't believe it so make plenty. These also freeze well.

Mixed Berry Cobbler

Makes: 6 servings   Prep Time: 30 minutes

Filling

3	cups	berries (mixture of blackberry, raspberry, blueberry or strawberry)
¼	cup	sugar
1	tablespoon	butter

Topping

1	cup	flour
1	tablespoon	sugar
1 ½	teaspoons	baking powder
¼	cup	butter, to make coarse crumbs
¼	cup	milk
1	whole	egg

Filling-Cook in saucepan for 5 minutes or until juices thickens a bit. Pour into greased 9"x 9" pan.

Topping-Mix together; flour, sugar and baking powder. Cut in butter to make coarse crumbs. Mix in milk and egg. Stir until just moistened. Drop by spoonful atop the hot fruit. Sprinkle with sugar. Bake for 20 minutes in a preheated 400 degree oven.

Blueberry Filling

Makes: 2 cups   Prep Time: 1 hour 30 minutes

4 ½	cups	blueberries
¾	cup	sugar
¼	cup	light corn syrup
1	teaspoon	lemon juice

Pick over blueberries. In a 3-quart heavy saucepan combine all ingredients and simmer, stirring, until reduced to about 2 cups, 25-30 minutes. Transfer filling to a bowl, chill covered at least 1 hour.

Cherry Filling

Makes: 2 cups   Prep Time: 20 minutes

1	cup	sugar
¼	cup	flour
½	cup	juice from berries
3	cups	cherries, sour, pitted
1	tablespoon	butter
2	drops	vanilla
¼	teaspoon	salt

Combine sugar, flour and salt. Stir in juice. Cook over medium heat until thick. Cook 1 minute longer. Add cherries, butter, vanilla and food coloring. Let stand for a few minutes.

I love this as a topping to the New York Cheesecake. Fresh picked cherries are best for this, but not always easy to get. You have to get up earlier than the birds because the second they turn ripe the birds swarm to the trees and they are gone in seconds. When we were lucky enough to get their before the birds, Mom and I would climb on top of the shed/chicken coop and pick.

Raspberry Filling

Makes: about 2 cups   Prep Time: 20 minutes

1	cup	sugar
½	cup	water
½	cup	cornstarch
4	cups	raspberries

Cook in saucepan on medium heat until thickened. You can use any of these fruit fillings as cheesecake toppings, to make bars or ice cream toppings. See Raspberry bar recipe and substitute cherries or blueberries for the raspberries. I have frozen this raspberry filling for 1 year and it was still very good.

Peach Crisp

Makes: 8 servings   Prep Time: 1 hour 15 minutes

1		pie crust

Almond Crumble Topping

1	cup	flour
3	tablespoons	sugar
½	cup	almonds, sliced
¼	teaspoon	cinnamon
6	tablespoons	butter, unsalted, melted

Filling

3	pounds (8-9 medium)	peaches, firm, ripe
½	cup	sugar
2	tablespoons	flour
½	teaspoon	almond extract
¼	teaspoon	cinnamon
2	tablespoons	butter, unsalted, cold

Roll out the bottom crust and arrange in a pie pan. Pre-heat the oven to 400 degrees.

Topping-Combine the flour, sugar and cinnamon in mixing bowl; stir well to combine and stir in the almonds. Stir in the butter evenly. Set aside for 5 minutes, then using your fingertips break the mixture into crumbs. Set aside while you prepare the filling. (This is the easiest and best crumb topping ever).

Filling-To make the filling, peel the peaches and cut into slices. Add the remaining ingredients except the butter, to the peaches and stir gently to combine. Pour the filling into the prepared pastry shell and dot with butter. Scatter the crumb topping evenly over the filling, then place the pie on the middle rack of the oven and bake for 15 minutes. Lower the temperature to 350 degrees and bake for another 30-45 minutes or until the crumble is deep golden and the juices are bubbling up.

Note: Sometimes I make these without a crust, in oven proof soup cups or small bowls for individual servings. The kids love it at our Sunday Dinners.

Pumpkin Pie

Makes: 2 pies   Prep Time: 1 hour 15 minutes

Filling

1 ½	cups	sugar
1	teaspoon	salt
2	teaspoons	cinnamon
1	teaspoon	ginger
½	teaspoon	cloves
4	large	eggs
1	large can (28 ounce)	100% pure pumpkin
2	12 ounce cans	evaporated milk
2	unbaked	pie crusts-deep dish

Ginger Streusel Topping

2	cups	flour
1	cup	brown sugar, packed
1	cup	walnuts or pecans, chopped
3	teaspoons	ground ginger
2	sticks	butter, cut into small pieces at room temperature

Filling-Mix sugar, salt, cinnamon, ginger and cloves together in small bowl. Beat eggs in large bowl. Stir in pumpkin and sugar spice mixture. Gradually stir in evaporated milk. Pour into shells, add topping (or not if you prefer the traditional pie), bake in preheated 425 oven for 15 minutes. Reduce temperature to 350; bake 40-50 minutes or until knife inserted comes out clean. Cool for 2 hours. Serve immediately or refrigerate.

Note: 3 ½ teaspoons pumpkin pie spice can be substituted for ginger, cloves and cinnamon. The taste will be slightly different.

Topping- Mix streusel together. Crumble on top of pie before baking.

Strawberry Pizza

Makes: 12 servings

Prep Time: 30 minutes

1	quart	strawberries, sliced
1	package	strawberry glaze
16	ounces	cream cheese, softened at room temperature
1	pound box	powdered sugar
4	ounces	pecans, chopped
2	cups	flour
2	sticks (1 cup)	butter (do not use margarine)

Melt butter, add to flour and pecans. Spread in bottom of sprayed 9"x13" pan. Bake at 350 degrees for 15 minutes and let cool. Mix softened cream cheese and powdered sugar, spread on top of cooled pecan mixture. Wash and slice strawberries, add glaze and spread on top of cream cheese mixture.

Patty Beam (AKA Beamer) gave me this recipe about 1982 and my family sure has enjoyed it. Thanks Patty!

Easter egg hunt- Sophie, Mason, Halle

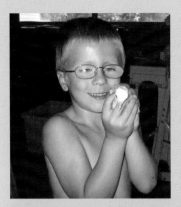

Mason and Halle with Baby Chicks

Dressings

Apricot Dressing
Balsamic Vinaigrette
Basil Dressing
Blackberry Dressing
Buttermilk Ranch Dressing
Caesar Salad Dressing
Creamy Dill Dressing
Hot Bacon Dressing
Italian Dressing
Lemon Basil Dressing
Orange Poppy Seed Dressing
Raspberry Dressing
Russian Dressing
Tomato Basil Vinaigrette
Watermelon Basil Vinaigrette

Apricot Dressing

Makes: 4 servings

1	tablespoon	apricot preserves
1 ½	tablespoons	apple cider or red wine vinegar
1	teaspoon	Dijon mustard
1	dash	salt
1	dash	pepper
¼	cup	canola oil

Combine all the ingredients together. Serve over mixed greens with chicken, raspberries, goat cheese and almonds.

Balsamic Vinaigrette

Makes: 1 cup

Prep Time: 10 minutes

½	cup	olive or canola oil
¼	cup	balsamic vinegar
2	tablespoons	Dijon mustard
2	tablespoons	fresh lemon juice
1	teaspoon	salt
1	dash	pepper
1	clove	garlic, minced

Combine all ingredients in a jar; cover tightly and shake to blend or process in food processor.

Basil Dressing

Makes: 8 servings

Prep Time: 15 minutes

2-3	cloves	garlic, minced
¼	cup	fresh basil, minced
¼	cup	parsley, fresh, minced
4	teaspoons	Dijon mustard
2	tablespoons	red wine vinegar
½	teaspoon	sugar
¾	cup	olive oil

Combine all ingredients in a food processor except the oil and process until smooth. With the food processor running slowly add the oil and process until well blended.

Blackberry Dressing

Makes: 4 cups   Prep Time: 15 minutes

1	cup	blackberries, fresh or frozen, thawed
¼	cup	red wine vinegar
⅛	cup	Dijon mustard
½	cup	sugar
1 ¾	cups	canola oil

Blend in food processor or blender until a smooth, thick consistency. This dressing is great served on spinach salad. Will keep in refrigerator up to four weeks. Wonderful served on fresh greens with berries, nuts and goat cheese.

Buttermilk Ranch Dressing

Makes: 2 cups   Prep Time: 8 hours

½	cup	sour cream
1	cup	mayonaisse
½	cup	buttermilk
1	teaspoon	garlic powder
2	tablespoons	parsley, fresh, chopped fine
1	tablespoon	onion, minced
¼	teaspoon	lemon juice
½	teaspoon	sugar
¼	teaspoon	salt
¼	teaspoon	pepper

Mix ingredients and let set overnight.

Caesar Salad Dressing

Makes: 8 servings   Prep Time: 15 minutes

1	teaspoon	garlic, chopped
1/8	teaspoon	kosher salt
¼	cup	parmesan cheese, finely grated
1	tablespoon	fresh lemon juice
1	tablespoon	mayonnaise
1	teaspoon	anchovy paste
1	teaspoon	Dijon mustard
1	teaspoon	Worcestershire sauce
1	teaspoon	Tabasco
¼	cup	olive oil
		salt and pepper

Mash garlic and kosher salt together. Add the remaining ingredients except the olive oil. Whisk in the olive oil in a slow steady stream. Chill.

Creamy Dill Dressing

Makes: 8 servings   Prep Time: 15 minutes

1 ¼	cups	mayonnaise
¾	cup	sour cream
5	tablespoons	lemon juice
3	teaspoons	fresh dill, snipped
½	teaspoon	salt

Mix all ingredients together and refrigerate until ready to use. This is great with a cucumber and seafood salad with crab, shrimp or salmon. You can use low fat or fat free mayo and sour cream or substitute sour cream with low fat yogurt.

Hot Bacon Dressing

Makes: 4 salads   Prep Time: 30 minutes

6	strips	bacon, diced
1	tablespoon	oil
¾	cup	red onion, sliced
¼	cup	apple cider vinegar
3	tablespoons	honey
1	tablespoon	Dijon mustard
⅓	cup	olive or canola oil
		salt and pepper to taste

Sauté bacon until crisp; drain. Pour off all but 1 tablespoon of drippings. Sauté onion for about 1 minute until crisp. Stir in vinegar, honey and mustard. Simmer until reduced about 1 minute. Remove from heat. Whisk in oil; season to taste. Toss with fresh spinach, mushroom slices, croutons and hard boiled eggs; wedged.

Italian Dressing

Makes: 1 ½ cups   Prep Time: 15 minutes

⅔	cup	olive or canola oil
¾	cup	red wine, apple cider or white wine vinegar
1	teaspoon	dried oregano or 2 teaspoons oregano, fresh, chopped
1	teaspoon	dried basil or 2 teaspoons basil, fresh, chopped
1	teaspoon	dried marjoram or 2 teaspoons marjoram, fresh, chopped
1	clove	garlic, diced
2	tablespoons	sugar
1	teaspoon	salt
1	dash	pepper

In a jar with a tight fitting lid shake ingredients or blend in blender or food processor.

Lemon Basil Dressing

2-3	cloves	garlic, minced
¼	cup	basil, fresh, minced
¼	cup	parsley, fresh, minced
4	teaspoons	Dijon mustard
2	tablespoons	lemon juice, fresh
½	teaspoon	sugar
1	dash	black pepper
¾	cup	olive oil

Combine all ingredients in a food processor except the oil and process until smooth. With the food processor running slowly add the oil and process until well blended.

Orange Poppy Seed Dressing

2	tablespoons	sugar
1	teaspoon	salt
1/3	cup	honey
2	tablespoons	Dijon mustard
2	tablespoons	white vinegar
2/3	cup	canola oil
1	tablespoon	onion, minced fine
1	tablespoon	poppy seeds
¼	cup	orange peel, zest

Mix all ingredients thoroughly in a food processor or blender. Refrigerate up to 2 weeks. This is one of my favorites. I love it on a green salad with fresh berries and nuts.

Raspberry Dressing

Makes: 4 cups   Prep Time: 15 minutes

1	cup	raspberries, fresh or frozen, thawed
¼	cup	red wine vinegar or raspberry flavored
⅛	cup	Dijon mustard
½	cup	sugar
1 ¾	cups	canola oil

Blend in food processor or blender until blended well. Should be thick and bright pink. Great served on spinach salad with fresh berries. Will keep in refrigerator up to four weeks.

Russian Dressing

Makes: 16 servings   Prep Time: 15 minutes

1 ½	cups	mayonnaise
1 ½	ounces	horseradish
2	ounces	onion, minced, blanched
½	teaspoon	salt
6	ounces	chili sauce
1 ½	teaspoons	Worcestershire sauce
¼	teaspoon	pepper

Mix well. Great served with reuben sandwiches. Will keep up to 1 week in refrigerator.

Tomato Basil Vinaigrette

Makes: 4 servings   Prep Time: 45 minutes

2	large	tomatoes, ripe
2	tablespoons	balsamic vinegar or lemon juice
1 ½	teaspoons	basil dried or 3 tablespoons basil, fresh, chopped
1	dash	pepper
1	dash	salt
¼	cup	extra virgin olive oil

In small sauce pan, bring 2 cups water to a boil. Put tomatoes in boiling water for 20 seconds or until their skins loosen. Remove them with a slotted spoon and rinse under cold water. Peel the skin from the tomatoes, cut them in half and squeeze out the seeds. Chop tomatoes. In a blender or food processor, combine tomatoes, vinegar, basil, salt and pepper. Blend on high until mixture is smooth. Reduce speed to low and add oil in a steady stream. Continue blending until dressing is smooth and fully incorporated. Let stand at room temperature for 30 minutes to absorb the flavors. Toss with salad greens and toasted walnuts or almonds.

Watermelon Basil Vinaigrette

Makes: 2 cups   Prep Time: 15 minutes

4	cups	watermelon, fresh, chopped and drained
¼	cup	red onion, diced small
2	tablespoons	honey
¼	cup	champagne vinegar
¾	cup	canola oil
2	tablespoons	basil, fresh, chopped
1	tablespoon	parsley, fresh, chopped
		salt and pepper to taste

Combine all ingredients in blender and blend for approximately 30 seconds. Drizzle over mixed salad greens and garnish with sliced watermelon.

Entrees

Beef
Beef and Noodles
Beef Brisket
Beef Bourguignon
Beef Stew
Corned Beef and Cabbage
Corned Beef with Jalapeño Pepper Jelly Glaze
Crock Pot, Pot Roast
Dad's Spaghetti Sauce
Filet of Beef Japanese
Grilled Tenderloin Tips
Herbed Beef Tenderloin with Tomato Relish
Lasagna
Meatloaf
Shredded Beef Fajitas
Swiss Steak

Chicken and Turkey
Cheese and Chicken Enchiladas
Chicken Alfredo Spinach Pizza
Chicken and Dumplings
Chicken and Noodles
Chicken and Pasta with Tomato Mushroom
  Pesto
Chicken Enchilada Casserole
Chicken Hash
Chicken Lasagna
Chicken Perisenne
Chicken with Blackberries
Chili Cheese Stuffed Chicken
Easy Chicken Enchiladas
Orange Pecan Chicken
Oven Roasted Chicken Breasts
Parmesan Chicken
Raspberry Chicken
Roasted Chicken
Southern Fried Chicken
Southwestern Chicken and Pasta
Summer Stuffed Chicken Breasts
Thanksgiving Turkey
  Gravy and Stuffing

Fish and Seafood
Baked Halibut with Avocado Salsa
Baked Salmon
Crab and Vegetable Pasta
Pecan Haddock
Salmon with Orange Glaze
Shrimp Scampi
Teriyka Glazed Salmon
Tomato, Basil Pasta with Shrimp
Tuna Noodle Casserole

Pork
Baked Ham
BBQ Baby Back Ribs
Cheese Tortellini Bake
Eggplant Casserole
Italian Crock Pot Pasta
Pork Roast with Sauerkraut
Roasted Pork Tenderloin with
  Apricot Glaze
Stuffed Acorn Squash
Zucchini Sausage Casserole

Vegetarian
Easy Broccoli Enchiladas
Eggplant Parmesan
Eggplant Pesto Crepes
Portobello Fajitas
Roasted Vegetable Pizza
Southwest Pasta

Beef & Noodles

Makes: 8-10 servings

Prep Time: 6-8 hours

2	pounds	beef chuck roast
1	teaspoon	oil
1	teaspoon	salt
1	teaspoon	pepper
2	cans	cream of mushroom soup (or homemade mushroom sauce/soup)
2-3	cups	water (depending on how much broth you like)
2	tablespoons	beef base
1	cup	onions, diced
½	teaspoon	garlic, minced
¼	cup	parsley, fresh, chopped or 2 tablespoons dried parsley
¼	cup	red wine (optional)
8	ounces	wide egg noodles, uncooked (I like the homemade Amish egg noodles for this)

Crock Pot Method-Wash meat and remove as much fat as possible; brown in hot skillet with oil. Place the roast in the crock pot and season with salt and pepper. Add all other ingredients with the beef except the noodles. Put the lid on the crock pot and cook on low for 6-8 hours or high for 4-6 hours until the meat is pull a part tender. When the roast is done, remove and pull apart into pieces. Turn the crock pot on high (if not already on high) and remove the lid. Add the noodles and cook until they are done. Approximately 30 minutes. The last 30 minutes you can add frozen peas, or mixed vegetables if you like. These are very good served over mashed potatoes.

Oven Method- Brown the meat in a hot skillet with oil. Then put all the ingredients except the noodles in a roasting pan, cover and slow roast on 325 degrees for about 3-4 hours. Cooking time depends on the size of the roast. When the meat is pull apart tender remove from the roasting pan and pull meat apart. Add noodles to the broth and put back into oven, until noodles are done. Add the meat.

Beef Brisket

Makes: 4-6 servings   Prep Time: 4 hours 30 minutes

2 ½ -3	pounds	beef brisket
1	dash	salt and pepper
3-4	tablespoons	olive or canola oil
2	cups	onions, chopped
1	cup	celery, chopped
½	cup	carrots, chopped
2	tablespoons	garlic, minced
¼	cup	parsley, fresh, chopped
4	sprigs	thyme, chopped
1	can	beef broth
1	12 ounce	bottle stout beer

Preheat oven to 350 degrees. Trim off the fat (or ask your butcher to do it for you). Make sure the meat is patted dry with paper towels then season with salt and pepper. Put the oil in a large heavy Dutch oven or stock pot to brown the meat. Heat the oil on medium-high heat. (Medium-high heat is the key to good browning). Brown both sides of seasoned beef about 5 minutes per side; remove. Add onions, celery, carrots and garlic. Cook 3 minutes. Stir in parsley and thyme. Return beef to pot. Add broth and beer, bring to a boil. Cover pot, place in the oven, and braise 1 ½ hours. Turn beef over and braise an additional 1 ½ hours or until fork tender. Remove beef from broth and let set for about 10 minutes before slicing. Slice against the grain and place on a serving platter. Drizzle with the herb topping. This is a delicious brisket.

Herb Topping

⅓	cup	shallots, minced
¼	cup	parsley, fresh, minced
¼	cup	thyme, fresh, minced
1-2	tablespoons	olive or canola oil
		Salt and pepper

Mix the herbs; add the oil, salt and pepper

Beef Bourguignon

Makes: 6-8 servings   Prep Time: 2 hours

1	tablespoon	oil
8	ounces	bacon, center cut, diced
2 ½	pounds	beef chuck roast or filet tenderloin, cut into 1 inch cubes
1	dash	kosher salt
1	dash	black pepper
1	pound	carrots, sliced diagonally into 1" chunks
2	medium	onions, sliced
2	teaspoons	garlic, fresh, chopped
1	bottle	good red wine (I have used pinot noir and cabernet; both work fine)
2	cups	beef broth
1	tablespoon	tomato paste
1	teaspoon	thyme leaves, fresh, chopped (or ½ teaspoon dried)
4	tablespoons	butter, unsalted, room temperature, divided
3	tablespoons	flour
1	pound	pearl or cipollini onions, peeled, fresh or frozen
1	pound	mushrooms, fresh, stems discarded, caps sliced thick

Preheat oven to 250 degrees. Heat the oil in a large Dutch oven. Add the bacon and cook over medium heat for 10 minutes, stirring occasionally, until the bacon is lightly browned. Add the garlic and cook 1 more minute. Add the bottle of wine and enough beef broth to almost cover the meat. Add the tomato paste and thyme. Bring to a simmer, cover the pot with a tight-fitting lid and place it in the oven for about 1 ¼ hours or until the meat and vegetables are very tender when pierced with a fork.

Combine 2 tablespoons of butter and the flour with a fork and stir into the stew. Add the onions. Sauté the mushrooms in 2 tablespoons of butter for 10 minutes until lightly browned and then add to the stew. Bring the stew to a boil on top of the stove, then lower the heat and simmer 15 minutes. Then season with salt and pepper to taste. Serve over noodles or rice.

This was a very popular holiday entrée that was special requested for caterings and carry-outs at Margy's Café.

Beef Stew

1	pound	chuck roast
1	tablespoon	canola oil
2-3	tablespoons	flour, seasoned with salt and pepper
2	cups	hot water
1	tablespoon	beef base
1	teaspoon	Worcestershire sauce
1	clove	garlic, minced
1	teaspoon	salt
¼	teaspoon	pepper
¼	cup	red wine; optional
3	large	potatoes, diced
1	cup	carrots, diced
1	cup	onions, diced

Stove top method- Dust meat with seasoned flour. In Dutch oven, thoroughly brown meat in hot oil turning once to make sure both sides is evenly browned. Add water and all other ingredients except the potatoes and carrots. Cover; simmer for 1 ½ hours until meat is pull apart tender. Remove the meat and pull it apart then add back to the pot with the vegetables. Cover and simmer 30-45 minutes until vegetables are tender.

Crock Pot method-Dust meat with seasoned flour. Thoroughly brown meat in hot oil turning once to make sure both sides is evenly browned. Put potatoes, onions and carrots in bottom of the crock pot and the roast on top of the vegetables. Add the remaining ingredients and cook on high for 4-6 hours or low for 6-8 hours.

Corned Beef and Cabbage

1	head	cabbage, quartered
4	pounds	corned beef brisket
8	whole	scallions, peeled
3	whole	carrots, cut into chunks
3	whole	red new potatoes
½	teaspoon	pepper
1	teaspoon	garlic, minced
1	cup	water

Put the vegetables in the bottom of the crock pot and lay the brisket on top. Add the remaining ingredients and cook on low for 6-8 hours or high for 4-6 hours. The meat should be pull apart tender. This makes a great broth. The flavor comes from the scallions blended with the sweetness of the new potatoes. If your scallions are small, use 12 of them. This can be cooked on the stove in a large pot. You will need to cover the meat and vegetables with water and cook on medium, covered for 2-3 hours medium heat.

Corned Beef with Jalapeño Pepper Jelly Glaze

Makes: 8 servings   Prep Time: 8 hours

4	pounds	corned beef brisket
1	jar	jalapeño jelly
1	cup	water

Rinse corned beef. Place in a roaster with a lid or baking dish covered with foil. Slow roast in a preheated 300 degrees oven for 3-4 hours or until tender. Cover the beef with jelly and slow roast, basting the beef every 15 minutes or so the last hour.

Crock Pot Method-Put in a crock pot and add water. Cook on low for 6 hours. Remove liquid in crock pot. Coat both sides of meat with jelly. Turn crock pot to high and cook 1-2 more hours uncovered. Keep glazing the meat with the jelly in the pot. Slice and serve. Great served with Irish soda bread and Irish mashed potatoes for St. Patty's Day. This makes great sandwiches. Do not add the pickling spice that comes with the corned beef.

Crock Pot, Pot Roast

Makes: 4-6 servings   Prep time: 6-8 hours

2	pounds	chuck roast, beef
1	tablespoon	butter
4	whole	potatoes, quartered
2	whole	carrots, sliced
1	whole	onion, quartered
1	teaspoon	Kitchen Bouquet
1	teaspoon	garlic, minced
1	teaspoon	seasoned salt
1	teaspoon	pepper

1	cup	water
1	teaspoon	beef base
½	cup	button mushrooms, sliced or whole

Brown both sides of the meat in butter in a large skillet. Put vegetables in the bottom of the crock pot. Season with ½ the seasonings. Place roast on top, season with remaining seasonings. Add 1 cup of water mixed with the beef base. Cook on low for 6-8 hours on high for 4-6 hours or until meat is pull apart tender.

Dad's Homemade Spaghetti Sauce

Makes: 8 servings   Prep Time: 2 hours 30 minutes

32	ounces	Hunts Tomato Sauce
4	tablespoons	Open Pit Original BBQ Sauce
2	tablespoons	yellow mustard
1-2	cups	ketchup
10-12	drops	Tabasco Sauce
2	teaspoons	garlic powder or salt
2	teaspoons	Italian seasonings
1	cup	diced onions
1	cup	diced green peppers
1	pound	ground beef, or meatballs

Brown the ground beef in a saucepan with the onions and peppers. Drain the grease and add the remaining ingredients. Add more ketchup and Italian seasonings as needed. Then simmer for 2 hours.

Everybody in the family loves Dad's Spaghetti Sauce. So I pinned him down one day for the recipe. It was difficult to do because he does what many of us do; a pinch of this and a pinch of that. So I had him make it a few times measuring as he went along. So now we have it. It really is a good sauce, but most of all, we feel special when Dad makes it for us as we all like to be pampered by our Dads.

Filet of Beef Japanese

Makes: 8-10 servings   Prep Time: 24 hours

1- 4	pounds	filet of beef, trimmed
1	cup	Japanese soy sauce
1	cup	olive oil
1	cup	sherry
6	cloves	garlic, minced
1	teaspoon	hot pepper sauce
		a few grindings of pepper

Marinate filet in combined ingredients for 24 hours, turning several times. Remove and dry. Rub with oil. Roast at 475 degrees (425 for convection) for 25 minutes, for very rare, 28-30 minutes for rare, 35-40 minutes for medium rare and 45 minutes for medium. Baste with marinade several times while roasting. Cool. Arrange on platter with watercress and cherry tomatoes. (During marinating, I put all in a large plastic zip lock bag, much easier to turn while marinating.)

Grilled Tenderloin Tips

Makes: 6 servings   Prep Time: 30 minutes

1	cup	soy sauce
½	cup	brown sugar
¼	cup	canola oil
¼	cup	cooking sherry
2	cloves	garlic, minced
2	pounds	beef tenderloin tips

Combine first 5 ingredients and pour over meat. Cover and refrigerate 2-3 hours. Stir occasionally. Cook on broiler or on grill. Don't over marinate or can get too salty from the soy sauce.

Herbed Beef Tenderloin with Tomato Relish

Makes: 10 servings   Prep Time: 1 hour

2 ½	pounds	beef tenderloin, trimmed
2	tablespoons	canola or olive oil
1	teaspoon	kosher salt
1	teaspoons	pepper
1	tablespoon	parsley, fresh, finely chopped
1	tablespoon	thyme, fresh, finely chopped
1	tablespoon	rosemary, fresh, finely chopped
2	cloves	garlic, diced fine

Tomato Relish

3	large	tomatoes, diced
1	small	sweet onion
3-4	tablespoons	canola or olive oil
1	teaspoon	lemon juice
		salt and pepper
2	tablespoons	basil, fresh, chopped

Preheat oven to 425 degrees. Mix oil, salt, pepper and herbs together. Rub beef with the herb mixture and bake for 30 minutes or until desired degree of doneness. Let rest 5 minutes before slicing. Mix the tomato relish ingredients together. Slice and put the tenderloin on a serving tray with a bowl of fresh tomato relish in the center.

Lasagna

Makes: 8 servings   Prep Time: 1 hour 30 minutes

1	pound	Italian sausage, or hamburger, cooked and drained
1	clove	garlic, minced
1	teaspoon	oil
10	leaves	basil, fresh, chopped
1	tablespoon	oregano, fresh, chopped
29	ounces	canned plum tomatoes, chopped
1	teaspoon	black pepper
1	teaspoon	salt
½	teaspoon	sugar

10	ounces	lasagna noodles, cooked
1	cup	ricotta or cottage cheese
½	cup	Parmigiano-Reggiano cheese
2	tablespoons	parsley, fresh, chopped
2	whole	eggs, beaten
1	pound	mozzarella cheese, sliced

Heat the oil in large skillet over medium-high heat. Add garlic, cook until soft and brown about 2 minutes. Add tomatoes and sugar. Simmer until thickens about 30 minutes. Season with salt, pepper, and add basil and oregano. Set aside to cool for a minute then add eggs to sauce.

In a large bowl combine ricotta, parmesan, parsley, dash salt and pepper. Stir. Set aside. Layer in a 9" x 13" inch sprayed pan, noodles, sauce, ricotta cheese, and mozzarella. Layer again 2 more times. Top with parmesan and parsley. Bake in a 375 degree oven for 45-60 minutes. Let cool for 10 minutes before cutting. This is also good meatless.

Meatloaf

Makes: 1 loaf or 4-6 servings   Prep Time: 1 hour 15 minutes

2	pounds	ground sirloin
1	large	egg
¾	cup	bread, crumbs
1	teaspoon	Worcestershire sauce
½	teaspoon	salt
½	teaspoon	pepper
½	tablespoon	garlic powder
¾	cup	onion, diced fine
		chili sauce
		ketchup

Mix together all ingredients except chili sauce and ketchup. Put in sprayed or greased loaf pan and top with chili sauce and ketchup mixed together. Bake covered 30 minutes at 350 degrees. Then uncovered the last 30 minutes. Pour off grease every ½ hour. Pour off grease when done.

Shredded Beef Fajitas

Makes: 12 Fajitas   Prep Time: 4-6 hours

Beef Ingredients

2	pounds	chuck roast
½	cup	water or beef broth
2	cloves	garlic, minced
3	whole	jalapeño peppers
3	whole	banana peppers
2	whole	onions, sliced
1		roasted red pepper, diced (optional)
		salt
		pepper

Serve with:

		Flour tortillas, warmed
½	cup	cilantro, chopped
1	whole	tomato, diced
½	cup	green onions, chopped
1	cup	Mexican white cheese, crumbled
1	cup	avocado, diced

Crock Pot Method-Brown the beef on both sides in a hot skillet with a tablespoon of butter. Put the beef in the crock pot and add the remaining beef ingredients and cook on high 4-6 hours or low 6-8 hours. When pull apart tender, remove the beef and shred. Serve on a platter with the cooked onions and peppers surrounding it. Serve with the above suggested sides.

Oven Method-Preheat oven to 350 degrees. Brown the beef on both sides in a hot skillet with a tablespoon of butter or oil. Add 1 cup beef broth; add the peppers, onions and garlic. Cover, place in the oven, and braise 1 ½ hours. Turn beef over and braise an additional 1½ hours or until fork tender. Remove beef from broth and let set for about 10 minutes before slicing.

Note: At the end of the garden season I freeze the left over jalapeños and banana peppers whole (I get tired of chopping them at this point). I created this recipe to use up these peppers. It is really delicious and very easy. It is not too spicy but very flavorful. I make this recipe with chicken breasts also.

These fajitas make a great summer time meal. I like to serve the Frosty Key Lime Pie or Mango Sorbet as a dessert with these.

Swiss Steak

4	pieces	cubed steak
¼	cup	flour, seasoned with salt and pepper
1	tablespoon	butter
½	cup	carrots, sliced
½	cup	celery, sliced
½	cup	onions, sliced
1	teaspoon	Kitchen Bouquet
1	can	cream of mushroom soup
1	teaspoon	garlic, minced
2	cups	water
2	teaspoons	beef base

Stove Top Method-Dust cubed steak with flour and in a large, hot skillet brown the cube steak in the butter. Place the carrots, sliced onion and celery in the skillet with the meat. Mix together the following and pour over the vegetables: 2 cups of water mixed with 2 teaspoons of beef base, 1 teaspoon Kitchen Bouquet, 1 can of Cream of Mushroom Soup and 1 teaspoon of minced garlic. Cover and simmer for about 45-60 minutes or until tender.

Crock Pot Method-Dust cubed steak with flour and in a large, hot skillet brown the cube steak in the butter. Place the carrots, sliced onion and celery in bottom of crock pot. Top with browned cube steak. Mix together the following and pour over the cube steaks: 2 cups of water mixed with 2 teaspoons of beef base, 1 teaspoon Kitchen Bouquet, 1 can of Cream of Mushroom Soup and 1 teaspoon of minced garlic. Cook on low 6-8 hours.

Cheese and Chicken Enchiladas

1	stick	butter
1	cup	onion, chopped
1	teaspoon	garlic, minced
½	cup	flour
2	cups	chicken broth
8	ounces	cream cheese, softened

16	ounces	Mexican cheese, shredded
2	cups	chicken, cooked, shredded
1	7 ounce can	chopped green chilies, drained
7	8"	flour tortillas, warmed
		Salsa

Preheat oven to 350 degrees. Spray 9" x 13" baking dish. Melt butter in medium saucepan over medium heat. Add onion and garlic; cook and stir until onion is tender. Add flour, cook and stir 1 minute. Gradually whisk in chicken broth. Cook and stir 2-3 minutes or until slightly thickened. Add cream cheese; stir until melted. Stir in 1 cup cheese, chicken and chilies. Spoon 1/3 cup mixture onto each tortilla. Roll up and place in prepared dish seam side down. Pour remaining mixture evenly on top and sprinkle with remaining cheese. Back 20-30 minutes or until bubbly and lightly browned. Serve with salsa.

Chicken Alfredo Spinach Pizza

Makes: 4 servings   Prep Time: 30 minutes

Pizza

1	large	whole wheat pizza crust or flat bread
½	cup	onion, diced
1	cup	spinach, fresh, diced
1	cup	chicken, cooked, diced
2	cups	mozzarella cheese, shredded

Alfredo sauce

2	tablespoons	butter
2	tablespoons	flour
½	teaspoon	garlic, minced
1	cup	milk (at least 2%)
½	cup	parmesan
½	teaspoon	chicken base

Melt butter; add flour and mix with wire whip for 2 minutes. Add milk, chicken base and garlic. Stir on medium heat until thickens. Add parmesan cheese and stir until melts.

Bake raw crust on pizza pan or baking sheet for 10 minutes in preheated 375 degree oven. Top crust with Alfredo sauce, then fresh chopped spinach, onions and chicken. Top with cheese and bake for 10-15 minutes until hot and cheese melted and browned.

Chicken & Dumplings

Makes: 8 servings   Prep Time: 2 hours 30 minutes

6	split	chicken breasts, bone in and skin on (Cooked and cubed)
3	tablespoons	oil
1	dash	kosher salt and pepper
5	cups	chicken stock (recipe follows-or you can use canned)
2	tablespoons	chicken paste
½	stick	butter, unsalted
2	whole	onions, chopped
¾	cup	flour
¼	cup	half and half
4	whole	carrots, chopped
2	cups	frozen peas
½	cup	parsley, fresh, chopped

Dumplings

2	cups	flour
4	teaspoons	baking powder
1	teaspoon	salt
¾	cup	milk

In a large pot or Dutch oven, melt the butter and sauté the onions over medium-low heat for 10-15 minutes, until translucent. Add the flour and cook over low heat stirring constantly for 2 minutes. Add the hot chicken stock to the sauce. Simmer over low heat for 1 more minute, stirring until thick. Add 2 teaspoons salt, ½ teaspoon pepper, and the half and half. Add the cubed chicken, carrots, peas and parsley. Mix well. Put the dumplings on top of the hot stew, cover and let simmer for 10 minutes, then remove lid and simmer for 10 more minutes.

Dumplings-Mix ingredients until combined.

Homemade Chicken Stock

6	whole	split chicken breasts
8	cups	water
1	whole	onion, cut into quarters
1	large	carrot, cut in half
2	stalks	celery with leaves
2	sprigs	fresh thyme
1	sprig	rosemary
2		bay leaves
2	tablespoons	chicken base

Rinse the chicken in cool water and place in a heavy stock pot with the remaining ingredients. Bring to a rolling boil, then turn down heat to medium and simmer for 1–1 ½ hours until the chicken is pull a part tender. Remove the chicken from the pot and from the bones and cut into cubes, set aside. Strain the stock into a clean pot and discard all the vegetables so the broth is clear. Add 2 tablespoons chicken base to the stock and continue to simmer for about 30 more minutes until the stock is a nice yellow.

These are also a big hit at Sunday family dinner time. This is an easy recipe it just looks difficult because there is so much reading to it. Once you try it you will know what I mean.

Chicken & Noodles

Makes: 8-10 servings   Prep Time: 3-8 hours

2	pounds	chicken breasts (preferably with the bone and skin for added flavor)
1	teaspoon	pepper
2	cans	cream of chicken soup
4-6	cups	water (depending on how much broth you like)
3	tablespoons	chicken base
1	cup	onions, diced
½	teaspoon	garlic, minced
¼	cup	parsley, fresh, chopped; or 2 tablespoons dried parsley
8	ounces	wide Amish egg noodles, uncooked

Crock Pot Method-Wash chicken and remove as much fat as possible. Place the chicken in the crock pot and season with salt and pepper. Add all other ingredients with the chicken except the noodles. Put the lid on the crock pot and cook on low for 6-8 hours or high for 4-6 hours until the chicken is pull a part tender. When the chicken is done, remove and pull apart into pieces. Turn the crock pot on high (if not already on high) and remove the lid. Add the noodles and cook until they are done. Approximately 30 minutes. Note: The last 30 minutes you can add frozen peas, or mixed vegetables if you like. These are very good served over mashed potatoes.

Oven Method -Put all the ingredients except the noodles in a roasting pan, cover and slow roast on 325 degrees for about 3 hours. When the meat is pull apart tender remove from the roasting pan and pull meat apart. Add noodles to the broth and put back into oven until noodles are done. Add the meat.These are very popular with the grandkids especially over mashed potatoes and when they don't feel good.

Chicken and Pasta with Tomato Mushroom Pesto

Makes: 4-6 servings   Prep Time: 30 minutes

3	6 ounce	chicken breasts (cut into strips)
¼	cup	olive oil
3	cloves	garlic, roasted, chopped
3	whole	shallots, chopped
½	cup	sun-dried tomatoes, sliced
2	ounces	basil, fresh, sliced
6	tablespoons	tomato and mushroom pesto
1	pound	cilantro fettuccine pasta, cooked (regular pasta will also work) salt and pepper to taste

Place oil in skillet; add chicken when oil is warm. Sauté chicken strips until done (approximately 4 minutes), add chopped roasted garlic, chopped shallot, sun-dried tomato (or regular diced tomato, seeded and peeled), fresh basil, tomato and mushroom pesto and toss with cooked pasta.

Chicken Enchilada Casserole

Makes: 4-6 servings   Prep Time: 1 hour

2	cups	chicken, cooked, diced
1	can	cream of mushroom or cream of chicken soup
2	cups	sour cream
1	4 ounce can	green chilies, diced
12	whole	corn tortillas
2	cups	cheddar or Colby cheese, shredded

Preheat oven to 350 degrees. Mix together the soup and sour cream. Spray a 9" x 13" baking dish and cover the bottom of it with ½ of the soup/sour cream mixture. Then put a layer of the tortillas on top of the soup mixture, then layer ½ the chicken, ½ the chilies and ½ the cheese. Do 1 more layer, soup/sour cream, tortillas, chicken, chilies and cheese. Bake for 30-45 minutes until hot throughout. Garnish with chopped green onion, diced tomatoes, fresh chopped cilantro and chopped avocado.

Note: As a variation I add 1 layer of black beans.

Chicken Hash

2	6 ounce	chicken breasts, cooked and cut into chunks (see oven roasted chicken breast recipe)
1	large	potato, cooked and cut into chunks
1	whole	green pepper, cut into chunks
1	whole	onion, cut into chunks
1/8-1/4	cup	canola or olive oil
		seasoned salt
		pepper

Cook potato in microwave as you were baking a potato or use a left over baked potato. Let set for about 5-10 minutes then cut into chunks. Heat the oil in the skillet starting with the smallest amount first. The oil should just cover the bottom of the skillet. Add seasoned salt and the chopped onion and peppers. Cook until they are almost done, about 3 minutes. You can add more oil if needed but just a little at a time. Add the chicken and potatoes and a little more seasoned salt and pepper if needed or to taste. Cook all the ingredients for about 5 minutes without turning on medium heat and then turn and cook for about another 5 minutes. If you prefer they are browned keep cooking for an extra 5 minutes each side.

Chicken Lasagna

1	pound	lasagna noodles, cooked
2	cups	chicken, cooked, diced
2	cups	mozzarella cheese, shredded
1/2	cup	parmesan cheese
2	tablespoons	butter
1/3	cup	tomatoes, fresh, diced or sun-dried tomatoes, chopped
1/4	cup	onion, chopped
1 1/2	cups	spinach, fresh, chopped
2-3	cups	Alfredo sauce (see recipe)
1	cup	mushrooms, sliced

Melt butter to sauté onion. Add spinach, tomatoes, mushrooms and Alfredo sauce. Place a small amount of sauce mixture in a greased 9" x 13" pan just to moisten the pan. Layer ½ noodles, ½ sauce, and ½ chicken and ½ cheeses. Repeat layering. Bake at 350 degrees for 45 minutes or until bubbly hot.

Chicken Perisenne

Makes: 4 servings   Prep Time: 1 hour 15 minutes

4	6 ounce	chicken breasts
1	can	cream of mushroom soup
1	cup	sour cream
¼	cup	sherry
2	teaspoons	chicken base
½	cup	onions, diced
1	cup	assorted mushrooms (oyster, shitake, portabella), sautéed
	dash	paprika
¾	cup	parmesan

Mix soup and sour cream together. Add sherry, chicken base, onions and mushrooms to soup mixture. Preheat oven to 375 degrees. Place chicken in a 9" x 13" baking dish and pour sauce over it; sprinkle with paprika; bake for 1 to 1¼ hour. Add ¾ cup of parmesan cheese the last 15 minutes and finish baking until cheese is melted and browned. I like to serve wild rice with this.

Chicken with Blackberries

Makes: 4 servings   Prep Time: 1 hour

½	cup	white wine, dry
4	6 ounce	chicken breasts, boneless
3	tablespoons	thyme, fresh, chopped
½	cup	chicken broth
2	tablespoons	brown sugar
2	tablespoons	blackberries, fresh, mashed
2	cloves	garlic, minced
1	teaspoon	canola or olive oil
¼	teaspoon	cumin, ground
½	cup	blackberries, fresh for garnish

Preheat oven to 375 degrees. Pour ¼ cup of the wine into a large baking dish. Arrange the chicken in the dish. Sprinkle with the thyme and season with salt and pepper. Bake for 35 minutes, adding the remaining ¼ cup of wine and then the chicken broth to the pan. Baste occassionally.

In a small bowl combine the brown sugar, mashed blackberries, garlic, oil and cumin. Spoon the mixture over the chicken and continue cooking for 10 minutes, basting occassionally until the juices run clear and chicken is tender. Transfer the chicken to a serving platter and cover with foil to keep hot.

Pour the cooking juices into a small saucepan and bring to a boil over moderate heat. Cook until reduced in half, about 2 minutes. Season the sauce with salt and pepper and spoon over the chicken. Garnish with the fresh blackberries.

Chili Cheese Stuffed Chicken

Makes: 12 servings   Prep Time: 30 minutes

6	6 ounce	chicken breasts, boneless, skinless
¾	teaspoon	salt
3	cups	tortilla chips, finely crushed
¾	teaspoons	cumin, ground
¾	teaspoon	chili powder
6	canned	whole green chilies, halved, seeded
12	pieces	jack cheese
¼	cup	buttermilk
		black pepper to taste
		(toothpicks)

Place the chicken breast, between sheets of plastic wrap; pound to ¼ inch thickness and season lightly with salt and pepper. Combine: tortilla chips, cumin, chili powder, spread on plate and set aside. Place 1 chili half and 1 slice of cheese in center of chicken. Roll up each piece from a narrow end and secure with a toothpick. Dip each piece of chicken in buttermilk, then coat generously with crumbs. Place in fold lined baking dish. Bake in preheated oven at 350 degrees for 35 minutes or until chicken tests done in the center. Slice and serve.

Easy Chicken Enchiladas

2	cups	chicken, cooked diced
2	cups	sour cream
1	can	cream of chicken soup
1 ½	cups	jack cheese, shredded
1 ½	cups	longhorn cheese or cheddar, shredded
1	4.5 ounce can	green chilies, chopped, drained
2	tablespoons	onion, chopped
1	dash	salt
1	dash	pepper
10	10"	flour tortillas
1	cup (4 ounces)	longhorn or cheddar cheese, shredded

Combine first 9 ingredients; mix well. Spread some of the sauce on the bottom of a 9" x 13" pan. Place a heaping ½ cup chicken mixture on each tortilla, and place seam side down in the pan. Cover and bake at 350 for 20 minutes. Sprinkle with 1 cup longhorn cheese and bake uncovered 5 additional minutes.

Orange Pecan Chicken

4	whole	chicken breasts, boneless, skinless
¼	cup	orange marmalade
¼	cup	honey
1	tablespoon	orange zest
		seasoned salt
		canola oil
¾	cup	pecan pieces

Preheat oven to 375 degrees. Mix together the marmalade, honey and zest. Coat a shallow baking sheet with the oil. Sprinkle both sides of chicken with salt. Coat each side of the chicken with the orange mixture and place on the baking sheet. Sprinkle the tops of the chicken with the pecans. Bake 12 minutes then turn chicken and sprinkle this side with pecans. Bake another 12-15 minutes until the chicken is done and tender. Glaze chicken with the orange sauce while it bakes. For more of an orange taste to the chicken you can make extra sauce and marinade the chicken in the sauce for a few hours before baking.

Oven Roasted Chicken Breasts

Makes: 4 servings   Prep Time: 35 minutes

4	6 ounce	chicken breasts, boneless, skinless
1-2	tablespoons	canola oil
¼	teaspoon	seasoned salt

Brush both sides of the chicken with canola oil then season with seasoned salt. Bake in preheated 375 degree oven 15 minutes on each side. This is great topped with a fresh summer salsa from veggies out of the garden. (See recipes.) This is my grandkid's favorite chicken and a great base for a lot of other recipes like the Chicken Hash, the Parmesan Chicken, many sandwich recipes in this book and the Herb Chicken breast. (See recipes).

Parmesan Chicken-Make the oven roasted chicken breasts, then cover with your favorite sauce, mozzarella and parmesan. Bake until cheese is melted.
Roasted Herb Chicken Breasts- add fresh chopped herbs to each side of the breasts after you have brushed the breasts with oil.

Raspberry Chicken

Makes: 12 servings   Prep Time: 30 minutes

1	cup	olive or canola
¼	cup	raspberry or red wine vinegar
6	sprigs	thyme, fresh
8	cloves	garlic, minced
1	cup	honey
1/8	teaspoon	pepper
½	teaspoon	salt
½	6 ounce	chicken breast, boneless, skinless

Mix well. Marinate chicken breasts for one hour. Then, bake, broil or grill. Top with Raspberry Sauce (see recipe), and garnish with fresh raspberries and a sprig of mint.

Roasted Chicken

Makes: 4 servings   Prep Time: 1 hour 15 minutes

1	whole	roasting chicken
1	teaspoon	Kitchen Bouquet (browning sauce)
¼	cup	butter, melted
1	teaspoon	garlic, minced
1	teaspoon	rosemary, fresh, minced
1	teaspoon	parsley, fresh, finely chopped
1	cup	fresh garden vegetables cut into chunks (zucchini, yellow squash, onions, celery)
		salt and pepper
¼	cup	water

Salt and pepper the vegetables. Remove the giblets from the chicken and wash the chicken inside and out with cold water. Stuff the chicken with the fresh vegetables. Add the fresh herbs to the melted butter then add the Kitchen Bouquet. Brush the chicken with the fresh herb butter. The butter will harden as you brush it on since the chicken is cold. Place the chicken in a roasting pan, add the water and cover with a lid or foil. Bake for 45-60 minutes in a 350 degree pre-heated oven. Remove the lid, baste with the juices and bake 15-30 minutes more uncovered until browned and chicken leg pulls away from the chicken.

I have people tell me they are intimidated to roast a whole chicken. This recipe is a very easy fool proof recipe so try it and you will not be intimidated any more. I promise. This is especially good with a free range, natural chicken from Seven Sons Farm.

Southern Fried Chicken

Makes: 4 servings   Prep Time: 1 hour 30 minutes

1	whole	chicken, cut up and washed
1	cup	flour
2	whole	eggs
¼	cup	buttermilk
½	teaspoon	salt
½	teaspoon	pepper
½	teaspoon	seasoned salt
¼	teaspoon	garlic powder
2	cups	canola oil

Wash chicken. Beat eggs and add salt and milk to eggs. Mix seasonings with flour in a separate bowl. Put 2 cups of canola oil in large skillet and heat on medium heat for 5-10 minutes. Dip chicken in egg wash and then flour mixture and repeat. Put chicken in skillet when oil is hot but not too hot. Cook chicken for 15 minutes then turn over and cook the other side for 15 minutes. Take chicken out and put on paper towels to drain. Put in the oven to keep warm or finish cooking if needed.

Southwestern Chicken and Pasta

Makes: 6 servings   Prep Time: 45 minutes

8	ounces	orzo pasta
1	large	tomato, diced
½	cup	zucchini, diced
2	green	onion, diced
½	green	pepper, diced
1	cup	black beans, cooked, drained
1	cooked	rotisserie chicken, diced
1	cup	mozzarella cheese, shredded
1	teaspoon	cumin
1	teaspoon	minced garlic
1	whole	avocado, diced
¼	cup	cilantro, fresh, chopped
1	teaspoon	mint, fresh, chopped
2	tablespoons	olive oil or canola oil

Cook pasta according to box directions, and rinse. Sauté green onion, green pepper and garlic in oil until soft. Toss pasta with vegetables. Add tomatoes, zucchini, black beans, chicken, cumin, cilantro, and mint and mozzarella cheese. Bake for 30 minutes at 350 degrees. Serve with avocado on top.

Summer Stuffed Chicken Breasts

Makes: 4 chicken breasts   Prep Time: 40 minutes

4	6 ounce	chicken breast, boneless, skinless
1	cup	feta cheese, crumbled
¾	cup	tomatoes, seeded, chopped
¼	cup	basil, fresh, chopped
⅛	cup	lemon juice
3	tablespoons	oil
1	tablespoon	galic, minced
		salt and pepper to taste

Pound chicken breasts and season with salt and pepper. Mix remaining ingredients together and put ¼ of the ingredients in the center of each chicken breast. Roll up chicken breast and secure with toothpicks. Brush each side of the chicken breast with oil and season with salt and pepper. Bake in a preheated 350 degree oven in a 9" x 13" pan or on the grill medium heat. Let chicken stand for 5 minutes. Slice each breast into about 4 slices. Serve. You can also roll the chicken breasts in Pancko bread crumbs before baking.

Thanksgiving Turkey

Makes: 12 servings   Prep Time: 5 hours

1	(12) pound	turkey, fresh or frozen, thawed
½	pound	butter, melted
1	teaspoon	Kitchen Bouquet
1	teaspoon	parsley, fresh, chopped
½	teaspoon	thyme, fresh, chopped
½	teaspoon	garlic powder
1	teaspoon	rosemary fresh, chopped
1	cup	water or chicken stock

These are the instructions and recipes I use for my Thanksgiving cooking classes. They are very detailed and may be more then what some of you need. If you are a first time Turkey roaster you will appreciate all the notes and details. There are many recipes and ways to roast a turkey which can be really confusing at first. Some bake with high temps some with low, some in 2 hours and some all night. But don't worry this is a fool proof recipe that I use for my family Thanksgiving dinner every year.

Thaw your turkey in its wrapper in the refrigerator 24 hours for each 5 pounds. It will take at least 2 to 2 ½ days to defrost your 12 pound turkey in the refrigerator. If you are cutting it close on time you can submerge the frozen turkey in cold water in the sink, changing the water frequently. It will take about 30 minutes per pound to defrost this way. The bird is thawed and ready for roasting when the giblets can be removed easily and there are no ice crystals in the body or neck. If the center is frozen the bird will cook unevenly.

If you want to stuff your turkey have your stuffing ready. Allow ¾ cup of stuffing per pound of bird. You will need 9 cups of stuffing for a 12 pound turkey.

Remove giblets from turkey. Pull off any remaining feathers. Clean and rinse inside and outside of turkey with cold water. Salt the cavity.

Melt butter with herbs & garlic in microwave. Add kitchen bouquet to herb butter.

Stuff and tie up the turkey.

Place the turkey in a large roasting pan with a rack (the rack will keep the turkey from sticking to the bottom of the pan especially if you spray it with a cooking spray) breast side up. A 2-3" deep roasting pan is important. Disposable aluminum pans are flimsy and can be dangerous.

Brush the melted herb butter on the turkey. Completely cover with the butter. The butter will harden on the turkey. Cover the turkey securely with foil or a tight fitting lid. Place on the lower rack, in the center of the oven and follow the roasting schedule below. You do not need to baste. The turkey will be done when the legs pull apart easily and the juices run clear or the meat thermometer reaches 175 degrees. When using the meat thermometer make sure it does not touch bone or you will get an incorrect reading. Check the turkey the last 30-60 minutes to see if it needs more browning. If so remove the foil/lid and continue baking.

Notes for a successful Turkey:
- Let turkey rest for 30 minutes before carving. This is very important for a juicy turkey.
- Keep oven door shut. Slow steady heat creates maximum flavor from the bird and produces a golden skin.
- Loosely stuff the turkey with stuffing. If you do not stuff your turkey you can fill the cavity with quartered onions, celery and carrots to add flavor to the drippings for the gravy.

- With 12 pounds or less allow 1 pound per person. With birds over 12 pound plan on ¾ pound per serving. For a boneless turkey breast plan ½ pound per person.
- Make sure to preheat the oven.

Cooking times:

Turkey Weight	Oven Temperature	Roasting Time
8 - 12 lbs.	325 degrees	3 - 3 ¾ hours
12 - 14 lbs.	325 degrees	3 ¼ - 4 ½ hours
14 - 18 lbs	325 degrees	4 - 5 hours
18 - 20 lbs	325 degrees	4 ½ - 5 ¼ hours
20 - 24 lbs	325 degrees	4 ¾ - 5 ¾ hours

*When baking in electric roaster I bake a 16 pound turkey on 275 for 4 hours.

Gravy

Makes: 12 servings

Prep Time: 3-4 hours

½	stick	butter
		turkey neck and giblet's
3	whole	celery stalks with leaves, cut in half
2	large	onions, quartered
4	whole	carrots, cut into chunks
¼	cup	parsley, fresh
1	teaspoon	garlic, minced
4	cups	water
3	tablespoons	chicken or turkey base (or use 4 cups of chicken broth instead of 4 c water and chicken base)
1 -2	teaspoons	Kitchen Bouquet (to make desired color)
1	cup	turkey drippings
		pepper to taste
¼	cup	corn starch or flour
¼	cup	water

Melt butter in large saucepan and add the next 6 ingredients and sauté until brown. Add the water, chicken base and kitchen bouquet. Simmer on low for 3-4 hours adding a little water if needed. You can cook in the crock pot on high for 6-8 hours instead of on the stove. Strain the stock so you have just broth left. Discard the veggies. Add turkey drippings and then pour into saucepan. Simmer on medium high heat for about 1 hour until it reduces. Mix the cornstarch and water together with wire whip until all lumps are gone. Slowly add the cornstarch to the broth with a whisk until gravy thickens about 3 minutes. Serve.

Note: I use the crock pot because cooking the stock takes hours and we go to my brother's house (with my other 5 siblings, kids and parents) for Thanksgiving at noon. Then we have our kids and grandkids over for Thanksgiving dinner in the evening. The stock can cook unattended in the crock pot while I am gone and I can finish it on the stove when I return home later afternoon. It works out great.

Stuffing

Makes: 12-15 serving

Prep Time: 1 hour

8	cups	bread, cubed or stuffing mix
1	tablespoon	chicken base
¼	pound	butter
1½	cups	water
1	cup	celery, chopped
1	cup	onion, chopped
1	teaspoon	garlic, minced or ½ teaspoon garlic powder
¼	cup	parsley, fresh, chopped
¼	cup	sage, fresh, chopped
1	teaspoon	thyme, fresh, chopped

Sauté celery, onion, garlic, parsley, sage and thyme in 1 tablespoon butter for about 3-4 minutes. Then add water and chicken base. Mix and bring to a boil on medium heat. Pour over bread cubes. Stuff the turkey. You can use poultry seasoning instead of the fresh herbs if you like. You can add chopped oysters, cooked chopped giblets, cranberries, golden raisins, apple pieces, walnuts, or whatever you like. You can also bake the stuffing in a baking pan if you prefer not to stuff the turkey or have extra stuffing. Refrigerate until ready to bake.

Baked Halibut with Avocado Salsa

Makes: 4 servings   Prep Time: 1 hour

2	pounds	halibut, fresh
4	tablespoons	olive oil
1	tablespoon	mint, fresh, chopped fine
1	tablespoon	lemon juice, fresh

Salsa

1	medium	tomato, diced small
¼	cup	jalapeño, diced fine
¼	cup	mild onion, diced fine
2	tablespoons	mint, fresh, chopped fine
1	dash	salt
1	dash	pepper
2	tablespoons	lime juice, fresh
½	cup	avocado, diced fine

Marinate the Halibut in the olive oil, fresh lemon juice and mint. Add a dash of salt and pepper. Marinate 15 minutes or more turning once to get marinate on both sides. While the Halibut is marinating, make the salsa. Add all the salsa ingredients together and toss gently. Let set in the refrigerator while the fish is baking. Spray or coat a baking dish with olive oil and bake the Halibut at 350 degrees for 20-30 minutes, depending on the thickness. The fish should be flakey when done. Serve the salsa on top of the fish.

Note: I use lemon mint whenever it is available.

Baked Salmon

Makes: 4 servings   Prep Time: 20 minutes

2	pounds	salmon
2	tablespoons	canola or olive oil
		salt
		pepper

Brush salmon with oil and season with salt and pepper. Bake at 350 degrees in a preheated oven for 15 minutes. I use this recipe for my salmon salads and salmon cakes. This is another recipe you can build on and is very good cooked on the grill as is or with the blackened seasoning spices and a bleu cheese sauce or topped with a fresh summer salsa. (See recipes.)

Crab and Vegetable Pasta

Makes: 4 servings   Prep Time: 15 minutes

1	pound	thin spaghetti, cooked
¾	cup	snow peas, cut in thirds
2	stalks	green onion, diced
½	cup	zucchini, diced
¾	cup	cherry tomatoes, halved
3	tablespoons	canola oil
½	teaspoon	salt
½	teaspoon	pepper
16	ounces	lump crab

Heat the oil with salt and pepper on medium heat. Add vegetables and crab meat. Sauté for about 1 minute; toss pasta in with the vegetables and crab, toss until mixed.

Pecan Haddock

Makes: 4 servings   Prep Time: 30 minutes

2	pounds	haddock, fresh
¼	cup	brown sugar
1	tablespoon	butter, melted
1	cup	pecans, chopped
Cayenne Butter Sauce		
¼	stick	butter, melted
½	teaspoon	cayenne pepper
¼	cup	red pepper, diced fine

Rinse and pat the fish dry. Place on a sprayed baking sheet pan. Brush the fish with the tablespoon of melted butter. Put the brown sugar on top of the fish. Press the pecans on the top of the sugar. Put the fish in the oven at 375 degrees and bake for 15 minutes until fish is flaky. Add the cayenne pepper to the ¼ stick of melted butter. Put a small amount of the cayenne butter sauce on each serving of Haddock. Garnish with the diced red pepper. This is really good and was a very popular weekend dinner special at Margy's.

Salmon with Orange Glaze

6	(6 ounce)	salmon fillets, skinned if desired
1	tablespoon	sesame oil, un-toasted
3	teaspoons	low-sodium soy sauce
¼	cup	white wine
1	cup	orange juice, fresh squeezed
1	teaspoon	orange zest, grated or minced
3	tablespoons	sherry
½	teaspoon	ginger root, peeled, grated or minced
2	thin	orange, unpeeled, sliced

Pat salmon dry. Preheat oven to 400 degrees. Have ready a glass baking dish large enough to hold salmon in a single layer. In a large skillet over medium-high heat, heat oil. Add salmon and sear, turning once, 1 minute on each side. You should hear fish sizzle. Transfer salmon to baking dish and drizzle with soy sauce and wine. Transfer to oven and roast 10 minutes until cooked through and flakes easily.

Meanwhile, in a non-reactive small saucepan over medium-high heat, heat orange juice and zest, sherry and ginger; simmer, stirring frequently, about 15 minutes until sauce is reduced by half and thickened. Add orange slices and cook, stirring once or twice. Remove from heat. Transfer salmon to individual plates, drizzle with sauce and serve immediately.

Shrimp Scampi

1	stick	butter, melted
2	cloves	garlic, minced
½	teaspoon	lemon juice, fresh
¼	teaspoon	cayenne pepper
1	pound	shrimp, 21-25 count, peeled, de-veined
¼	cup	dry white wine

Melt butter in skillet over medium-high heat. Add shrimp and sauté 2 minutes, add garlic, lemon juice and pepper. Cook 30 seconds then add wine, scraping the bottom of the pan. Simmer until it reduces, about 2 minutes. Serve over rice or crusty bread.

Teriyaki Glazed Salmon

Makes: 4 servings   Prep Time: 20 minutes

2	pounds	salmon, fresh
1	tablespoon	canola oil for pan
2-3	tablespoons	teriyaki sauce

Brush salmon with Teriyaki sauce and place on an oiled baking sheet. Bake at 350 degrees in a preheated oven for 15 minutes or until salmon flakes.

Note: This is also very good cooked on the grill.

Tomato Basil Pasta with Shrimp

Makes: 6 servings   Prep Time: 30 minutes

1	pound	raw shrimp, peeled, de-veined
½	cup	olive oil
1	clove	garlic, chopped
1 ½	pounds	tomatoes, peeled, seeded, diced
1	each	shallot, chopped
1	pound	lemon linguini, cooked (or any pasta)
2	ounces	basil, fresh, sliced

Heat the oil in a large skillet over medium heat. When oil is warm, add shrimp and sauté 2-3 minutes. Turn to other side and sauté 3 minutes more or until the shrimp are almost cooked. Add chopped shallot and garlic and sauté for 2 minutes. Then add diced tomatoes and fresh basil to skillet and season with salt and pepper; toss with pasta.

Tuna Noodle Casserole

Makes: 4-6 servings   Prep Time: 1 hour

8	ounces	egg noodles, cooked
1	can	cream of mushroom soup
6	ounces	tuna, all white albacore, drained
½	cup	frozen peas
1	cup	sour cream
½	cup	green onion, chopped
1	cup	cheddar cheese, shredded

Topping

½	stick	butter, melted
¾	cup	bread crumbs

Mix egg noodles, soup, tuna, peas, sour cream, green onion and shredded cheddar. Put in a sprayed casserole dish. Mix topping ingredients together and put on top of casserole. Bake at 350 degrees for 30-45 minutes or until hot throughout and topping is browned.

Baked Ham

Makes: 2-3 servings per pound   Prep Time: 15 minutes per pound

Mustard Glaze

1	cup	brown sugar
1	teaspoon	dry mustard
2-3	tablespoons	ham drippings, or fruit juice

Honey-Orange Glaze

1	cup	brown sugar
½	cup	honey
½	cup	orange juice

Peach Glaze

1 ½	cups	brown sugar
⅓	cup	syrup from peaches
3	tablespoons	apple cider vinegar
¾	teaspoon	cloves

Cherry Sauce

4	teaspoons	cornstarch
½	cup	sugar
½	teaspoon	salt
2	1 pound cans or 3 cups	red sour cherries, fresh, pitted or dark sweet cherries
2	tablespoons	lemon juice
2	tablespoons	vanilla

Baking the ham- Place the ham fat side up on a rack in a shallow pan. Score ham in diamonds-cut ¼ inch deep. Do not cover, add ½ cup water. Insert meat thermometer. Bake in slow oven at 325. Bake 15-17 minutes per pound until reaches an internal temperature of 130. Half an hour before time is up, remove from oven and pour fat drippings from pan. Stud the ham with whole cloves at this time, if desired. Spoon glaze over ham; continue baking 30 more minutes basting occasionally.

Mustard, Orange and Peach Glaze: Mix ingredients together and glaze.
Cherry Sauce: Put starch, sugar and salt in saucepan. Mix well. Gradually add the juice from the cherries, 1 ½ cups. Cook over low heat until thick. Remove from heat and add lemon juice and vanilla. Serve over ham.

BBQ Baby Back Ribs

Makes: 8 servings   Prep Time: 2 hours

4	pounds	pork back ribs
1	gallon	water, boiling
2	whole	bay leaves
1	tablespoon	Tabasco sauce
1	cup	barbecue sauce

Put the ribs in the pot of boiling water with the bay leaves and Tabasco sauce. Boil 20 minutes. Remove from the pot. Turn the ribs over and put them back in the pot and boil 20 more minutes. Remove from the pot and put on a baking dish. Cover both sides with barbecue sauce and bake or grill for 10-15 minutes or until the sauce is baked on.

Cheese Tortellini Bake

Makes: 4 servings   Prep Time: 1 hour

1	pound	Italian sausage links, cooked, sliced
1	pound	cheese tortellini, cooked
1	whole	green pepper, chopped
1	whole	sweet onion, chopped
1	clove	garlic, minced
1	whole	zucchini, chopped (optional)
1	tablespoon	canola or olive oil
4	cups	of your favorite pasta sauce
8	ounces	Italian cheese, shredded

Preheat oven to 350 degrees. Sauté onion, pepper and zucchini in oil until onion is translucent. Mix all ingredients but the cheese together and put in a greased 9" x 13" baking dish. Sprinkle the cheese on top and bake covered for 30 minutes then uncovered for 15 minutes; until hot throughout and cheese is lightly brown and melted. You can add olives or mushrooms if you like.

For a vegetarian spin on this I use eggplant or Portabella mushrooms instead of the sausage. They can either be sautéed with the other vegetables or roasted in the oven.

Eggplant Casserole

Makes: 4 servings   Prep Time: 1 hour

2	tablespoons	oil
1	tablespoon	kosher salt
1	pound	Italian sausage links
1	15 ounce can	tomatoes, diced
1	dash	Italian seasonings
8	ounces	provolone cheese, sliced
1	whole	green pepper, cut into medium size chunks
1	large	onion, cut into medium size chunks
1	large	eggplant, skin removed, cut into medium size chunks

Cook sausage in large skillet. When sausage is almost done add the onions and peppers and continue cooking until sausage is done. Remove sausage from skillet, slice and put back in skillet. Add 1 can tomatoes and Italian seasoning.

Mix eggplant and salt. Put in strainer and rinse eggplant with cool water after 30 minutes. Pat it dry on paper towels. Put on baking sheet and coat with oil; bake at 400 degrees for 25 minutes, or until eggplant is soft and brown.

Mix eggplant with the tomatoes and sausage then put into greased 9" x 13" casserole dish. Cover with cheese and bake until hot through-out and cheese is browned.

Italian Crock Pot Pasta

Makes: 4 servings   Prep Time: 6-8 hours

1	pound	Italian sausage links, uncooked (Italian turkey sausage also works)
1	medium	yellow onion, sliced
1	medium	green pepper, sliced
1	teaspoon	Italian seasonings, dried
1	cup	mushrooms, sliced or small left whole
3	cups	spaghetti sauce (no meat)
1	pound	pasta, cooked
		parmesan cheese

Brown the sausage in skillet. Put all ingredients, except pasta in the crock pot and cook on low for 6-8 hours. Slice links and serve sauce/sausage over pasta. Top with parmesan cheese.

Vegetarian-Eliminate the sausage and add sliced zucchini and yellow squash, cubed eggplant and or any variety of vegetables you prefer.

Pork Roast with Sauerkraut

Makes: 6 servings   Prep Time: 2 hours

2	pounds	pork roast
1	teaspoon	salt
1	teaspoon	pepper
1	teaspoon	garlic powder
1 ½	cups	sauerkraut, drained and rinsed
½	cup	apple juice
1	teaspoon	brown sugar

Oven Method- Season the roast with salt, pepper and garlic. Put in a roasting pan or baking dish add sauerkraut, juice and sugar. Cover, and bake at 300 degrees for 2-3 hours or until fork tender.

Crock Pot method- Season the roast with salt and pepper. Brown pork in skillet. Place pork in crock pot. Add sauerkraut, juice and sugar to crock pot. Cook on low for 6-8 hours or high for 4-5 hours.

Roasted Pork Tenderloin with Apricot Glaze

Makes: 6-8 servings   Prep Time: 45 minutes

2-3	pounds	pork tenderloin
1	teaspoon	garlic, minced
1 ½	cups	apricot preserves
2	tablespoons	white vinegar
1	teaspoon	rosemary, fresh, chopped
1	teaspoon	oregano, fresh, chopped or ½ teaspoon dried
1	tablespoon	oil

Preheat oven to 425 degrees. Heat a small sauce pan over medium heat. Coat pan with oil. Add garlic; cook 30 seconds. Stir in preserves and the next 4 ingredients (through oregano); bring mixture to a boil. Reduce heat and cook for 5 minutes; stirring occasionally. Stir in ¼ teaspoon of salt and ⅛ teaspoon pepper.

Rub pork roast with oil, then season with salt and pepper. Bake roast on baking sheet and sear in oven for 15 minutes. Remove from oven and glaze with the apricot glaze. Bake for another 20-30 minutes until reaching an internal temperature of 160 degrees. Let set for 5 minutes then slice and serve. This is a very easy and delicious dish. Guys especially love this one. Slice and place on tray; garnish with fresh rosemary twigs.

Stuffed Acorn Squash

Makes: 6 servings   Prep Time: 45 minutes

1	pound	sausage, ground
2	cups	brown rice, cooked
½	cup	onion, diced
½	cup	red or green pepper, diced
¼	cup	green onion, diced
½	teaspoon	seasoned salt
1	teaspoon	garlic, minced
3	whole	acorn squash, halved
1	cup	mozzarella cheese, shredded

Cut acorn squash in half, remove seeds. Place in microwave and/or bake in oven at 350 degrees for 10-15 minutes, until soft. Cook sausage. When done, add onion, pepper, garlic, rice and seasoned salt. Stuff squash with the sausage, rice mixture. Put cheese on top and bake 15 minutes on 350 degrees, or until cheese is hot and bubbly. This was a very popular fall, lunch special at the restaurant. It also makes great leftovers as it reheats well.

Zucchini Sausage Casserole

Makes: 8 servings   Prep Time: 1 hour

1	pound	sausage meat, ground, cooked
1	tablespoon	oil
1	whole	onion, sliced
2	small	zucchini, cubed, uncooked
1	small	yellow squash, cubed
2	cloves	garlic, minced
¼	cup	basil, fresh, chopped
2	cups	marinara sauce
1	cup	parmesan cheese
8	ounces	mozzarella or provolone cheese

Sauté zucchini, yellow squash, garlic and onion. Mix all ingredients together except cheeses and put in greased casserole dish. Cover with cheeses and bake at 350 degrees for 30-45 minutes or until zucchini is tender.

Easy Broccoli Enchiladas

Makes: 4-6 servings   Prep Time: 45 minutes

1	bunch	broccoli, chopped
1	can	cream of chicken soup
1	8 ounce package	cream cheese
1	small can (4.5 ounce)	chopped green chilies
¼	cup	green onions, chopped
10-12	10"	flour tortillas
8	ounces	jack and cheddar mix, shredded

Cook 1 bunch chopped broccoli in microwave

Mix the soup, cream cheese, green chilies and onions together and heat in microwave; stir.

Add the broccoli to ingredients above.

Fill tortillas with about ½ cup of filling.

Put in sprayed 9" x 13" pan, cover with shredded cheese. Bake at 350 for 20- 30 minutes until hot throughout. You can add salad shrimp, mushrooms, cooked chicken etc.

Eggplant Parmesan

Makes: 4 servings

Prep Time: 1 hour

2	medium	eggplants, peeled, sliced thin
		Kosher salt
2	whole	eggs, beaten
½	cup	milk
1	cup	flour
½ -¾	cup	oil; heated on medium heat
3	cups	pasta sauce
2	cups	mozzarella cheese, shredded
1	cup	parmesan cheese, shredded

Prepare the eggplant: Place eggplant slices on paper towels and sprinkle with salt. Let stand 15-30 minutes then rinse with cool water.

Mix eggs and milk to make an egg wash. Add a dash of salt and pepper to flour. Dip eggplant in egg wash then flour. Cook in oil until brown on both sides. Drain on paper towels.

Spray a 9" x 13" casserole dish. Put a thin layer of sauce on the bottom and layer the bottom with eggplant. Cover the eggplant with a thin layer of sauce, shredded mozzarella and parmesan; layer 2 more times with eggplant, sauce and cheese, ending with cheese. Bake in a 375 degree preheated oven for 20-30 minutes until hot throughout and the cheese is brown and bubbly.

Eggplant Pesto Crepes

Makes: 4-6 servings   Prep Time: 1 hour

2	whole	eggplants
¼	cup	basil pesto (see recipe)
12-16	slices	mozzarella cheese
		oil

Filling

1	whole	shallot, minced
2	cups	ricotta cheese
½	cup	parmesan, grated
½	cup	parsley, fresh, chopped
½	cup	parmesan cheese, grated

Sauce

¼	cup	butter
1	tablespoon	shallot, minced
¼	cup	flour
1 ¾	cups	milk or cream
2	each	egg yolks, beaten
1	teaspoon	thyme, fresh, chopped
¼	cup	parsley, fresh, chopped
¼	cup	parmesan, grated
1 ½	tablespoons	pesto

Topping

¼	cup	parmesan, grated
¼	cup	bread crumbs

Prepare eggplant-Slice eggplant lengthwise into even ¼ inch thick slices. Brush with oil and bake in preheated 400 degree oven for 10 minutes.

Filling- Mix ricotta, shallot, parsley, parmesan and salt and pepper.

Sauce-Melt butter then sauté shallots in butter. Add flour and make a roux, whisk for 3 minutes. Slowly add the milk and whisk until starts to thicken. Add egg yolks and continue to whisk. Add remaining ingredients and whisk until all is incorporated.

Topping-Mix the bread crumbs and cheese together.

Assemble- Spread the pesto on eggplant, then a slice of mozzarella cheese. Spread the ricotta mixture on top of the mozzarella cheese then roll up the eggplant like you would roll up a crepe. Place the eggplant rolls in a 9" x13" greased baking dish. Cover with sauce, sprinkle with topping and bake 25 minutes until lightly brown. This recipe is from my chef friend, Bun Lim.

Portobello Fajitas

Makes: 1 serving

Prep Time: 25 minutes

2	medium	flour tortillas, warmed
1	whole	portobello mushroom
1	tablespoon	Mushroom Marinade, see recipe
¼	cup	lettuce, shredded
¼	cup	tomatoes, diced
1	tablespoon	green onion, chopped
1	teaspoon	cilantro, fresh, chopped
¼	cup	salsa
¼	cup	jack cheese, shredded

Marinate the mushroom for a few minutes then bake, broil or grill until mushroom is cooked to soft. Cut mushroom into strips and place on the tortillas. Half a mushroom on each tortilla. Top the mushroom with the remaining ingredients except serve the salsa on the side. You can use Mexican white cheese or farmers cheese instead of the jack. Don't cook the mushroom on a high heat, it will burn. I bake them in the oven on 350 degrees or medium heat on the grill for about 15.

Roasted Vegetable Pizza

Makes: 2 serving

Prep Time: 45 minutes

Pizza

1	large	whole wheat pizza crust or flatbread
1	whole	eggplant, peeled, cubed
1	bunch	asparagus, cut into 1" pieces
1	whole	onion, cubed
1	cup	mini portabella mushrooms, sliced thick
½	cup	fresh tomatoes, diced
1	cup	feta cheese
1-2	tablespoons	canola or olive oil

Roast vegetables- Peel and cube eggplant. Cut asparagus into 1 inch pieces. Cut onion into cubes. Slice mushrooms, thick. Put the oil and salt on the vegetables and roast on baking sheet for 25 minutes in preheated 375 degree oven. Bake raw crust on sheet pan for 12 minutes in preheated 375 degree oven. Top crust with roasted veggies, and fresh diced tomatoes then top with the feta cheese. Bake for 15 minutes until cheese is melted and lightly brown.

Southwest Pasta

2	cups	spinach pasta, cooked
1/8	cup	olive oil
1	teaspoon	garlic, minced
1/4	teaspoon	seasoned salt
1	dash	pepper
1/2	cup	black beans, cooked, drained
1/2	cup	red peppers, chopped into 1 inch pieces
1	bunch	asparagus, fresh, chopped into 1 inch pieces
1/2	pound	smoked sausage, sliced (raw shrimp can be substituted for the sausage)
1	teaspoon	southwest seasonings

Topping

1/2	cup	avocado, diced
1/4	cup	cilantro, chopped
1	cup	Mexican white cheese, jack, crumbled or shredded

Heat the oil in large skillet with garlic, salt and pepper. Add asparagus and red peppers, and cook about 2 minutes stirring them in the seasoned oil. Add sausage or shrimp and black beans. Toss until heated. Add pasta and southwest seasoning. Toss as it heats. Serve topped with cheese, avocado and cilantro.

Farm to Fork Recipes

Appetizers
Caprese Kebabs
Fresh Garden Eggplant Sauce
Tomato and Basil Topped Bruschetta
Tomato and Goat Cheese Bruschetta
Zucchini Dip

Beverages
Apple Carrot Cucumber Smoothie
Vegetable Cocktail

Entrees
Garden Shrimp Creole
Grilled Fish with Tomato Basil Sauce
Italian Garden Vegetable Stew
Summer Lasagna with Spinach Pesto
Vegetable Frittata
Vegetable Garden Pasta
Vegetable Stuffed Portobello Mushrooms

Relish, Salsas, and Seasonings
Arugula Vegetable Topping
Garden Vegetable Relish
Italian Seasoning Mix
Summer Relish
Watermelon Salsa

Salads and Sides
Cole Slaw with Apples and Raisins
Cole Slaw with Bacon and Tomato
Corn and Tomato Salad
Egg Salad with Veggies
Fresh Garden Green Beans
Fresh Tomato Salad
Garden Fresh Vegetable Salad
Ice Box Slaw
Marinated Tomato, Mozzarella &
   Cucumber Salad
Zucchini and Tomatoes Au Gratin
Zucchini Tomato Salad

Soups and Sandwiches
Fresh Vegetable Broth
Gazpacho Soup
Grilled Garden Sandwich

Caprese Kebabs

Makes: 6 servings Prep Time: 20 minutes

6	wooden skewers	trimmed to 6" lengths
18	grape tomatoes	about 1 cup
18	mozzarella cheese	cubes (about 4 oz)
¾	cup	basil pesto (see recipe)

Thread skewers with tomatoes and cheese cubes alternating the tomatoes and cheese with 3 of each on each kebabs. Serve skewers with pesto for dipping.

Fresh Garden Eggplant Sauce

Makes: 3 cups Prep Time: 30 minutes

2	whole	green peppers, seeded, diced
2	whole	eggplants, peeled, cut into chunks
3	cloves	garlic, minced
3	tablespoons	oil
6	whole	tomatoes, fresh, peeled, seeded, diced
1	dash	salt
1	teaspoon	paprika

Cook eggplant, peppers and garlic in oil until lightly brown then add tomatoes and seasoning. Continue cooking until the eggplant is done. Stir and serve hot with nice crusty bread toasted.

Tomato and Basil Topped Bruschetta

Makes: 4 servings Prep Time: 20 minutes

(8)	1 ounce	slices of Italian Bread
1	clove	garlic, halved
3	cups	tomatoes, chopped
3	tablespoons	basil, fresh, thinly sliced
4	teaspoons	olive oil
¼	teaspoon	salt
⅛	teaspoon	pepper

Preheat oven to 425 degrees. Arrange bread slices in a single layer on a baking sheet, bake at 425 for 8 minutes, turning after 4 minutes. Rub 1 side of toast with garlic clove; set toast aside. Mix together the tomatoes, basil, olive oil, salt and pepper. Spoon the tomato mixture on top of the toast. Serve immediately.

Tomato and Goat Cheese Bruschetta-Spread goat cheese on the bread and then top with the tomato basil mixture.

Zucchini Dip

Makes: 4 servings   Prep Time: 15 minutes

1 ½	cups	zucchini, finely shredded, squeezed dry
1	cup	cheddar cheese, shredded
3	ounces	cream cheese, softened
½	teaspoon	lemon juice
½	teaspoon	garlic powder
¼	teaspoon	salt
¼	teaspoon	pepper
2	tablespoons	mayonnaise
½	cup	walnuts, chopped
		Assorted vegetables or crackers for dipping

In a bowl, combine all the ingredients. Cover and refrigerate.

Apple, Carrot Cucumber Smoothie

Makes: 1 serving   Prep Time: 10 minutes

¼	cup	apple juice
1	tablespoon	lemon juice, fresh squeezed
1	whole	carrot, cut into chunks
½	cup	cucumber, cut into chunks

In a blender, combine juices, carrot and cucumber. Blend until smooth. This is a very refreshing drink.

Vegetable Cocktail

Makes: 6 servings   Prep Time: 15 minutes

2	pounds	ripe tomato, peeled, seeded
½	pound	spinach, fresh, chopped
1	whole	red pepper, diced
1	whole	cucumber, diced
2	teaspoons	lemon juice, fresh
1	dash	salt and pepper
1	dash	Tabasco sauce
¼	cup	carrot, diced
¼	cup	celery, diced

Put through a juicer or puree in a blender and serve over ice. This fresh vegetable juice was a popular drink at Margy's. You can eliminate the cucumber to make a vegetable juice to use in chili or soup.

Garden Shrimp Creole

Makes: 8 servings   Prep Time: 1 hour

8	medium	tomatoes, peeled, chopped and seeded or 2-15 ounce cans diced tomatoes
1	medium	onion, diced
2	small	green peppers, diced
2	small	jalapeño peppers , diced
1	medium	banana pepper, diced
½	cup	celery, diced
3	whole	garlic gloves, diced
2	whole	bay leaves
1	tablespoon	butter
1	teaspoon	salt
1	teaspoon	sugar
1	small can	tomato paste
1	pound	shrimp, large, uncooked
3	cups	rice, cooked

Sauté onion, peppers, celery and garlic in butter until vegetables are softened. Add tomatoes, salt, tomato paste, sugar and bay leaves. Simmer 30-45 minutes on medium high heat until thickens then add shrimp, stir and cook for 3-5 minutes or until shrimp is pink. Add salt and pepper to taste. Remove the bay leaves and serve over rice.

Grilled Fish with Tomato Basil Sauce

Makes: 4 servings   Prep Time: 30 minutes

4	pieces	fish, fresh for grilling
1	recipe	Fresh Fish Marinade (see recipe)

Sauce

3	cups	tomatoes, seeded and diced
20	whole	basil leaves, thinly sliced
2	cloves	garlic, minced
½	cup	olive oil
2	tablespoons	lemon juice
		salt and pepper to taste

Marinate fresh fish for 1 to 24 hours before grilling. I like a mild whitefish for this recipe like tilapia, walleye, sea bass etc. Use what ever you like that is fresh and available at the time. Mix together the sauce ingredients and refrigerate until ready to serve. Grill on a medium heat for about 10-15 minutes or until fish flakes. Put on platter and top with sauce.

Italian Garden Vegetable Stew

Makes: 6 servings   Prep Time: 1 hour

1	pound	Italian sausage links, sweet
2	whole	red potatoes, diced
½	cup	onion, diced
¼	cup	red and green bell peppers, diced
1	cup	water
3	whole	tomatoes, fresh, diced
2	medium	zucchini, diced
1	head	cabbage, sliced
3	tablespoons	basil, fresh, chopped
1	teaspoon	oregano, fresh, chopped
2	tablespoons	parsley, fresh, chopped

This is especially good when using fresh vegetables from the garden. Brown the sausage. Add onions, peppers, and potatoes. Add the rest of the ingredients. Simmer low until meat and potatoes are done. Top with Parmesan cheese. This makes a great broth.

Summer Lasagna with Spinach Pesto

Makes: 4 servings   Prep Time: 45 minutes

1	recipe	Spinach Pesto (see recipe)
¼	pound	egg noodles, large
2	cups	corn, fresh off the cob
1½	cups	green beans, fresh, trimmed, cut in half
1	cup	tomatoes fresh, diced
1	tablespoon	oil
		salt and pepper to taste
1	cup	ricotta cheese, heated
½	cup	parmesan cheese, grated

Cook pasta, corn and beans in salted, boiling water together. Drain.
Place ricotta cheese in the bottom of a large serving bowl; season with salt and pepper.
Top with pasta and vegetables. Pour pesto over pasta and cheese. Top with parmesan and tomatoes, finish with olive oil, salt and pepper; toss together and serve.

Vegetable Frittata

Makes: 12 servings   Prep Time: 1 hour

2	tablespoons	canola oil
1	each	yellow onion, sliced
1	each	zucchini, sliced
1	each	yellow squash, sliced
1	each	red pepper, sliced
¼	cup	swiss cheese, shredded
1	tablespoon	parsley, fresh, chopped
¼	teaspoon	salt
¼	teaspoon	pepper
6	whole	eggs, beaten
¼	cup	cheddar cheese, shredded

Pre-heat oven to 450 degrees. Pour oil into a 9" x 13" baking dish and arrange onions in the bottom. Bake for 5 minutes. Remove dish from oven. Arrange the other vegetables on top of the onions. Sprinkle with cheese and parsley, salt and pepper. Reduce heat to 400 degrees. Pour the eggs over the vegetables and cheese. Bake approximately 20 minutes until the eggs have puffed and the center of the frittata is set. Do not over cook. Can use any combinations of meats or vegetables.

Vegetable Garden Pasta

Makes: 6 servings   Prep Time: 30 min

½	head	broccoli, blanched
½	head	cauliflower, blanched
¼	cup	olive oil
2	cloves	garlic, chopped
1	whole	shallot, chopped
½	teaspoon	red pepper flakes
1	tablespoon	thyme, fresh (optional)
1	whole	small zucchini, julienned
1	whole	small yellow squash, julienned
1	whole	carrot, julienned
¼	pound	sugar snap peas
1	pound	pasta, cooked

Place oil in saucepan over medium heat. When oil is warm, add garlic and sauté until lightly golden (about 1 minute). Add shallot, zucchini, yellow squash, carrot, and sugar snap peas; season with salt, pepper, fresh thyme and red pepper flakes. Sauté for 2 to 3 minutes, toss with broccoli, cauliflower and cooked pasta.

Vegetable Stuffed Portobello Mushrooms

Makes: 6 mushrooms   Prep Time: 30 minutes

6	whole	portobello mushrooms (stems and gills removed)
1	tablespoon	oil
		Salt and pepper
1	cup	onion, diced
1	cup	green or red papper, diced
4	cups	spinach, fresh, chopped
1	cup	tomatoes, fresh, chopped
2	teaspoons	garlic, minced
1	teaspoon	crushed red pepper flakes
1	dash	salt
1	dash	pepper
1 ½	cups	mozzarella cheese, cubed
¼	cup	parmesan cheese

Remove stems and scrape out the gills with a spoon (they make everything brown if not removed). Brush mushroom with oil and season with salt and pepper inside and out. Preheat oven at 350 or grill on medium heat. Sauté the onion and pepper in oil add the spinach, tomatoes, garlic and seasonings. Fold in the mozzarella cubes, stuff the mushroom caps; sprinkle with parmesan and grill for about 5-10 minutes or bake in the oven for 15-20 minutes.

Arugula Vegetable Topping

Makes: 4 servings   Prep Time: 15 minutes

2	cups	arugula, fresh, chopped
1	whole	tomato, fresh, chopped
1	whole	cucumber, chopped, seeded
1	whole	zucchini, chopped
2	tablespoons	balsamic vinegar
		salt and pepper to taste

Toss all ingredients together and use as a topping for burgers, chicken or fish or serve as a side salad.

Garden Vegetable Relish

Makes: 4 servings   Prep Time: 15 minutes

1	large	cucumber, peeled, seeded, diced
2	large	tomatoes, diced
1	large	green pepper, diced
1	small	yellow onion
1	small	zucchini
3-4	tablespoons	canola or olive oil
1	teaspoon	lemon juice
		salt and pepper

Finely dice all vegetables to approximately the same size. Mix all veggies then toss in canola oil and lemon juice; season with salt and pepper. This is great served on top of a grilled chicken breast, pork tenderloin, steak or hamburger or as a side salad.

Italian Seasoning Mix

Makes: 24 servings   Prep Time: 1 month

2	tablespoons	oregano, dried
3	tablespoons	marjoram, dried
2	tablespoons	thyme, dried
3	tablespoons	basil, dried
2	tablespoons	rosemary, dried

Mix all the ingredients together and store in an airtight container. If you don't have all the above herbs you can use oregano, basil and marjoram. This can be used as seasoning for Italian tomato sauce, meat loaf, soup or mix with butter and toss with vegetables. You can also put the dried herbs in a nice jar and give as gifts. My father looks forward to receiving his every year. He says the herbs dried from my garden have much more flavor than store bought. See notes on how to dry herbs in the canning and freezing chapter.

Summer Relish

Makes: 4 servings   Prep Time: 15 minutes

¼	cup	white wine vinegar
1	tablespoon	sugar
2	cups	grape tomatoes halved
1	cup	yellow corn, fresh, blanched (about 2 ears of corn)
½	cup	red onion, diced fine
2	tablespoons	parsley, fresh, chopped
1	tablespoon	basil, fresh, thinly sliced
		salt and pepper to taste

Combine vinegar and sugar in a large bowl, whisking until sugar is dissolved. Add tomatoes, corn, onion, and herbs to the vinegar mixture: season with salt and pepper and toss to coat. Cover and chill relish until ready to serve. This is wonderful topped on a roasted pork tenderloin or chicken. Also great served as a side salad.

Watermelon Salsa

Makes: 8 servings   Prep Time: 15 minutes

2	cups	watermelon, diced, small cubes
1	tablespoon	brown sugar
1/8	cup	lime juice, fresh
1	small	jalapeño pepper, diced fine
1/2	cup	cucumber, seeded, peeled, diced
1/4	cup	red onion, diced fine
1/4	cup	cilantro, chopped
1/4	cup	mint, fresh, chopped
		salt and pepper to taste

Mix the brown sugar and lime juice together then stir in the remaining ingredients. This salsa is wonderful served on top of a grilled chicken breast or fish in the summer time.

Cole Slaw with Apples and Raisins

Makes: 4-6 servings   Prep Time: 15 minutes

Slaw

16	ounces	slaw mix or 4 cups cabbage, fresh, grated
1	whole	apple, diced with peel on
1/2	cup	raisins

Dressing

3/4	cup	mayonnaise
3	tablespoons	milk
2	tablespoons	apple cider vinegar
2	tablespoons	sugar

Mix dressing ingredients together then mix with the slaw ingredients.

Cole Slaw with Bacon and Tomato

Makes: 4-6 servings   Prep Time: 15 minutes

Slaw Mix

16	ounces	*slaw mix or 4 cups cabbage, fresh, grated*
1	cup	*cherry tomatoes, halved*
½	cup	*bacon, cooked, diced*

Dressing

¾	cup	*mayonnaise*
3	tablespoons	*milk*
2	tablespoons	*apple cider vinegar*
2	tablespoons	*sugar*

Mix dressing ingredients together then mix with the slaw ingredients.

Corn and Tomato Salad

Makes: 6 servings   Prep Time: 15 minutes

6	ears	*corn, cooked and removed from cob*
1	whole	*tomato, diced*
½	cup	*green onion, diced*
½	cup	*Basil dressing (see recipe)*

Cut the corn from the cob, put in a bowl, cover with water and saran wrap. Cook 5 minutes in the microwave. Drain and rinse with cold water. Add remaining ingredients and toss.

Egg Salad with Veggies

Makes: 6 servings   Prep Time: 15 minutes

10	whole	*eggs, hard boiled, chopped*
1	small	*zucchini, diced*
¼	cup	*celery, diced*
¼	cup	*carrot, diced*
2	tablespoons	*green onion, chopped fine*
2	tablespoons	*red peppers, diced*
⅓	cup	*mayonnaise*

2	tablespoons	Italian Creamy salad dressing or Buttermilk Ranch (see recipe)
1	tablespoon	dill weed, fresh, finely chopped
1	teaspoon	mustard
1/8	teaspoon	salt

Combine eggs and vegetables. Stir in mayonnaise, dressing, dill, mustard and salt. Cover and chill 1-2 hours. This is a delicious egg salad and was very popular at Margy's.

Fresh Garden Green Beans

1. Clean and cut ends of beans. Cut in desired size pieces or leave whole. Prepare pan of boiling water then add the beans (1 cup of water per pound of green beans.) Cook until desired doneness. Drain immediately and add butter and seasoned salt. Toss.

2. Follow directions above except cook until still somewhat firm. Drain. Melt butter in skillet and sautéed green beans in skillet until desired doneness. Toss with seasoned salt.

3. Follow directions in step 1 then set beans aside. Brown butter in sauce pan and melt until brown. Add bread crumbs and mix. Toss in green beans and add seasoned salt. Use ½ stick butter to 1 cup bread crumbs.

Fresh Tomato Salad

Makes: 2 cups   Prep Time: 10 minutes

2	cups	cherry or grape tomatoes, halved
2	tablespoons	red wine or balsamic vinegar
1	tablespoon	olive or canola oil
1	teaspoon	sugar
		salt and pepper to taste
¼	cup	basil, cut into strips

Toss tomatoes, vinegar, oil, sugar and seasonings together. Add basil just before serving.

Garden Fresh Vegetable Salad

Makes: 8 servings

Prep Time: 20 minutes

2	large	cucumbers, peeled, seeded
2	large	tomatoes
2	large	green peppers, seeded
1	small	yellow onion
1	bunch	broccoli
1	small	zucchini
1	small	yellow squash
¼ -½	cup	Basil or Italian dressing (see recipes)

Finely dice all vegetables to approximately the same size. Mix all veggies except tomatoes with dressing and refrigerate. Stir in diced tomatoes right before serving. Keeps refrigerated 2-3 days.

Ice Box Slaw

Makes: 10 servings

Prep Time: 45 minutes

4	cups	cabbage, shredded
1	cup	carrot, shredded
½	cup	green pepper, diced fine
½	cup	red pepper, diced fine
1 ¼	cups	sugar
¼	cup	cider vinegar
¼	cup	canola oil
1	teaspoon	salt
½	teaspoon	celery salt

Bring sugar, vinegar, oil, salt, and celery salt to a boil. Mix cabbage, carrots, and peppers together in a bowl. Pour boiling mixture over cabbage mixture while hot and let set. Cover with lid to let flavors absorb. This will keep in the refrigerature 3-4 days. This recipe is from my mother-in-law, Mary Barnes and was our signature side salad at Margy's Café.

Marinated Tomato, Mozzarella & Cucumber Salad

Makes: 4 servings   Prep Time: 15 minutes

2	medium	tomatoes, sliced thin (can use a combination of red and yellow tomatoes)
1	whole	cucumber, sliced thin
¼	pound	fresh water mozzarella, sliced thin
⅛	cup	Italian dressing (see recipe)

Layer vegetables and cheese and cover with dressing. Can add mushrooms and/or sliced onions if desired.

Zucchini and Tomatoes Au Gratin

Makes: 6-8 servings   Prep Time: 30 minutes

2	pounds	zucchini, cut into ¼ inch pieces
¼	cup	onion, chopped
3	tablespoons	canola oil
2	cups	tomatoes, peeled, seeded
1	dash	salt
1	dash	pepper
¾	cup	parmesan cheese, grated

Put oil in pan and heat to medium. Add onion and zucchini and cook slowly for 5 minutes. Stir frequently; add tomato, salt and pepper. Cover and cook 5 minutes. Turn into greased baking dish. Sprinkle with cheese and bake at 375 degrees for 20 minutes.

Zucchini, Tomato Salad

Makes: 8 servings   Prep Time: 15 minutes

4	cups	zucchini, thinly sliced
2	medium	tomatoes, cut into wedges
¼	cup	green onions, thinly sliced
1	recipe	Italian dressing (see recipe)

Combine the ingredients and toss with the Italian dressing. Refrigerate at least 2 hours before serving.

Fresh Vegetable Broth

Makes: 4 cups   Prep Time: 2 hours

1	medium	onion, peel left on
2	cloves	garlic, peel on
2		ribs celery, with leaves
2	whole	carrots, peel on, cut into chunks
2	whole	leeks, trimmed, cut into chunks
4		scallions, peel on, cut in half
2	medium	tomatoes, quartered
4	medium	red potatoes, halved with peel
8	sprigs	parsley
1		bay leaf
8	whole	black peppercorns
1	teaspoon	kosher salt
10	cups	water

Rinse all vegetables. Place all the broth ingredients in a large heavy pot. Bring to a boil, reduce heat and simmer uncovered for 1 hour. Adjust the seasonings to taste and simmer for 30 more minutes. Strain the broth, let set at room temperature to cool. Refrigerate or freeze. Fresh broth will keep about 4 days.

Note: You can add additional vegetables. When I trim asparagus or broccoli, I freeze the trimmings and the next time I am ready to make vegetable broth I add them to it.

Gazpacho Soup

Makes: 4-6 servings   Prep Time: 25 minutes

Soup

1	whole	cucumber, halved, seeded
1	whole	red bell pepper, cored, seeded
1	whole	green bell pepper, cored, seeded
4	whole	tomatoes
1	medium	onion
3	cloves	garlic, minced
3	cups	tomato juice
3	tablespoons	cilantro, fresh, chopped
2	whole	limes, juiced

½	teaspoon	chili flakes
¼	cup	white wine vinegar
¼	cup	olive oil
½	tablespoon	salt
1	teaspoon	black pepper
2	whole	peppers left whole, cored, seeded, top removed

Dice the cucumbers, 1 red and 1 green bell pepper, tomatoes and onions into 1 inch cubes. Put vegetables separately into a food processor and pulse until coarsely chopped. After each vegetable is processed, combine them in a large bowl and add the remaining ingredients. Mix well and chill before serving. I like to serve the Gazpacho in the whole peppers; top removed and inside seeded. It makes a pretty presentation and adds to the flavor.

Grilled Garden Sandwich

Makes: 6 sandwiches   Prep Time: 45 minutes

12	pieces	French bread, sliced ¼ inch (ciabatta or focaccia also work)
1	whole	eggplant, sliced ¼ inch length way
1	whole	zucchini, sliced ¼ inch length way
1	whole	red pepper, cut in strips
2	whole	Portobello mushrooms, sliced in strips
1	whole	onion, sliced ¼ inch
1-2	tablespoons	canola or olive oil
1	teaspoon	garlic, minced
2	cups	spinach, fresh, chopped
6-8	whole	cherry tomatoes, halved
2	teaspoons	balsamic vinegar

Lightly oil vegetables and toss with seasonings. Grill vegetables on the grill or roast in the oven at 375 degrees for 20-30 minutes. Grill or toast the French bread. Toss the spinach, tomatoes, salt and pepper with the balsamic vinegar right before grilling the vegetables.

Stack the grilled/roasted veggies on the toasted French bread and top with the spinach mixture and top piece of bread. Cut in half and serve.

Note: You can use other vegetables from the garden, melt Feta cheese on the veggies the last few minutes of cooking or replace the mushrooms with sliced cooked chicken breast or beef. This is our family favorite fresh from the garden sandwich.

Salads

Bean Salads
Black Bean Salad
Easy Bean Salad

Chicken Salads
BLT Chicken Salad
Classic Chicken Salad
Cobb Chicken Salad
Curry Chicken Salad
Tarragon Chicken Salad
Tropical Chicken Salad
Waldorf Chicken Salad

Lettuce Salads
Caesar Salad
Chow Mein Chicken Salad
House Salad
Margy's Signature Spinach Salad
Salmon Cucumber Salad
Seven Layer Salad
Taco Salad

Miscellanious Salads
Crab, Corn and Tomato Salad
Ham Salad
Italian Turkey Salad
Shrimp and Crab Salad
Shrimp Salad
Tuna Salad

Pasta Salads
Broccoli Chicken Pasta Salad
Cheese Tortellini Pasta Salad
Chicken Club Pasta Salad
Chicken Pasta Salad
Greek Pasta Salad
Macaroni Salad
Shrimp and Pasta Salad
Southwestern Chicken Pasta

Potato Salads
Caesar Potato Salad
Creamy Dilled Potato Salad
Garden Bean and Potato Salad
German Potato Salad
Margy's Potato Salad
Potato Salad with Bacon Dressing
Spicy Sweet Potato Salad

Vegetable Salads
Broccoli Salad
Broccoli, Cauliflower, Cheddar
Carrot Salad
Cucumbers in Dilled Sour
  Cream Sauce
Greek Cucumber Salad
Spring Pea Salad
Tomato, Feta & Cucumber Salad

Black Bean Salad

Makes: 4-6 servings   Prep Time: 30 minutes

2	cups	black beans, cooked
1	cup	corn
½	cup	red pepper, diced
½	cup	green pepper, diced
1	cup	tomatoes, diced
½	cup	mild onion, diced
½	cup	Italian dressing (see recipe)
¼	cup	cilantro, fresh, chopped

If using canned black beans make sure to rinse first. Mix all ingredients together and refrigerate until ready to serve.

Easy Bean Salad

Makes: 8 servings   Prep Time: 4 hours

1	15 ounce can	green beans, drained
1	15 ounce can	wax beans, drained
1	15 ounce can	dark red kidney beans, drained
1	15 ounce can	lima beans, drained
1	small	green pepper, diced
1	medium	onion, sliced thin or diced
½ to ⅔	cup	Italian dressing (see recipe)

Mix all the beans together, rinse and drain. Add dressing and refrigerate for at least 4-6 hours. You can use the following dressing recipe below if you prefer the standard bean salad dressing. This salad can be made ahead as it tastes the best on day 2. I prefer to use fresh beans for this but it's not always possible. So in a pinch I use canned, no salt added or rinse the beans which removes a lot of the salt added.

Dressing

¾	cup	sugar
½	cup	canola oil
½	cup	white vinegar
½	teaspoon	salt
½	teaspoon	pepper

Combine ingredients in a small saucepan; bring to a boil over low heat stirring until sugar dissolves. Pour hot dressing over bean mixture; stir gently. Cover and chill at least 4 hours.

BLT Chicken Salad

Makes: 6-8 servings   Prep Time: 1 hour

½	cup	mayonnaise
¼	cup	BBQ sauce
2	tablespoons	onion, grated
1	tablespoon	lemon juice
½	teaspoon	pepper
2	large	tomatoes, chopped
3	cups	chicken, cooked, diced
10	slices	bacon, cooked, crumbled

Combine first 5 ingredients; stir well. Cover and chill dressing. Combine remaining ingredients and mix with dressing.

Classic Chicken Salad

Makes: 6-8 servings   Prep Time: 2 hours 15 minutes

4	cups	chicken, all white, diced
¼	cup	celery, diced
½	teaspoon	salt
¼	teaspoon	pepper
2	tablespoons	lemon juice
¾	cup	mayonnaise

Classic Chicken Salad Panini-Classic Chicken Salad on toasted foccaci bread.
Put a scoop of classic chicken salad on the bottom slice of foccacia bread, top with slices of sun-dried tomatoes or fresh tomato slices and jack cheese. Put the top of the foccacia bread on and toast in the oven until hot throughout, or cook in a Panini press.

Cobb Chicken Salad

Makes: 4-6 servings   Prep Time: 15 minutes

3	cups	chicken, cooked, diced
¾	cup	bacon, cooked, diced
4	whole	eggs, hard boiled
½	cup	tomatoes, diced
¼	cup	green onions, diced
½	cup	bleu cheese, crumbled
1	cup	Ranch salad dressing

Toss all ingredients and chill. Can serve a slice of tomato with the chicken salad instead of adding the diced tomatoes. Great as a sandwich or served on a bed of lettuce.

Curry Chicken Salad

Makes: 4-6 servings   Prep Time: 15 minutes

3	cups	chicken, cooked, diced
1	cup	mayonnaise
2	tablespoons	chutney, Major Greys
1	teaspoon	curry powder
¼	cup	celery, diced fine
¼	cup	golden raisins, seedless

Mix mayonnaise, curry and chutney to make a dressing. Put chicken, celery, and raisins in a bowl and add dressing.

Tarragon Chicken Salad

Makes: 8 servings   Prep Time: 15 minutes

4	cups	chicken, all white meat, diced
1	cup	mayonnaise
⅛	cup	Dijon mustard
¼	cup	green onion, diced
⅛	cup	cooking sherry
½	cup	toasted pinenuts or almond slivers
¼	teaspoon	tarragon, fresh

½	teaspoon	garlic powder
⅛	teaspoon	pepper
⅛	cup	Worcestershire sauce

Mix mayonnaise, dijon mustard, sherry, garlic powder, pepper, Worcestershire sauce and tarragon. Add chicken and onions to mayonnaise mixture. Put toasted nuts on chicken salad right before serving. To toast the nuts, put on a baking sheet and bake 350 until golden, about 5-10 minutes.

Tropical Chicken Salad

Makes: 8 servings   Prep Time: 1 hour

4	cups	chicken, all white meat, cooked, diced
1	15 ounce can	pineapple, crushed, drained
1	15 ounce can	Mandarin oranges, drained, chopped
½	cup	coconut, shredded
1	cup	mayonnaise

Mix all ingredients making sure pineapple and oranges are drained well. You may need less or more mayonnaise. Put in a ½ cup at a time. This is a great summer salad or sandwich served on a croissant. This was very popular at Margy's and is my Mother's favorite.

Waldorf Chicken Salad

Makes: 4 servings   Prep Time: 30 minutes

2	cups	chicken, all white meat, cooked, diced
¾	cup	apple, chopped fine
¼	cup	celery, chopped fine
½	cup	walnuts, chopped
¼	cup	raisins, seedless
¾	cup	mayonnaise
1	tablespoon	lemon juice

In a medium bowl, toss together chicken, apple, celery, walnuts, and raisins. Mix mayonnaise and lemon juice together then mix with the chicken mixture. Great as a sandwich.

Caesar Salad

Makes: 1 serving   Prep Time: 5 minutes

1	cup	romaine lettuce, chopped
1/8	cup	bacon or pancetta, cooked, diced
1/8	cup	parmesan cheese, grated
1/4	cup	croutons
1-2	tablespoons	Caesar Dressing (see recipe)

Toss all together. The bacon can be substituted with grilled chicken strips, shrimp, grilled portobello mushroom strips or prosciutto.

Chow Mein Chicken Salad

Makes: 4 servings   Prep Time: 15 minutes

4	cups	lettuce
1	cup	chow mein noodles
2/3	cup	chicken, cooked, diced
2	each	green onions, chopped
6	teaspoons	almonds, sliced, toasted
1	small can	mandarin oranges, drained

Vinaigrette

1/4	cup	vegetable oil or canola
4 1/2	teaspoons	white vinegar
1	tablespoon	sugar
1/4	teaspoon	pepper
1/8	teaspoon	salt

In large salad bowl, combine the lettuce, chow mein noodles, chicken, onions, almonds and mandarin oranges. In a jar with a tight fitting lid, combine all the vinaigrette ingredients; shake well. Drizzle over salad; toss to coat. Serve immediately.

House Salad

Makes: 6 servings   Prep Time: 30 minutes

Cheese Mix

2	ounces	mozzarella cheese, shredded
2	ounces	feta cheese, crumbled
¼	cup	parmesan cheese, shredded

Dressing

½	cup	white vinegar
½	cup	vegetable oil
1/8	cup	sugar
½	teaspoon	garlic powder
1	tablespoon	basil, dried
½	teaspoon	oregano, dried

Salad

6	cups	romaine lettuce, chopped
½	cup	cheese mix
2	tablespoons	red onion, diced
1/8	cup	black olives, sliced
¼	cup	croutons
½	cup	house dressing

Mix first three ingredients (cheeses) together to make the house cheese mix. Mix the next six ingredients together to make the vinaigrette dressing. Mix the last six ingredients together to make the salad mix. Toss the cheese mix, dressing and salad mix all together and serve immediately.

Margy's Signature Spinach Salad

Makes: 1 serving   Prep Time: 10 minutes

1	cup	spinach, fresh, stems removed, chopped
¼	cup	strawberries, sliced, fresh
¼	cup	blueberries or blackberries, fresh
¼	cup	raspberries, fresh
1/8	cup	gorgonzola or blue cheese crumbles
¼	cup	walnuts or pecans, toasted

Sprinkle cheese on top of spinach, then berries and nuts and serve with Raspberry or Blackberry Dressing (see recipe).

Salmon Cucumber Salad

Makes: 1 salad   Prep Time: 15 minutes

1	cup	mixed greens
4	ounces	baked salmon (see recipe)
4	slices	cucumbers, thin
1/8	cup	red peppers, diced
1	sprig	dill, fresh
2	tablespoons	Creamy Dill Dressing (see recipe)

Put greens on a plate, top with salmon. Place cucumbers, peppers and dill nicely on top of the salmon. Serve the dressing on the side or drizzle over the top of the salad.

Seven Layer Salad

Makes: 6-8 servings   Prep Time: 15 minutes

3	cups	lettuce, shredded
1/2	cup	broccoli, chopped
1/2	cup	cauliflower, chopped
1/2	cup	peas, frozen or fresh, blanched
1/4	cup	green onion, chopped
1	pound	bacon, cooked, chopped
4	whole	eggs, hard boiled, diced
1/4	cup	parmesan cheese, shredded
1	cup	cheddar cheese, shredded
1	cup	mayonnaise
1/8	cup	sugar

Mix mayonnaise and sugar together. Mix the remaining ingredients together and toss with mayonnaise.

Taco Salad

Prep Time: 15 minutes

½	head	lettuce, chopped
1½	cups	green onion, chopped
1	cup	cheddar cheese, shredded
1	teaspoon	cumin
1	pound	ground beef, extra lean, cooked
½	cup	tortilla chips, crumbled
½	cup	sour cream
1	teaspoon	chili powder
1	whole	tomato, diced

Cook ground beef with cumin and chili powder. Put lettuce in bowls and top with equal portions of hamburger mixture, green onions, cheddar cheese, ground chips and top with sour cream and diced tomatoes. Serve immediately. Can add sliced, black olives.

Crab, Corn and Tomato Salad

Makes: 4 servings   Prep Time: 15 minutes

1	cup	fresh corn kernals (about 2 ears), blanched
¼	cup	basil, fresh leaves, sliced
¼	cup	red pepper, diced
2	tablespoons	green onion, diced
1	pound	lump crabmeat
2	cups	cherry or grape tomatoes, halved
¼ - ½	cup	Lemon Basil Dressing (see recipe).

Toss all ingredients together. This is a wonderful summer salad with the fresh corn and tomatoes from the garden.

Ham Salad

Makes: 6 servings   Prep Time: 30 minutes

1	pound	ham, smoked lean, ground
1	cup	mayonnaise
¼	cup	sweet relish (zucchini relish-see recipe)
¼	cup	celery, diced
¼	cup	sweet onion, diced
4	whole	eggs, hard boiled, diced
1	cup	cheddar cheese, shredded

Mix all ingredients. Serve on croissants, with crackers or on wheat toast.

Italian Turkey Salad

Makes: 4-6 servings   Prep Time: 15 minutes

2	cups	turkey breast, diced
1/8	cup	green onions, diced
¼	cup	red pepper or roasted red peppers, diced
¼	cup	green pepper, diced
1/8-¼	cup	Italian dressing (see recipe)

Mix all ingredients and refrigerate. This is good as a salad or sandwich

Shrimp and Crab Salad

Makes: 4 servings   Prep Time: 30 minutes

8	ounces	shrimp, small, cooked
¼	cup	celery, diced fine
1	cup	crab, diced
¾	cup	mayonnaise
1 ½	tablespoons	dill, fresh, chopped
1	tablespoon	lemon juice
1	dash	salt and pepper
½	teaspoon	Dijon mustard

Mix all ingredients. This salad is great just as a salad, on a croissant or to make a Shrimp and Crab Melt sandwich (see recipe).

Shrimp Salad

Makes: 4-6 servings   Prep Time: 30 minutes

Salad

1	pound	shrimp, salad, cooked 45-50 ct.
1	whole	cucumber, seeded, diced
¼	cup	cilantro, chopped
¼	cup	green onion, chopped
1	whole	jalapeño, diced
1	whole	tomato, diced
¼	cup	mint, fresh, chopped

Dressing

2	tablespoons	lemon juice
⅛	cup	canola oil
½	teaspoon	salt
½	teaspoon	pepper

Mix dressing ingredients together and toss together with salad ingredients. You can add cooked pasta and or crab meat if you like. If adding pasta, make extra dressing.

Tuna Salad

Makes: 6 servings   Prep Time: 10 minutes

2	6-ounce cans	tuna in water, all white albacore, drained
¼	cup	celery, diced
1	teaspoon	lemon juice
½	cup	mayonnaise
¼	cup	relish, sweet
⅛	cup	onion, diced
1	dash	white pepper

Mix all ingredients. I always receive rave reviews from this tuna salad recipe. The key is the all white meat, albacore tuna. Please make sure to use a quality name brand tuna and drain it well.

Broccoli Chicken Pasta Salad

Makes: 8 serving   Prep Time: 30 minutes

1 ½	cups	chicken, cooked, white meat, diced
1 ½	cups	broccoli florets
2	cups	pasta, cooked
1	cup	Peppercorn ranch salad dressing
1	tablespoon	basil, fresh, chopped fine
¼	cup	sun-dried tomatoes, not in oil, julienned

Mix all ingredients and refrigerate. The pasta will absorb the dressing as it sets so you may need to add more. You can add different meats, vegetables or cheeses.

Cheese Tortellini Pasta Salad

Makes: 6-8 servings   Prep Time: 30 minutes

2 ½	pounds	pasta, tortellini, cooked
½ -1	cup	sun-dried tomatoes, no oil, julienned
1	cup	broccoli, cut
½	cup	green onion, diced
½ -¾	cup	Greek vinaigrette dressing

Mix all ingredients. Pasta will absorb much of the dressing after setting so you may need to add more. Start with ½ cup at a time. Use sun-dried tomatoes that are not oil packed. They will absorb the oil in the dressing.

Chicken Club Pasta Salad

Makes: 8-10 servings   Prep Time: 30 minutes

4	cups	pasta, cooked
1	pound	bacon, cooked, chopped
6	whole	eggs, hard boiled, diced
¾	cup	tomato, diced
1¼	cups	green onion, diced
8	ounces	cheddar cheese, shredded
1-1 ½	cups	Ranch salad dressing
1 ½	cups	chicken, cooked, diced avacado for garnish

Mix all ingredients and refrigerate. May need to add more dressing after it sets. Serve with avocado slices on the top for garnish.

Chicken Pasta Salad

Makes: 8-10 servings   Prep Time: 45 minutes

1	pound	pasta shells, cooked
1 ½	cups	chicken, all white meat, diced
1	cup	red grapes, seedless, washed, stems removed
¼	cup	celery, diced fine
1 ½	cups	Ken's Buttermilk Ranch salad dressing
½	teaspoon	black pepper
¼	cup	walnuts, chopped

Mix all ingredients except walnuts. Refrigerate. Sprinkle walnuts on top before serving. The pasta soaks up the dressing as it sets, so you may need to add more. The secret to this recipe is to use *Buttermilk* ranch dressing - I use Ken's. My second choice would be Kroger's Buttermilk Ranch.

This was Margy's number one selling menu item. When my first cook book was released the grocery stores on the southwest of Fort Wayne, ran out of Ken's Buttermilk Ranch dressing.

Greek Pasta Salad

Makes: 4-6 servings   Prep Time: 30 minutes

2	cups	mostaccioli, cooked
2	cups	spinach, fresh, chopped
1	whole	cucumber, diced
1	whole	tomato, fresh, chopped
¼	cup	black olives, sliced
1	tablespoon	dill, fresh, chopped
1	cup	chicken, cooked, diced
1	cup	greek salad dressing
½	cup	feta cheese, crumbled

Cool pasta. Mix all ingredients. Pasta soaks up the dressing so you may need to add more dressing after it sets awhile.

Macaroni Salad

Makes: 8-10 servings   Prep Time: 2 hours

1	pound box	macaroni pasta, cooked, cooled
1	pound	bacon, cooked, chopped
½	cup	green onions, chopped
12	ounces	cheddar cheese, shredded
6	each	hard boiled eggs, sliced

Dressing

1 ½	packages	Hidden Valley Ranch dry seasoning mix
1	cup	milk
¾	cup	mayonnaise
¾	cup	sour cream

Mix the dressing ingredients together. Pour the dressing over the cooked pasta and mix in with the remaining ingredients. Refrigerate for 1 hour before serving. Top with sliced eggs to make a pretty presentation. My sister-in-law Tammy brings this to family gatherings and it is so good I asked her for the recipe. This recipe is from her friend, Bonnie Hecht.

Shrimp and Pasta Salad

Makes: 6-8 servings   Prep Time: 30 minutes

Cilantro Lime Vinaigrette Dressing

3	cloves	garlic, minced
¼	cup	cilantro, minced
2	tablespoons	Dijon mustard
1	teaspoon	salt
½	teaspoon	pepper
⅔	cup	canola oil

Combine all ingredients except oil in food processor. Then slowly add the oil. Chill until ready to serve.

Salad

8	ounces	bow tie pasta, uncooked
1	tablespoon	canola oil
2	tablespoons	parsley, fresh, chopped
2	tablespoons	cilantro, fresh, chopped
2	tablespoons	red onion, minced

Chicken Pasta Salad, Black Bean Soup, Strawberry Bread, Double Chocolate Chip Cookies

Our goats, Bell and Rosie and friends

1	cup	red bell pepper, julienne
1	cup	cucumbers, sliced
1	cup	cherry tomatoes, halved
10	ounces	spinach, fresh, chopped
1	pound or more	salad shrimp, fresh, cooked

Cook the pasta, rinse with cold water, drain and toss with canola oil in large bowl. Add the rest of the ingredients and toss lightly with the dressing. Add salt and pepper if needed.

Southwestern Chicken Pasta Salad

Makes: 6-8 servings   Prep Time: 30 minutes

Salad

1	pound	small mostaccioli pasta, cooked and cooled
¼	cup	green onions, chopped
¼	cup	green pepper, chopped
¼	cup	cilantro, chopped
1	cup	corn, drained or 1 cup fresh blanched
1	cup	black beans, drained and rinsed
1	cup	cherry tomatoes, halved
8	ounces	Colby jack cheese, shredded
1 ½	cup	chicken, cooked diced
1	whole	avocado sliced for garnish

Dressing

1	16 ounces	buttermilk Ranch dressing
1	8 ounces	mild salsa

Salad- Mix the salad ingredients together in a large bowl.

Note: for a variation I like to add chopped zucchini, yellow squash and red pepper to this recipe.

Dressing-Mix the ranch and salsa together and pour over the salad. Save ¼-½ of the dressing to add later as the pasta will soak up the dressing at it sets. Add crushed tortilla chips on the top of the salad before serving.

Caesar Potato Salad

Makes: 6 cups   Prep Time: 30 minutes

1 ½	pounds	red potatoes, unpeeled
2	whole	eggs
1	cup	romaine lettuce, cut
1	cup	croutons

Boil potatoes with eggs until potatoes are tender; 12-15 minutes. Drain; set eggs aside and cool. Dice potatoes and toss while hot with ¾ cup of Caesar Dressing (see recipe). Let set for 10 minutes. Mash eggs with a pastry blender. Add romaine, croutons and eggs to potatoes. Serve warm or at room temperature.

Creamy Dilled Potato Salad

Makes: 8 servings   Prep Time: 2 hours

2 ½	pounds	small red potatoes, unpeeled
1	medium	onion, chopped
¼	cup	celery, chopped
6	each	hard boil eggs, peeled, chopped
1	cup	dill pickles, chopped
1	cup	mayonnaise
3	tablespoons	dill pickle juice
¼	teaspoon	black pepper
2	tablespoons	dill, fresh, chopped
3-4	whole	radishes, sliced thin for garnish

Place potatoes in a large pot of water. Boil for 15 minutes or until fork tender. Drain well.

Cut the potatoes in half (cut larger potatoes in quarters) so all pieces are about the same size. Place the potatoes in a large bowl while still warm. Pour the dill pickle juice on the potatoes, add the onions, celery, eggs and diced pickles and stir gently to combine.
In small bowl, stir together, mayonnaise, pepper and dill. Spoon mayonnaise mixture into potato mixture and stir gently. Cover and refrigerate 2-4 hours. Place sliced radishes on top as a garnish right before serving.

Garden Bean and Potato Salad

Makes: 6 servings   Prep Time: 25 minutes

1 ½	pounds	red potato
¾	pound	fresh green beans, trimmed
1	small	red onion, chopped
¼	cup	basil, fresh, chopped
⅛-¼	cup	balsamic vinegar

Boil potatoes until tender. Place potatoes in a large serving bowl. Boil beans in a pot of boiling water until tender; about 7-10 minutes. Halve the potatoes; add beans, onions and basil. Add balsamic vinaigrette to potato mixture and toss gently. Serve immediately or cover and chill. For a variation you can add diced cooked bacon.

German Potato Salad

Makes: 6-8 servings   Prep Time: 30 minutes

1 ½	pounds	red potatoes, sliced ¼ inch thick
½	pound	smoked kielbasa sausage, sliced ¼ inch thick
1	tablespoon	oil
½	cup	onions, diced
⅓	cup	apple cider vinegar
2	tablespoons	oil
2	tablespoons	sugar
		salt and pepper to taste

Boil potatoes in water until tender; about 12 minutes. Drain well. Sauté kielbasa in 1 tablespoon oil in a large skillet over medium high heat. Brown on both sides for about 5 minutes. Add onion and sauté until soft, 3 minutes. Stir in vinegar, 2 tablespoons oil and sugar, simmer 2 minutes. Gently stir potatoes into the sauce to make sure potatoes are well coated. Serve warm.

Note: you can substitute kielbasa with bacon.

Margy's Potato Salad

Makes: 4-6 servings   Prep Time: 30 minutes

2	pounds	potatoes (red potatoes are my preference)
8	whole	eggs, hard boiled, 6 chopped and 2 sliced (for garnish)
¼	cup	sweet pickle juice
½-¾	cup	mayonnaise
½	cup	sweet baby gherkin pickles, chopped
¼	cup	green onions, chopped
2	tablespoons	yellow mustard
1	teaspoon	sugar
		Paprika for garnish

Cook potatoes with skin until tender about 15 min (I boil the eggs with the potatoes). Drain and separate eggs. Let potatoes cool for a few minutes. Cube potatoes while still warm and toss with pickle juice in a bowl; cool to room temperature. Add green onions, chopped eggs and pickles to cooled potatoes. Combine mayonnaise, mustard and sugar to make the dressing. Gently toss the dressing with the potato mixture. When ready to serve put salad in a serving bowl and top with sliced eggs then a sprinkle of paprika. Serve immediately or chill for 1 hour. This potato salad is just as good at room temperature. I always make a double recipe as this potato salad is very popular as are the requests for seconds.

Potato Salad with Bacon Dressing

Makes: 8-10 servings   Prep Time: 45 minutes

5	pounds	potatoes
1	dozen	eggs
½	cup	celery, diced
½	cup	onion, diced
1	pound	bacon
1	jar	Kraft Miracle Whip salad dressing
1/3	cup	sugar
1	tablespoon	vinegar (white or cider)

Boil potatoes and eggs together. Cool, peel and dice. Dice bacon and cook in large skillet. Leave bacon and ¼ cup drippings in skillet; and lower heat to low-medium. In medium bowl add ½-¾ jar of Miracle Whip, ⅓ cup sugar and 1 tablespoon vinegar. Mix well then add to bacon and drippings in skillet and stir constantly until smooth and starts to bubble. Do not heat too much or the sauce will break. Pour sauce over potatoes and eggs. Serve warm or chilled.

Spicy Sweet Potato Salad

Makes 4 -6 servings   Prep Time: 30 minutes

5	strips	bacon, thick cut, diced
½	cup	red onion, diced
¼	cup	jalapeño pepper jelly (see recipe-or use store bought)
2	tablespoons	apple cider vinegar
1	dash	salt
1 ½	pounds	sweet potatoes, diced small

Preheat oven to 400 degrees. Line a baking sheet with foil and spray with Pam. Sauté bacon in skillet until crisp. Pour off fat; leave bacon in the pan. Add onion and sauté until soft about 5 minutes. Whisk in jelly, vinegar and salt; simmer until smooth. Stir in potatoes to coat with sauce. Transfer to foil lined pan. Place another sheet of foil over the pan with the potatoes and bake in the oven until potatoes are tender about 20-25 minutes. Remove foil and bake 5 minutes more. Transfer to serving dish. Serve salad warm or room temperature.

Broccoli Salad

Makes: 4-6 servings   Prep Time: 30 minutes

3	cups	broccoli florets
½	pound	bacon, cooked, diced
¼	cup	red onion, diced
½	cup	raisins
¾	cup	mayonnaise
⅛	cup	sugar
2	tablespoons	cider vinegar
½	cup	sunflower seeds

In a large bowl combine broccoli, bacon, onion and raisins. In a small bowl, whisk together mayonnaise, sugar and vinegar. Combine dressing with the vegetables, and refrigerate. Mix in sunflower seeds right before serving. For a vegetarian or lower fat salad I leave out the bacon and it is just as delicious.

Broccoli, Cauliflower, Cheddar Salad

Makes: 4-6 servings   Prep Time: 20 minutes

1	bunch	broccoli
1	head	cauliflower
1	cup	mayonnaise
½	cup	sour cream
2	tablespoons	sugar
2	cups	cheddar cheese, shredded

Mix sugar, sour cream and mayonnaise together. Put broccoli and cauliflower in the food processor and chop to fine but still with some chunks. Put cheese in with vegetables and then mix in the mayonnaise dressing.

Carrot Salad

Makes: 4-6 servings   Prep Time: 15 minutes

2	cups	carrots, grated (about 5 carrots)
1	8 ounce can	pineapple tidbits in heavy syrup, un-drained
½	cup	raisins
½	cup	walnuts, chopped
¼	cup	mayonnaise
1	tablespoon	lemon juice, fresh
1	dash	salt

Toss all ingredients together in a medium bowl. Cover and chill.

Cucumbers in Dilled Sour Cream Sauce

Makes: 6 servings   Prep Time: 30 minutes

4	large	cucumbers, halved length wise, seeded and sliced
4	teaspoons	salt
¾	cup	mayonnaise
¾	cup	sour cream
¾	cup	red onion, diced
½	cup	white vinegar
¼	cup	sugar
3	tablespoons	fresh dill, chopped or 2 tablespoons dried

Place cucumber slices in a colander and sprinkle with salt. Let stand for 15 minutes and then rinse. Combine mayonnaise, sour cream, onion, vinegar, sugar and dill in a bowl. Add cucumber slices and toss to coat. Let stand for 5 minutes before serving or make 1 day ahead.

Greek Cucumber Salad

Makes: 4-6 servings   Prep Time: 30 minutes

1	cup	cucumber, diced
1	cup	tomatoes, chopped
½	cup	chickpeas, canned, drained, rinsed
¼	cup	kalamata olives, pitted
¼	cup	green onions, sliced
¼	cup	parsley, fresh, chopped
1	whole	lemon, juiced
1	clove	garlic, minced
1	teaspoon	sugar
		salt and pepper to taste
2	tablespoons	olive or canola oil
3	tablespoons	mint, fresh, chopped
½	cup	feta cheese, crumbled

Combine the cucumbers, tomatoes, chickpeas, olives, green onions, and parsley in a large bowl. Whisk together lemon juice, garlic, sugar, salt and pepper in a separate bowl. Drizzle oil into lemon juice mixture slowly. Stir in mint. Toss the dressing into the salad mixture. Refrigerate until ready to serve. Sprinkle the feta cheese on top right before serving.

Spring Pea Salad

Makes: 4 servings   Prep Time: 15 minutes

2	cups	peas, fresh or frozen (if using fresh make sure to blanch them for a few minutes)
¼	cup	sweet onions, chopped
2	whole	hard boiled eggs, crumbled
2-3	tablespoons	mayonnaise
¾	cup	cheddar cheese, cubed

Mix together and chill for about 1 hour.

Tomato, Feta & Cucumber Salad

Makes: 4 servings   Prep Time: 15 minutes

1	cup	grape or cherry tomatoes
1	whole	cucumber, seeded, cut into thick slices
¼	pound	feta cheese, crumbled
1	cup	button mushrooms, mini, whole
¼	cup	Italian Dressing (see recipe)

Toss together and refrigerate until ready to serve.

Sandwiches

Hot
Chicken Pesto Focaccia
Chicken Salad Panini
Crab Cake on Croissant
Eggplant and Goat Cheese
Hawaiian Chicken
Honey Mustard Chicken
Italian Grilled Cheese Flat Bread
Malibu Chicken
Pulled Pork
Rueben Bake
Shrimp and Crab Melt
Tuna Melt
Turkey Rueben
Ultimate Grilled Cheese

Cold
Apple Walnut Turkey
Egg Salad BLT
Shrimp Wrap
Turkey Club Wrap

Chicken Pesto Focaccia

Makes: 1 sandwich   Prep Time: 30 minutes

1	teaspoon	basil pesto (see recipe)
1	tablespoon	mayonnaise
1	slice	jack cheese
1	6-ounce	chicken breast, boneless, skinless, roasted (see recipe)
1	focaccia	bread, sliced and toasted
1	slice	tomato

Roast a chicken breast (see recipe). Add the jack cheese and continue to bake until melted. Toast the bread in the oven on a baking dish. Spread the pesto mayonnaise on the toasted bread, add the chicken and sliced tomato.

Chicken Salad Panini

Makes: 1 sandwich   Prep Time: 15 minutes

½	cup	classic chicken salad (see recipe)
1	piece	focaccia bread, sliced, cut in half or quarters
⅛	cup	sun-dried tomatoes
1	slice	jack cheese

Put a scoop of classic chicken salad on the bottom slice of the focaccia bread, top with sun-dried tomatoes or fresh tomato slices and Monterey jack cheese. Put on the top of the focaccia bread and toast in the Panini press or in the oven until hot through-out. This was a popular lunch special at Margy's.

Crab Cake on Croissant

Makes: 1 sandwich   Prep Time: 15 minutes

2	each	crab cakes (see recipe)
2	tablespoons	jalapeño mayonnaise (see recipe)
1	regular	size croissant
1	slice	lettuce leaf

Cook crab cakes and toast croissant. Put jalapeño mayonnaise on top of crabcake add lettuce. This was also very popular at the café, especially during lent.

Eggplant and Goat Cheese Sandwich

Makes: 2 sandwiches   Prep Time: 45 minutes

8	(1/2 inch thick)	eggplant slices cut long wise, with or without skin
2	teaspoons	olive or canola oil
1	large	red bell pepper, halved and seeded
4	slices	ciabatta bread
2	tablespoons	pesto (see recipe)
1	cup	baby arugula
¼	cup	goat cheese

Preheat oven to 400 degrees. Arrange eggplant in a single layer on baking sheet. Brush both sides of eggplant with teaspoon of oil. Arrange pepper halves, skin side down on baking sheet. Bake 25-30 minutes. Toast bread or broil in oven until toasted turning once. Spread 1 tablespoon of pesto on one slice of bread; add 4 slices of eggplant and ½ pepper. Toss arugula with remaining teaspoon of oil and black pepper. Divide arugula and place on top of peppers. Spread goat cheese on remaining bread slice.

Hawaiian Chicken Sandwich

Makes: 1 serving   Prep Time: 30 minutes

1	tablespoon	Teriyaki sauce
1	ounce	pineapple, sliced
1	ounce	Swiss cheese, sliced
1	6-ounce	chicken breast, boneless, roasted (see recipe)
		hamburger bun, mixed grain, toasted

Roast your chicken breast according to recipe. Five minutes before it's done, put teriyaki sauce on both sides of the chicken. Put the pineapple and Swiss cheese on top and continue to bake until cheese melts. Serve on a warm toasted bun. For a variation, you can eliminate pineapple and add sautéd onions and mushrooms.

Honey Mustard Chicken Sandwiches

Makes: 4 sandwiches   Prep Time: 40 minutes

Honey Mustard Marinade

½	cup	Dijon mustard
½	cup	honey
1 ½	cups	vegetable oil
½	teaspoon	lemon juice
4	6 ounce	chicken breasts, boneless
8	slices	bacon, cooked
½	cup	jack cheese, shredded
½	cup	cheddar cheese, shredded
4		wheat buns, toasted

Use electric mixer or food processor to combine the honey mustard marinates ingredients. Whip for 30 seconds. Pour about ⅔ of the marinade over the chicken breasts and marinade, covered, for about 2 hours. Chill the remaining marinade until later. After the chicken is marinated, preheat oven to 375. Put chicken on sprayed baking sheet and bake for 12 minutes on each side. When the chicken is done, crisscross 2 pieces of bacon on top of each piece of chicken, and top with the shredded jack and cheddar. Bake for 7-10 minutes, or until the cheese is melted. Serve the remaining honey mustard chicken to dip the sandwich in. Serve the chicken on toasted wheat buns. This also makes a wonderful entrée.

Italian Grilled Cheese Flat Bread

Makes: 1 sandwich   Prep Time: 15 minutes

2	slices	provolone cheese
4	tablespoons	Italian cheese or blend of Italian cheeses like Asiago, Ramano & Parmesan, shredded or grated
1	piece	flatbread, cut in half (I use rosemary flatout)
2-3	slices	tomato
½	tablespoon	butter, unsalted
½	clove	garlic, minced

Melt the butter with garlic. Heat skillet on medium high heat until hot. Brush melted butter on 1 side of each flatbread piece and put butter side down in skillet. Top each piece of flatbread with a slice of provolone cheese and 2 tablespoons of the Italian cheese. Place the tomato slices in the skillet to heat on both sides then place them on top of one side of the flatbread. When the cheese is half melted flip the flatbread together and let it finish melting. Cut in half. This is a perfect complement to my Tomato Bisque or Italian Vegetable Meatball soup. (See recipes).

Malibu Chicken Sandwich

Makes: 1 sandwich   Prep Time: 15 minutes

1	6 ounce	chicken breast, boneless, skinless
¼	cup	Italian salad dressing, creamy
2	slices	Monterey jack cheese
1	each	hamburger bun
2	slices	bacon, cooked

Marinate the chicken breast in the Italian dressing for 5-10 minutes. Shake off the excess dressing and broil or bake the chicken at 350 degrees for 15 minutes on each side. Put the bacon and cheese on the chicken and put back in the oven long enough to melt the cheese. Serve on a toasted bun.

Pulled Pork Sandwich

Makes: 6 serving   Prep Time: 6 hours

2	pounds	pork roast
1	teaspoon	oil
½	cup	water
½	teaspoon	seasoned salt
½	teaspoon	pepper
1	teaspoon	garlic, minced
1	cup	bbq sauce

Rinse the meat and brown in a hot skillet on all sides. Place the meat in a crock pot. Add the water and seasonings except the BBQ sauce. Cook on low 6-8 hours or high 4-6 hours until the meat is pull apart tender. Remove the meat from the crock pot and discard the liquid. Pull the meat and put back in the crock pot. Add the bbq sauce and heat until ready to serve. This is really good served with the Iced Box Slaw on top. (See recipe).

Rueben Bake

Makes: 8 servings   Prep Time: 30 minutes

2	sheets	Puff Pastry (groceries freezer section)
1	pound	Swiss cheese, sliced
1 ¼	pounds	deli corned beef, sliced (or turkey to make a turkey Rueben)
1	14 ounce can	sauerkraut, rinsed, well drained.
⅔	cup	Thousand Island dressing
1	each	egg white, beaten
3	teaspoons	caraway seeds

Unroll 1 sheet of puff pastry and press into bottom of 9" x 13" baking dish. Press to cover the bottom of the baking dish. Bake in a preheated 375 degree oven for 8-10 minutes or until golden brown. Then layer with half the cheese and all of the meat. Combine sauerkraut and dressing; spread over meat. Top with remaining cheese. On lightly floured surface press or roll out the second sheet of pastry to fit the 9" x 13" pan. Place over the cheese. Brush with egg white; sprinkle with caraway seeds. Bake for 12-16 minutes or until heated through and crust is golden brown. Let stand 5 minutes before cutting.

Shrimp and Crab Melt

Makes: 1 serving   Prep Time: 15 minutes

½	cup	shrimp and crab salad (see recipe)
2	slices	tomato
2	slices	jack cheese
1	whole	english muffin, halved

Toast the English muffin halves. Place a tomato slice, topped with a scoop of shrimp and crab salad then a slice of jack cheese in the oven, toaster oven or microwave until hot and cheese is melted. Place the tomato, shrimp and crab with cheese on top of the toasted English muffin and serve open face.

Tuna Melt

Makes: 1 serving   Prep Time: 15 minutes

½	cup	tuna salad (See recipe)
2	slices	tomato
2	slices	jack or cheddar cheese
1		english muffin, halved

Toast the English muffin halves. Place a tomato slice, topped with a scoop of tuna salad then a slice of jack cheese in the oven, toaster oven or microwave until hot and cheese is melted. Place the tomato, tuna and cheese on top of the toasted English muffin and serve open face. This was a very popular sandwich at Margy's.

Turkey Rueben

Makes: 1 serving   Prep Time: 10 minutes

2	slices	marble rye bread
4	ounces	turkey, oven roasted or smoked, sliced
¼	cup	saurkraut, drained
2	ounces (slices)	Swiss cheese
2	tablespoons	Russian dressing (see recipe) or store bought Thousand Island dressing

Toast the bread in a toaster or toaster oven. Place the turkey topped with saurkraut, and cheese in the toaster oven, oven or microwave and heat until hot through out and cheese is melted. Top with the dressing and put on the toast. Cut in half and serve. This was a huge seller at Margy's. Substitute corned beef if you prefer it to Turkey. You can grill this sandwich versus toasting if you like.

Ultimate Grilled Cheese Sandwich

Makes: 1 sandwich   Prep Time: 15 minutes

2	ounces (1/2 cup)	white cheddar cheese, shredded or sliced
4	tablespoons	Italian or blend of Italian cheeses like Asiago, Romano & Parmesan, shredded or grated
2	slices	hearty white or wheat bread
2	slices	tomato
1	slice	red onion, sliced thin
½	tablespoon	butter, unsalted
½	clove	garlic, minced
2	slices	bacon, center cut, cooked
¼	cup	spinach leaves, sliced

Melt the butter with garlic. Heat skillet on medium high heat until hot. Brush melted garlic butter on 1 side of each piece of bread and put the bread butter side down in the skillet. Top each piece of bread with the cheese. Place the tomato slices and onion in the skillet to heat on both sides then place them on top of one piece of the bread. Then top the tomato, onion with the spinach and bacon. Flip the two pieces of bread together and let the cheese finish melting. Cut in half. This is a perfect complement to my Tomato Bisque soup.

Apple Walnut Turkey Sandwich

Makes: 4 servings   Prep Time: 15 minutes

1-¾	cups	mayonnaise
¼	cup	celery, chopped
¼	cup	cranberries, dried
¼	cup	walnuts, chopped
1	medium	tart apple, chopped
1	pound	turkey, sliced
8	slices	sourdough bread
8	leaves	lettuce

Combine mayonnaise, celery, cranberries and walnuts. Stir in apple and set aside. Place turkey on bread and top with apple mixture and lettuce. This is an excellent sandwich and perfect on mini croissants for a tea, bridal shower or brunch.

Photos taken by Swikar Patel, The Journal Gazette, Fort Wayne, Indiana. Copyright 2011.
Italian Grilled Cheese Flatbread, Raspberry Bread, Garden Vegetable Soup

A variety of our Family Meal pictures

Egg Salad BLT

Makes: 1 sandwich

Prep Time: 30 minutes

½	cup	egg salad (see recipe)
2	slices	center cut bacon, cooked
1	leaf	leaf lettuce
1	large	tomato, fresh, sliced
2	pieces	nice white or wheat bread

Place the lettuce on 1 slice of the bread, top with the egg salad, bacon and tomato. Slice in half and enjoy.

Shrimp Wrap

Makes: 4 servings

Prep Time: 15 minutes

4	wraps	spinach, tomato or wheat
4	tablespoons	chive and onion cream cheese spread
1	whole	cucumber, sliced thin
½	whole	red pepper, sliced thin
½	cup	cooked salad shrimp, cleaned
1	whole	avacado, sliced thin

Spread cream cheese on each wrap. Place in the center of each wrap the following and in this order: cucumbers, red peppers, shrimp then avacado. Roll up the wrap and slice in half. You can sub the cream cheese with ranch dressing.

Turkey Club Wrap

Makes: 4 wraps

Prep Time: 15 minutes

4	10"	flour tortillas (I like to use spinach or tomato tortillas for this)
4	tablespoons	Ranch dressing
1	pound	deli turkey, sliced
8	slices	bacon, cooked
4	leaves	leaf lettuce
4	slices	tomato

Spread 1 tablespoon of dressing on each tortilla. Put lettuce in center of the tortilla, top with the turkey, bacon and tomatoes. Roll up and cut in half.

Sauces

Blackened Seasoning

Butters
Cinnamon Honey
Orange Honey
Strawberry

Cranberry Chutney

Cranberry Relish

Fresh Fish Marinade

Mushroom Marinade

Mayonnaise
Ginger
Jalapeño
Orange Rosemary
Tarragon

Pesto
Basil
Lemon Thyme
Red Pepper
Spinach
Sun-dried Tomato Basil
Tomato and Mushroom

Sauces
Alfredo
Apricot Horseradish
BBQ
Caramel
Cocktail
Coney
Raspberry
White Sauce

Blackened Seasoning

Makes: 12 servings   Prep Time: 5 minutes

1 ½	tablespoons	salt
1 ½	tablespoons	white pepper
1 ½	tablespoons	whole fennel seeds
1 ½	tablespoons	black pepper
2 ½	teaspoons	dry mustard
2 ½	teaspoons	cayenne pepper, ground

Mix all ingredients together. This recipe is great for blackening chicken, steaks, burgers, fish, shrimp etc. Brush with oil or marinate then rub with seasoning; bake sauté or grill. Make sure you ventilate well when blackening. This seasoning will keep for months stored in an air tight container.

Cinnamon Honey Butter

Makes: 12 servings   Prep Time: 15 minutes

1	pound	butter, softened
1	teaspoon	cinnamon
½	cup	honey
¼	cup	brown sugar

Mix well in mixer or food processor. Great on baked sweet potatoes, apple scones or carrot cake pancakes (see recipes).

Orange Honey Butter

Makes: 12 servings   Prep Time: 30 minutes

1	pound	butter, softened
¼	cup	honey
⅛	cup	orange peel, grated fine

Blend well adding honey slowly. This is the butter recipe from the café and is perfect served with my signature sweet potato or cinnamon rolls.

Strawberry Butter

Makes: 12 servings   Prep Time: 15 minutes

½	cup	strawberries, fresh, sliced
1	cup	butter, softened
½	cup	powdered sugar
8	ounces	cream cheese, softened

Mix in food processor or blender. Great served with strawberry bread or scones.

Cranberry Chutney

Makes: 4 servings   Prep Time: 1 hour 40 minutes

½	cup	cranberries, fresh or frozen, thawed
¼	cup	water
3	tablespoons	sugar
1	tablespoon	brown sugar
½	teaspoon	cinnamon
½	teaspoon	ginger
½	teaspoon	cloves
¼	cup	water
¼	cup	celery, chopped fine
1	medium	apple, peeled, diced
2	tablespoons	raisins, seedless

In a medium sauce pan, bring water to a boil. Add all above ingredients except apples and raisins. Simmer 15 minutes. Add apples and simmer additional 10 minutes or until apples are soft. Remove from heat and stir in raisins while sauce is hot. Cool thoroughly. Serve with turkey burgers or carved turkey.

Cranberry Relish

Makes: 12 servings   Prep Time: 15 minutes

1	15-ounce can	cranberry sauce
2	tablespoons	golden seedless raisins
2	tablespoons	thyme, fresh, chopped
1	cup	mandarin oranges, drained

Chop oranges. Mix all ingredients. Great served with turkey sandwiches or turkey burgers.

Fresh Fish Marinade

Makes: 8 servings   Prep Time: 10 minutes

1	cup	olive oil
1	tablespoon	rosemary, fresh, chopped
1	teaspoon	kosher salt
1	teaspoon	lemon juice, fresh

Mix all ingredients. Marinate your fresh fish for 1-24 hours. Again, this is one of those basic recipes you can build on, add additional herbs, different toppings etc. You can bake, grill, broil or sauté fish marinated in this recipe. This marinade goes great with a fresh salsa topping. (See recipes.)

Mushroom Marinade

Makes: 12 servings   Prep Time: 15 minutes

1 ½	cups	soy sauce
1	teaspoon	ginger, ground
4	cloves	garlic, minced
1	cup	olive oil, extra virgin

Mix well and pour over your favorite mushrooms. Marinate for at least one hour. Roast mushrooms on a sprayed baking pan at 375 degrees for 30 minutes or on the grill. This is a very popular and delicious recipe. This is also what I use for a roasted portobella sandwich and portabella fajitas.

Ginger Mayonnaise

Makes: 12 servings   Prep Time: 5 minutes

1	cup	mayonnaise
1	teaspoon	ginger, dried
½	teaspoon	soy sauce
½	teaspoon	garlic powder

Mix all ingredients. This is great served with a fish sandwich or salmon cakes.

Jalapeño Mayonnaise

Makes: 12 servings   Prep Time: 15 minutes

1	cup	mayonnaise
2	tablespoons	lemon juice
2	tablespoons	Dijon mustard
1	whole	jalapeño, chopped
½	teaspoon	paprika
3	tablespoons	honey

Blend until smooth. This sauce is GREAT served with crab cakes. For lunch during lent we would make crab cake sandwiches on croissants with jalapeño mayo. What a hit they were. This is also great on fish sandwiches or burgers and will keep in refrigerator for 4-5 days.

Orange Rosemary Mayonnaise

Makes: 4 servings   Prep Time: 10 minutes

¼	cup	orange marmalade
½	cup	mayonnaise
¾	teaspoon	rosemary, fresh, chopped fine
1	dash	salt

Mix all ingredients and let set in refrigerator for one hour. Great served with chicken sandwiches or a sauce to make chicken salad.

Tarragon Mayonnaise

Makes: 8 servings   Prep Time: 15 minutes

1	cup	mayonnaise
4	tablespoons	tarragon, fresh, chopped
1	dash	salt
1	dash	pepper
2	tablespoon	orange peel, grated

Mix all ingredients. Refrigerate, covered. Don't make more than one day ahead. Great served on chicken sandwiches, burgers, turkey or used as a dressing for chicken salad.

Basil Pesto

Makes: 12 serving   Prep Time: 15 minutes

2	cups	basil leaves, fresh
¼	cup	pine nuts or walnuts
¼	cup	parmesan cheese, freshly grated
4	cloves	garlic, fresh, minced
¼	cup	olive or canola oil
		salt and pepper to taste

Combine all ingredients in a food processor. Blend until a stiff puree has been made. Add more oil if needed but only a tablespoon at a time. Pesto is great on so many things; tossed with pasta, roasted veggies, chicken breasts, fish, mixed in with mashed potatoes, on a chicken sandwich or served on toasted french bread.

Lemon Thyme Pesto

Makes: 12 servings   Prep Time: 30 minutes

½	cup	parsley, fresh, chopped
½	cup	pine nuts or walnuts
1	tablespoon	thyme, fresh, chopped
2	tablespoons	lemon peel
2	tablespoons	lemon juice, fresh
½	cup	olive or canola oil
1	dash	salt
1	dash	pepper

In food processor or blender, blend the first 5 ingredients until almost smooth. With machine running, slowly add olive oil and process until smooth. If pesto is dry, add more olive oil by the tablespoon. Add salt and pepper to taste. Cover and refrigerate. Will keep in refrigerator for up to one week or in the freezer for up to one month. This is great to put on fish to bake, grill or broil such as tilapia. Rub pesto on both sides of fish.

Red Pepper Pesto

Makes: 3 cups   Prep Time: 30 minutes

4	whole	red bell peppers (roasted)
1	cup	parmesan cheese
2	tablespoons	olive oil
4	cloves	garlic, roasted
2	tablespoons	thyme, fresh
1/8	teaspoon	salt
		white pepper to taste

Add ingredients all at once in a food processor and process until incorporated. This is great tossed with pasta or used as a sauce over fish or a variety of meats.

Roasting Peppers-Coat with oil, put in 375 degree oven for 30 minutes; 15 minutes on each side. Put in cold pan, wrap and put in refrigerator to cool. Peel.

Spinach Pesto

Makes: 4-6 servings   Prep Time: 15 minutes

3	cups	spinach, fresh, stems removed
½	cup	basil, fresh
½	cup	parmesan
1/8-¼	cups	olive or canola oil
½	teaspoon	salt
2	cloves	garlic, minced
½	cup	pine nuts or walnuts (optional)

Chop in food processor. Refrigerate up to 1 week. This is great tossed with fresh cooked pasta and veggies as a hot entrée or tossed with roasted veggies as a salad dressing.

Sun-dried Tomato Basil Pesto

Makes: 16 servings   Prep Time: 45 minutes

2	cups	sun-dried tomatoes, not in oil
4	cloves	garlic, minced
2	tablespoons	basil, fresh, chopped
½	teaspoon	salt
½	teaspoon	crushed red pepper
½	cup	olive oil, extra virgin
½	cup	parsley, fresh, chopped
½	cup	parmesan cheese, shredded

Cover sun-dried tomatoes with hot water and let set for 20 minutes. Drain tomatoes and squeeze out excess water. In food processor, put in tomatoes, garlic, basil, salt, crushed red peppers, parsley and parmesan cheese. With food processor running, add olive oil. Do not make pesto smooth, should have a choppy texture to it. Just mix long enough to incorporate. If pesto seems dry, add more olive oil, 1 tablespoon at a time. Pesto will keep in refrigerator up to one week. Can be frozen up to one month. This pesto is great tossed with spinach pasta and chicken strips.

Tomato and Mushroom Pesto

Makes: 4 servings   Prep Time: 30 minutes

12	ounces	shitake or button mushrooms
5	whole	shallots or ½ of onion
1	tablespoon	thyme, fresh
4	tablespoons	olive oil
2	cloves	garlic
4	tablespoons	butter
1	pound	tomatoes, seeded, chopped
		salt and pepper to taste

Rinse mushrooms thoroughly with water, drain and clean to remove all sand. Chop mushrooms, onion, garlic and the fresh thyme finely, using a food processor. Place the butter and oil in skillet. When oil is warm, add the chopped ingredients and sauté for 15 minutes, stirring constantly with a spoon. Meanwhile, run the chopped tomatoes in the food processor, and then add it to other ingredients, season with salt and pepper to taste, and simmer for 5 minutes. Toss with pasta. (See recipe in entrée chapter.)

Alfredo Sauce

Makes: 8 servings

Prep Time: 15 minutes

4	tablespoons	butter
4	tablespoons	flour
1	teaspoon	garlic, fresh, minced
1	dash	pepper
1	pint (2 cups)	heavy whipping cream
1	teaspoon	chicken base
1 ½ -2	cups	milk
2	5.2 oz packages	boursin cheese
½	cup	parmesan, fresh, grated

Melt butter, add garlic on medium heat. Stir in flour and whisk for 1 minute. Keeping on medium heat, whisk in heavy cream and then milk. Heat whisking constantly then add chicken base and boursin cheese, stirring until melted. Add parmesan and whisk until heated through and cheese is melted. Add milk to create desired consistency.

Varied uses for this sauce: My friend, Bun Lim, the chef at Sycamore Hills Country Club, uses Alfredo Sauce to make his verson of the best scalloped potatoes you have ever had. As a change from the traditional lasagna, I make a variation with a layer or red sauce and a layer of alfredo sauce. This sauce also works great for chicken lasagna.

Note: this sauce holds up well in a chaffing dish or crock pot for a pasta bar event. We do an occasional Pasta Bar for our Sunday family dinners. The kids and grandkids love it!

Apricot Horseradish Sauce

Makes: 12 servings

Prep Time: 15 minutes

12	ounces	apricot jam
¼	cup	orange juice
1/8	cup	horseradish

Mix. This is the perfect sauce for either blackened or the coconut shrimp.

BBQ Sauce

2	tablespoons	lemon juice
1	tablespoon	Worcestershire sauce
1	cup	ketchup
½	cup	honey
¼	cup	butter
1/8	teaspoon	garlic, powder
½	teaspoon	cumin

Bring all ingredients to a boil then remove from heat and serve.

Caramel Sauce

1	pound	butter
¾	cup	sugar
2	cups	heavy whipping cream

Melt butter half way and add sugar, let brown, stirring constantly. Add cream when butter and sugar start to separate. Bring to a boil and remove from heat and let set to cool. Can store in refrigerator up to one week. Great served on bread pudding, pecan waffles, pancakes and anything else you like.

Cocktail Sauce

½	cup	chili sauce
½	cup	ketchup
3	tablespoons	prepared horseradish
1	teaspoon	lemon juice
½	teaspoon	Worcestershire sauce
¼	teaspoon	hot sauce

Mix together and let set for a few minutes in refrigerator. Serve with shrimp cocktail (see recipe).

Coney Sauce

1	tablespoon	canola oil
1	large	onion, chopped fine
3	pounds	ground sirloin
5/8	cup	chili powder
2	teaspoons	salt
1	tablespoon	red pepper
1	tablespoon	all spice
1	tablespoon	oregano
1	cup	tomato sauce
5	cups	water
1	tablespoon	crushed red pepper

Heat large pan then add oil and onion. Cook onion until translucent or starts to turn brown. Add ground beef and cook until pink is gone. Drain grease. Add all the spices except the crushed red pepper, mix well. Add tomato sauce and water bring to a boil, turn off and add crushed red pepper. Put the mixture through a blender or food processor for a few seconds. This recipe is a big hit with the guys on game night and is a much healthier version than the original.

Raspberry Sauce

3	cups	raspberries, fresh
1/2	cup	sugar
1/3	cup	water

Mix together in sauce pan and cook for five minutes. Put through sieve to strain seeds. Will keep in refrigerator for up to two weeks. Can use as a sauce for desserts or on chicken breasts with fresh berries.

White Sauce

Medium

2	tablespoons	butter
2	tablespoons	flour
¼	teaspoon, each	salt and pepper
1	cup	milk

Thick

3	tablespoons	butter
4	tablespoons	flour
¼	teaspoon, each	salt and pepper
1	cup	milk

Thin

1	tablespoon	butter
1	tablespoon	flour
¼	teaspoon, each	salt and pepper
1	cup	milk

A basic white sauce can be used for many other recipes. Soups, sauce for macaroni and cheese, alfredo sauce, bechamel sauce etc.

Melt butter in saucepan and whisk in flour and salt. Cook paste for 1 minute on low heat. Add milk slowly, stirring constantly to avoid lumps. The sauce thickens as it cooks. If you find lumps press them out with the back of a spoon. Use medium white sauce for sauces, scalloped and creamed dishes. Use thin sauce for soups and creamed vegetables and thick sauce for souffles.

Cheese Sauces-To 1 cup hot medium white sauce, add 1 cup shredded sharp cheddar cheese; stir to melt. Or to 1 cup hot medium white sauce, add ½ cup shredded sharp cheddar cheese and ½ cup shredded swiss cheese; stir to melt.

Soups

The Basics of Making Soup

Beef
American Chowder
Cheeseburger
Chili
Italian Vegetable Meatball
Rueben
Vegetable Beef

Chicken
Chicken Broth
Chicken Corn Rival
Chicken, Tomato Rice Florentine
Creamy Broccoli Chicken
Easy Chicken Tortilla
White Chicken Chili

Pork
Brazilian Black Bean
Cabbage
Cream of Potato made with
  Left over Mashed Potatoes
Cream of Potato with
  Sausage and Cheese
Cream of Sausage
Ham and Bean
Italian Vegetable Sausage
Smoked Sausage
Split Pea with Ham
Lasagna

Seafood
Cioppino
Clam Chowder
Shrimp and Crab Bisque

Vegetable
Black Bean
Broccoli Cheese
Butternut Squash with
  Toasted Pumpkin Seeds
Corn Chowder
Cream of Artichoke
Cream of Mushroom
Fresh Vegetable Broth
Italian Garden Vegetable
Portobello Mushroom with Leek
Pumpkin with Jalapeño Pesto
Quick Vegetarian Chili
Quick Vegetable
Roasted Red Pepper
Tomato Bisque
Vegetarian Lentil
White Cheddar Cheese
Wild Rice and Mushroom

There is nothing more inviting to the table then a nice hot bowl of soup in the cold of winter, especially when the vegetables in the soup are from your summer garden.

Following are a few basic tips to get you started with making great soups.

There are three types of soup:

Broth soup-A clear soup made from meats, poultry, fish or vegetables. Broths can be used to make other soups. Unlike other soups broth can be served "as is". For broth soups you can use chicken, beef, vegetable, ham, mushroom, seafood or tomato broth as a base for other soups. You can also use a combination of broths; one of my favorites is a combination of chicken broth and tomato paste, especially with bean or tortilla soups. You can make the broths from scratch, use a canned broth, base/paste, bouillon cubes or granules. To make a great soup you need to start with a great broth and great ingredients. I make broth from scratch when I have the time but when I don't I use a soup base called "Better than Bouillon". It is made from real meats and vegetables, is very concentrated and has much more flavor than bouillon and granules, contains no fat or MSG and is lower in sodium than other broths. You can buy it in any of the groceries or buy it at their web site www.superiortouch.com. They have a large variety including the basics; chicken, beef, vegetable, mushroom, seafood etc. and organic, gluten free, vegan, kosher, and a variety of naturally reduced sodium. In reading my recipes you will notice I always use base (sometimes called paste) and I always use the *Better than Bouillon* brand or my homemade broth or both.

Cream soups-A cream soup is based on a white sauce - milk thickened with roux. (Roux–pronounced Roo), is a mixture of melted fat and flour, cooked to remove the starchy taste of flour; used to thicken soups and stews and to make gravy. See white sauce recipe in the sauce chapter.

Puree soups-Are thicker than a cream soup and have a courser texture. They are often based on dried peas, lentils, beans or starchy vegetables like carrots, potatoes and squashes.

Note: You will notice with some of my soup recipes, I do not sauté the onions and other vegetables; instead I add them to the boiling broth. The reason I do this is to make the soup healthier by eliminating the use of oil.

American Chowder

Makes: 8-10 servings

Prep Time: 1 hour

1	pound	ground beef
½	cup	onions, diced
½	cup	celery, diced
½	cup	green pepper, diced
½	cup	red pepper, diced
3	cups	water
3	tablespoons	beef base
3	cups	potatoes, diced
1	cup	milk
3	cups	half and half
1	teaspoon	hot sauce
1	pound	cheddar cheese, shredded or Velvetta cheese, cubed

Stove Top Method-In a large stock pot, sauté onions, celery, and peppers together with uncooked ground beef. Drain grease. Add water and beef base, bring to a low boil; add potatoes. Cook on a low simmer until potatoes are almost done then add the milk, half and half and hot sauce. Heat, then add the cheese and stir until melts. Do not over heat the cheese or it will break. Salt and pepper to taste.

Crock Pot Method-Cook the ground beef and drain the grease. Add the remaining ingredients into a crock pot except the cheese and cook on low 4-6 hours until the vegetables are cooked. Add the cheese and stir. Heat until cheese is melted and then turn down the temperature.

Cheeseburger Soup

Makes: 8 servings

Prep Time: 45 minutes

2 ¼	cups	water
3	cups	potatoes, cubed
¼	cup	carrots, diced
½	cup	onions, diced
1	teaspoon	garlic, minced
1 ½	tablespoons	beef base
1	pound	ground lean beef, cooked and drained
3 ¾	cups	milk (use at least 2% so the soup doesn't break)
4 ½	tablespoons	flour
½	pound	cheddar cheese, cubed
½	teaspoon	cayenne pepper

Combine the first 6 ingredients and bring to a boil. Reduce heat. Cover and simmer for 15-20 minutes or until potatoes are tender. Stir in beef and 2 cups of milk. Heat through. Combine flour & remaining milk until smooth, gradually stir into soup. Bring to a boil, cook & stir for 2 minutes until thickened and bubbly; reduce heat, stir in cheese until melted. Add cayenne.

Chili

Makes: 6-8 servings   Prep Time: 1 hour

1	pound	ground lean beef, cooked (drain grease)
1	medium	onion, diced
1	15 ounce can	tomatoes, diced, or fresh, peeled and seeded
2	15 ounce cans	dark red kidney beans
2	cups	vegetable juice
2	packages	French's chili seasoning mix (I use mild or regular)
½	cup	green chilies, diced or fresh banana peppers or jalapeños
2	tablespoons	molasses
2	tablespoons	brown sugar

Crock Pot Method- Put all ingredients in crock pot and cook on low for 6-8 hours or high for 4-6 hours.

Stove Top Method- Cook ground beef with onions and peppers; drain grease and add remaining ingredients. Simmer for 1 hour.

Chili Bar -you can put out chopped green or white onions, shredded jack or cheddar cheese, sour cream, corn chips, macaroni noodles etc.

Note: You can simmer the soup with whole peppers vs. dicing them.

Italian Vegetable Meatball Soup

Makes: 6-8 servings   Prep Time: 45 minutes

1	whole	carrot, diced
2	stalks	celery, diced
1	whole	onion, diced
1	tablespoon	oil
6	cups	chicken stock
2	cups	water
1	can or 2 cups	tomatoes, diced
1	cup	green beans, fresh, cut into 1" pieces
1	cup	zucchini, fresh, diced or shredded
2	cups	spinach, fresh, chopped

Meatballs

1	pound	ground beef (extra lean)
¼	cup	bread crumbs
½	cup	parmesan cheese
1	dash	salt
1	dash	pepper
1	teaspoon	garlic, minced
		Use small scoop to make mini meatballs.
1	pound	pasta noodles, small.

Sauté carrot, celery and onion in oil until transparent. Add chicken stock and water; bring to a boil. Add tomatoes, green beans and zucchini. Bring to a boil.

Mix meatball ingredients together. Put meatballs in boiling stock and add pasta. Cover and cook until pasta is done. Add the fresh chopped spinach at the last minute just until wilts.

If you prefer the traditional Italian wedding ring soup you would eliminate the following from this recipe: Tomatoes, green beans, zucchini.

Rueben Soup

Makes: 8 servings

Prep Time: 30 minutes

1	cup	onion, diced
½	cup	celery, diced
3	tablespoons	butter
1 ½	cups	chicken broth
1 ½	cups	beef broth
¾	teaspoon	baking soda
3	tablespoons	cornstarch
3	tablespoons	cold water
1 ¼	cups	sauerkraut, drained, rinsed
3	cups	half and half
3	cups	corned beef, cooked, diced
1 ½	cups	Swiss cheese, shredded
		salt and pepper to taste

Sauté onion and celery in butter until tender. Add broth and baking soda. Combine cornstarch and water, add to pan. Bring to a boil; boil for 2 minutes, stirring occasionally. Reduce heat. Add sauerkraut, cream and corned beef, simmer and stir for 15 minutes. Add cheese, heat until melted. Add salt and pepper. Garnish with croutons if desired.

Vegetable Beef Soup

Makes: 8-10 servings

Prep Time: 5 hours

2	pounds	beef chuck or English roast
48	ounces	vegetable juice or tomato juice
2	tablespoons	beef base
1	teaspoon	garlic powder
1	teaspoon	Lawry's Seasoned Salt
1	teaspoon	pepper
2	cups	water

Wash roast. Season both sides with salt and pepper. Brown both sides in a skillet. Put in a large roasting pan. Add vegetable juice, beef base, water and garlic. Roast in a preheated oven covered at 325 degrees for 3-4 hours. When meat is pull apart tender, remove from oven and put on top of stove. Add whatever vegetables you desire. Cook until vegetables are done. Pull meat into pieces. You can also cook in the crock pot on low for 6-8 hours but start the vegetables with the meat on top. You will still need to brown the meat.

Chicken Broth

1	whole	chicken, cut up, or 3 pounds chicken breasts with skin and bone
2	stalks	celery, with leaves, cut into chunks
2	whole	carrots, with peels cut into chunks
2	medium	onions, with skins, halved
4	cloves	garlic, whole
2	sprigs	parsley
1	large	thyme, branch, fresh
1	whole	bay leaf
2	quarts (8 cups)	water
2-4	tablespoons	chicken base

Clean chicken parts, remove fat and wash in cool water. Put all ingredients in a deep stock pot and bring to a simmer on medium heat, uncovered. Keep it at a steady simmer until chicken is tender, about 1 to 1-½ hours. Remove chicken, let cool. Put broth through a strainer and discard the vegetables. Let broth cool (if not serving right away) and refrigerate. Remove the hardened layer of fat from the top before using. For chicken soup, remove chicken from bones and set aside. Return strained broth to stock pot and continue simmering to reduce the broth until it is rich. This will take about 30 minutes. Add the noodles and diced chicken. You can freeze the broth in 1 cup containers. I make a large batch and freeze it for future recipes calling for chicken broth.

Chicken Corn Rival Soup

1	whole	chicken, cut up, or 3 pounds chicken breasts with skin and bone
4-5	cups	chicken broth (see recipe)
1-½	cups	corn (from the cob)
1	whole	egg, beaten
1	cup	flour
½	teaspoon each	salt and pepper

Cook the chicken to make the broth following the chicken broth recipe. Remove the chicken from the bones and cut into bite size pieces. Set aside. To make the rivels add the flour, salt and pepper to the beaten egg. The largest pieces should be no bigger than a pea. Bring broth to a boil then add rivels with a fork. Stirring constantly but gently. Reduce heat to medium, cover and simmer about 8-10 minutes. After the rivels are done add the corn and the chicken. This is from my mother-in-law, Mary Barnes.

Chicken, Tomato Rice Florentine

Makes: 6 servings   Prep Time: 15 minutes

3	cups	chicken broth
1	can	tomatoes, diced, or fresh, peeled and seeded
½	cup	onion, chopped
1	cup	chicken, cooked, diced
1	tablespoon	basil, fresh, diced or 1 teaspoon dried basil
½	teaspoon	oregano
1	tablespoon	parsley, fresh, chopped or 1 teaspoon dried parsley
2	cups	spinach, fresh, chopped
1	cup	cooked rice

Put all of the above ingredients (except the spinach & rice) in a large soup pot and bring to a boil. Turn down the heat as soon as it boils and simmer on low for 10 minutes; add the spinach and rice.

Creamy Broccoli Chicken Soup

Makes: 8 servings   Prep Time: 45 minutes

1 ½	cups	broccoli, florets, small
½	cup	carrots, shredded
¼	cup	onion, chopped
¼	cup	butter
¼	cup	flour
1 ½	teaspoons	basil, fresh, chopped fine
¼	teaspoon	pepper
3	cups	milk
1	cup	half and half, or light cream
1	tablespoon	Worcestershire Sauce
1 ½	teaspoons	chicken base
1 ½	cups	chicken, diced

In a medium sauce pan, cook and stir broccoli, carrots and onion in butter for 6-8 minutes or until tender but not brown. Stir in flour, basil, and pepper. Add milk and half and half all at once. Add Worcestershire sauce and chicken base. Cook and stir until thickened and bubbly. Stir in chicken, heat through.

Easy Chicken Tortilla Soup

Makes: 4-6 servings   Prep Time: 30 minutes

1	can (15 ounces)	diced tomatoes, or fresh, peeled and seeded
1	can	corn, or 2 cups off the cob
1	can	black beans
¼	cup	cilantro, chopped
1	cup	onion, diced
2	cups	chicken, cooked, diced
½	cup	green pepper, diced
2	cups	water
2	tablespoons	chicken base
1	tablespoon	butter

Sauté onions and green pepper in butter until soft. Add remaining ingredients and bring to a gentle boil on medium heat. Simmer on low for about 30 minutes. Serve with shredded cheddar and tortilla chips on top.

White Chicken Chili Soup

Makes: 4-6 servings   Prep Time: 1 hour

4-5	cups	navy beans, cooked
½	cup	water
2	cups	chicken, cooked, diced
1	tablespoon	chicken base
1	small can	green chilies, chopped
1	teaspoon	cumin
1	teaspoon	oregano, dried
½	teaspoon	red pepper flakes
1	cup	onion, diced
¼	cup	chives, chopped
		Sour cream

Crock Pot Method- Put all ingredients in crock pot; cook on low 6-8 hours or high 4-6 hours. Serve with a dollop of sour cream on top and chopped chives.

Stove Top Method- Put all ingredients in a large stock pot and bring to a low boil then simmer on low for 30 minutes or until onions are tender. This recipe is from my daughter, Candas DeHoff, thanks Candas.

Brazilian Black Bean Soup

1	pound	kielbasa sausage, sliced
½	cup	onion, chopped
4	cups	water
4	tablespoons	chicken base
1	clove	garlic, minced
2	cans (or 3 cups, cooked)	black beans, drained, rinsed
2	teaspoons	chili powder
1	can	diced tomatoes, or fresh, peeled and seeded
2	cups	spinach, fresh, stemmed, chopped
1	whole	jalapeño pepper, left whole
2	cups	cooked rice

Put all ingredients except rice and spinach in a large pot and bring to boil and then simmer for about 30-60 minutes. Add rice and spinach and simmer a few more minutes until spinach is wilted.

Cabbage Soup

1	tablespoon	butter
½	cup	onions, diced
¼	cup	carrots, diced
½	cup	celery, diced
1	pound	sliced smoked sausage, or diced ham
½	teaspoon	garlic, minced
4	cups	chicken broth
2	cups	potatoes, peeled, diced
½	teaspoon	dried thyme
4	cups	cabbage, diced
½	teaspoon	salt and pepper

Melt the butter in a stock pot; sauté the onions, carrots and celery for about 2 minutes. Add the garlic and sausage and sauté for another 2-3 minutes. Add the broth and bring to a boil, add the potatoes, thyme salt and pepper. Simmer on medium low heat for about 15 minutes and add the cabbage. Continue to simmer for about 15-30 more minutes until the cabbage is done.

Cream of Potato made with left over Mashed Potatoes

Makes: 4-6 servings   Prep Time: 15 minutes

3	cups	mashed potatoes, see recipe or leftovers
1	cup	half and half, or milk
1	tablespoon	chicken base
1	cup	sausage or bacon cooked, ground or diced
1	cup	cheddar cheese
¼	cup	sour cream
1	cup	spinach, fresh, chopped

Put potatoes in a large soup pot; add half and half, chicken base and meat. Heat soup slowly and on low, stirring occasionally. Taste and add salt and pepper if needed. You may need a little more milk and chicken base. Add cheese, sour cream and spinach; heat throughout on low. The consistency should not be too thick nor to thin. We ran this as a soup special on Monday at the restaurant if we had left over mashed potatoes and sausage or bacon from Sunday brunch. This was one of our most popular soups and very easy to make.

Cream of Potato with Sausage and Cheese

Makes: 8 servings   Prep Time: 1 hour

3	pounds	potatoes, peeled, diced
1	large	carrot, peeled, diced
2	tablespoons	chicken base
1	pound	smoked or Italian sausage, cooked, sliced or crumbled
2	cups	half and half, or milk
1	cup	onions, diced
1	cup	spinach, fresh, chopped
½	teaspoon	pepper
8	ounces	cheddar cheese, cubed or shredded
⅓	cup	sour cream, regular or lite, don't use no-fat

Put potatoes, carrots and onions in large pot and just cover with water. Add chicken base. Let boil until potatoes are tender. Mash potatoes, carrots and onions in pot with potato masher. Add approximately 2 cups of half and half or milk - depends on consistency. Add remaining ingredients. Simmer on low and stir until cheese is melted. Do not boil or heat to high or cheese may break.

Cream of Sausage Soup

1	pound	sausage, ground
½	cup	onion, diced
2	tablespoons	chicken base
1	clove	garlic, minced
2	tablespoons	butter
3	tablespoons	flour
¼	teaspoons	white pepper
1 ½	cups	heavy cream, or half and half
1	pound	cream cheese
1	cup	water

Brown and drain sausage, cool slightly then grind in food processor. Place onions, garlic, chicken base and water in a 3-quart sauce pan and bring to a boil. Melt butter in large sauce pan over medium heat and stir in flour. Cook two minutes stirring constantly. Add pepper and cream and cook on low heat until thickened and hot. Add sausage, onion and garlic. Cut cream cheese into chunks and add. Cook until cheese is melted. This soup can be made thicker and then used for sausage and biscuits. Use only 1 cup heavy cream to make thicker for sausage and biscuits.

Ham and Bean Soup

1	20-ounce bag	beans, 15 bean mix or navy beans
1	tablespoon	chicken base
1	tablespoon	ham base
1	cup	onion, diced
2	whole	carrots, diced
½	cup	celery, diced
1	teaspoon	thyme, fresh, chopped
1	teaspoon	garlic, minced
6	ounces	tomato paste, canned
1 ½	pound	ham bone with meat

Soak beans overnight in the refrigerator. Rinse and put in large pot. Cover beans with water. Add all ingredients except tomato paste. Simmer, and stir occasionally for 1½-2 hours or until beans are very soft. With potato masher, mash the beans a little and add tomato paste and stir until incorporated. Make sure while beans are cooking that they're covered with water the entire time. You may need to occasionally add a little water.

Italian Vegetable Sausage Soup

Makes: 6-8 servings   Prep Time: 1 hour

1	whole	onion, diced
1	can	tomatoes, diced, or fresh, peeled and seeded
1-2	cups	water
1	tablespoon	beef base
1	tablespoon	chicken base
1	bunch	broccoli, chopped
1	cup	cauliflower, chopped
2	whole	zucchini, diced
1	clove	garlic, chopped or ½ teaspoon garlic powder
¼	cup	parsley, fresh, chopped or 1 teaspoon dried
1	teaspoon	dried basil or 1 tablespoon basil, fresh, chopped
½	teaspoon	dried oregano or 1 tablespoon fresh, chopped
1	small can	tomato paste
1	pound	Italian sausage links (browned)

Put the following in a soup pot and bring to a boil: onion, tomatoes, water; beef and chicken base. Turn the heat down to medium and add the remaining ingredients; simmer for 30 minutes. (Put the sausage links in whole). When the sausage is done remove it from the soup, slice it and add it back in.

Notes: you can add green beans instead of the broccoli and cauliflower. Serve with toasted Italian bread and sprinkle parmesan on top.

Smoked Sausage Soup

Makes: 4-6 servings   Prep Time: 1-8 hours

1	pound	smoked sausage, sliced
3	cups	water
2	tablespoons	chicken base
1	teaspoon	garlic
½	cup	onion, diced
2	cups	potatoes, diced
1	head	broccoli cut in florets

Stove Top Method-Bring water to boil with chicken base, garlic and onion; simmer and add sausage, potatoes and broccoli. Cook until vegetables are tender.

Crock Pot Method-Put all ingredients in crock pot and cover with water. Cook on low 6-8 hours or high 4-6 hours until potatoes and broccoli are cooked.

Split Pea with Ham

Makes: 8 servings   Prep Time: 2 hours

1	pound	split peas
1	pound	ham hocks or ham with bone
1	cup	onion, diced
½	cup	carrots, diced
1	tablespoon	chicken or ham base
1	cup	water
1	each	bay leaf

Put peas in a crock pot and cover with one inch of water. Add all ingredients. Cook on high for 4-5 hours or low for 6-8 hours. Check occasionally to make sure the beans are covered with water. You may need to add a little. When it is done, the soup will be creamy and thick. If you like it thinner, add more water. I like to cook in the crock pot because when cooking on the stove you have to keep a close eye on it so it doesn't burn.

Lasagna Soup

Makes: 8 cups   Prep Time: 45 minutes

1	pound	Italian sausage, bulk
2	cups	onion, chopped
1	cup	carrots, diced
2	tablespoons	garlic, minced
4	cups	chicken broth
1	14 ½ ounce can	Italian tomatoes, chopped
1	10 ¾ ounce can	tomato sauce
1	cup	lasagna noodles, broken up
2	cups	spinach, fresh, chopped
1	cup	provolone cheese or mozzarella, diced
4	teaspoons	basil, fresh, sliced

Brown sausage in a large saucepan over medium-high heat. Add onions and carrots; sauté 3 minutes. Stir in garlic and sauté another 3 minutes. Add broth, tomatoes and sauce and bring to a boil. Drop in pasta and simmer until cooked, about 10 minutes. Stir in spinach and cook until wilted. Place ¼ cup of cheese into each serving bowl and pour hot soup over it. Garnish with parmesan and basil strips. You can add mushrooms if you like. Add them with the garlic and sauté with garlic.

Cioppino Soup

¼	cup	butter
1	large	onion, diced
1	cup	celery, diced
3-4	cups	water
2-3	tablespoons	chicken base
1	large (30-32 ounce)	can tomatoes, diced
¼	cup	basil, fresh, chopped or 1/8 cup dried
¼	cup	parsley, fresh, chopped or 1/8 cup dried
2	cups	cod or other white fish, cut in cubes (approx. 2 pieces)
1	15 ounce can	clams with juice
2	cups	shrimp, tails removed, uncooked
		(small to medium size)

This is a delicious fish soup that was very popular during Lent at the restaurant.
Sauté onion & celery in butter until onion is clear. Put water, onions and celery, chicken base, tomatoes, basil and parsley in a large stock pot and bring to a boil. Once the broth is boiling turn down heat to simmer. Add the fish to the simmering broth and let simmer for 5 minutes then add the clams and shrimp. Simmer for another 5 minutes until the fish is cooked.

Note: As a variation you can add fresh chopped spinach when you add the shrimp. You can also add cooked rice when serving.

Clam Chowder

¼	cup	onions, chopped
2	tablespoons	butter
2	tablespoons	flour
2	6.5 ounce cans	clams
2	cups	half and half
1/8	cup	white wine or cooking sherry
1	whole	potato, cooked, diced

Melt butter, add onion and cook until translucent. Add flour, cook and stir 2 minutes. Add clam juice from the canned clams. Then add clams, half and half, wine and potato. Cook until hot, throughout. You can add cooked, diced bacon for additional flavor.

Shrimp and Crab Bisque

Makes: 4-6 servings   Prep Time: 1 hour

¼	cup	onion, diced
¼	cup	butter
1	sprig	thyme, fresh
1		bay leaf
2	tablespoons	parsley, fresh, chopped
2 -2 ½	pounds	shrimp and crab meat
¼	cup	sherry
1	cup	dry white wine
6	cups	fish stock
1	cup	heavy cream
1	dash	cayenne pepper

Sauté onion in butter; add thyme, bay leaf and parsley. Add seafood and cook for a few minutes. Add fish stock, sherry and white wine. Reduce heat and simmer for 10 minutes. Add heavy cream to broth and simmer 3-5 minutes. Season with salt and pepper.

Black Bean Soup

Makes: 12 serving   Prep Time: 3 hours

4	cups	black beans, dried, do not soak
¼	cup	chicken base
1	cup	onions, chopped
2	small	jalapeño, chopped (or leave them whole)
2	whole	carrots, chopped
½	cup	cilantro, fresh, chopped
¼	cup	garlic, fresh, chopped

Put black beans in large pot. Cover beans 2-3 inches with water and cook on low. Add all the ingredients and stir. Check soup every 15 minutes and stir. Use a heavy pot or black beans could burn. May need to add additional water. Make sure beans are always covered with water. When the soup is done the beans will be very soft and even start to mash when stirring. When done, take half the beans out of the pot and blend in food processor until smooth. (This is an example of a pureed soup). Put back in pot with the rest of the beans. If you don't have a food processor, use a blender or potato masher. Serve soup with tortilla chips, fresh chopped cilantro, fresh chopped tomatoes and a crumbled, white Mexican Cheese or Jack cheese.

Broccoli Cheese Soup

Makes: 6 servings

Prep Time: 30 minutes

1	head	broccoli, florets
1/3	cup	onion, chopped
2	cups	water
2-3	teaspoons	chicken base
1	clove	garlic, minced
1/2	teaspoon	thyme
2	tablespoons	butter
3	tablespoons	flour
1/4	teaspoon	pepper, white
1 1/2	cups	half and half
2	tablespoons	chives, chopped
12	ounces	cheddar cheese

Place broccoli, onion, water, chicken base, garlic and thyme in 3 quart sauce pan. Cover and bring to a boil. Reduce heat and simmer 15 minutes until broccoli is tender. Cool slightly. Puree broccoli in blender or food processor. Set puree mixture aside. Melt butter in large sauce pan over medium heat. Stir in flour. Cook two minutes stirring constantly. Add pepper and cream and cook until thickened, stirring constantly for two minutes. Stir in broccoli puree and cheddar cheese. Heat until cheese is melted. Do not boil the soup or the cheese will break.

Butternut Squash with Toasted Pumpkin Seeds

Makes: 6 servings

Prep Time: 30 minutes

1	large	butternut squash, skinned, diced
1	large	sweet onion, diced
2	large	carrots, diced
2 1/2	cups	vegetable or chicken broth
1	tablespoon	butter
1/4	cup	parsley, fresh, chopped
1/4	cup	milk
1/2	teaspoon	ginger, fresh, grated (optional)

Toasted Pumpkin Seeds

1	tablespoon	sugar
1	tablespoon	brown sugar
1	each	egg white, lightly beaten
¼	teaspoon	water
⅛	teaspoon	salt
⅛	teaspoon	cinnamon
1	dash	cayenne pepper, ground
¾	cup	pumpkin seeds, unsalted
		cooking spray

Soup-Melt butter in large saucepan over medium heat. Add squash, carrot and onion; sauté for 15 minutes stirring constantly. Add broth and ginger bring to a boil. Cover, reduce heat and simmer 30 minutes. Remove from heat; stir in milk and add salt. Place squash in food processor or blender. Serve with toasted breads or topped with toasted pumpkin seeds. This soup freezes well.

Pumpkin Seeds-Preheat oven to 300 degrees. Toss the first 7 ingredients in a small bowl. Add seeds and stir to coat. Spread seed mixture evenly on a baking sheet coated with cooking spray. Bake at 300 for 15 minutes. Stir mixture, bake an additional 15 minutes. Cool and break into pieces.

Corn Chowder

Makes: 4-6 servings   Prep Time: 15 minutes

2	cans	corn, drained, or 4 cups fresh, blanched, corn from the cob
½	cup	sweet onion, diced
2	cups	half and half
¼	teaspoon	cayenne pepper
1	whole	red pepper, diced
1	tablespoon	chicken base

This is a wonderfully fresh soup especially made with corn right off the cobb. Puree all ingredients together in food processor or blender except the red peppers. Add peppers after blending. Heat and serve. Adjust chicken base and salt and pepper, as needed. For variations of this recipe you can add crabmeat, cooked diced bacon, fresh tomatoes or cooked, diced potatoes.

Cream of Artichoke Soup

2	15 ounce cans	artichokes
4	cups	half and half
1	teaspoon	garlic, minced
1/8	cup	Dijon mustard
2	tablespoons	chicken base
1	tablespoon	cooking sherry

Puree drained artichokes and all other ingredients in food processor or blender. Heat until hot. For a variation you can add diced chicken, fresh spinach or crab meat.

Cream of Mushroom Soup

¼	cup	butter, unsalted, room temperature
½	cup	onion, chopped
½	cup	green onion, chopped
4	cups	mushrooms, portobella, button, shitake, cremini or a combination, sliced
¼	cup	flour
3	cups	chicken or vegetable stock
4	tablespoons	dry sherry
2	cups	half and half
1	dash	pepper
1	dash	salt

Melt butter in pot on medium heat. Sauté onions in butter until tender. Add mushrooms and sauté until done. Stir flour into onion and mushroom mixture. Add stock, half and half and sherry. Bring to a boil, reduce heat and simmer until thickened. Add salt and pepper. Bring to a boil, reduce heat and simmer until thickened.

Note: To make your own cream of mushroom soup for casserole dishes use this recipe with only 2 cups of chicken stock instead of 3 and dice mushrooms versus slicing them. Button mushrooms work best for casserole dishes.

Fresh Vegetable Broth

1	*medium*	*onion, peel on*
2	*cloves*	*garlic, peel on*
2	*ribs*	*celery, with leaves*
2	*whole*	*carrots, peel on, cut into chunks*
2	*whole*	*leeks, trimmed, cut into chunks*
4	*whole*	*scallions, peel on, cut in half*
2	*medium*	*tomatoes, quartered*
4	*medium*	*red potatoes, peel on, halved*
8	*sprigs*	*parsley*
1	*whole*	*bay leaf*
8	*whole*	*black peppercorns*
1	*teaspoon*	*kosher salt*
10	*cups*	*water*

Rinse all vegetables. Place all the broth ingredients in a large heavy pot. Bring to a boil, reduce heat and simmer uncovered for 1 hour. Adjust the seasonings to taste and simmer for 30 more minutes. Strain the broth, let set at room temperature to cool. Refrigerate or freeze. Fresh broth will keep about 4 days. Note you can add additional vegetables. When I trim asparagus or broccoli, I freeze the trimmings and the next time I am ready to make vegetable broth I add them to it.

Italian Garden Vegetable Soup

2	*cups*	*tomatoes, diced*
4	*cups*	*water*
¼	*cup*	*vegetable base*
1	*clove*	*garlic, diced*
½	*cup*	*onion, diced*
¼	*cup*	*parsley, fresh, chopped*
1	*teaspoon*	*oregano, dried*
1	*teaspoon*	*Italian seasoning, dried*
3	*whole*	*potatoes, diced*
1	*large*	*carrot, diced*
1	*cup*	*green beans, fresh or frozen*
1	*whole*	*zucchini, diced*

Bring tomatoes, water and vegetable base to a boil; add garlic, onion, parsley, oregano, Italian seasonings, carrots, potatoes and green beans; simmer until they are tender. Once potatoes, carrots and green beans are tender add the zucchini.

I use this recipe a lot in the winter time with the frozen vegetables from my summer garden; frozen tomatoes, green beans, onions and zucchini. I also use my dried herbs from the garden (the Italian Seasoning Mix in the *Farm to Fork Chapter*).

Portobello Mushroom with Leek

Makes: 6 servings   Prep Time: 1 hour

¼	cup	butter, unsalted
5	whole	leeks, chopped (white and light green parts only- about 3 cups)
1	medium	onion, chopped
10	ounces	Portobello mushrooms, sliced (4 cups)
¼	cup	flour
3	cups	chicken stock
4	tablespoons	dry sherry
2	cups	half and half
¼	teaspoon	cayenne pepper

Melt butter in large heavy pot over medium heat. Add leeks and onion, sauté until tender, 10 minutes. Add mushrooms and sauté 5 minutes. Reduce heat to low. Add flour, cook until mixture is thick, stirring occasionally, about 3 minutes. Gradually stir in stock and 2 tablespoon sherry. Bring soup to a boil, stirring. Reduce heat and simmer until thickened, about 10 minutes. Stir in half and half. Simmer until slightly thickened, about 10 minutes. Stir in cayenne pepper, season to taste with salt and pepper. Stir remaining 2 tablespoons sherry into soup and simmer 5 more minutes. Serve.

This recipe is from Romana Lee. Thanks so much for sharing this great recipe with us.

Pumpkin Soup with Jalapeño Pesto

Makes: 8-10 servings   Prep Time: 1 hour

Jalapeño Pesto

1	cup	cilantro, fresh
1	cup	parsley, fresh
½	cup	pine nuts, lightly toasted (can substitute walnuts for pine nuts)
½	cup	parmesan
5	cloves	garlic, minced
4	whole	jalapeño peppers, chopped
1	teaspoon	lime juice
½	teaspoon	lime peel, grated
¾	cup	olive oil (can use canola)

In food processor, combine cilantro, parsley, nuts, cheese and garlic; process 10-15 seconds to chop. Add jalapeños, lime juice and lime peel, process 5-10 seconds to blend. With machine running, add oil in slow steady stream just until well blended. Set Pesto aside.

Pumpkin Soup

4	14 ½ ounce cans	chicken broth
¼	cup	onion, chopped
2	tablespoons	jalapeño peppers, finely chopped
1	16 ounce can	pumpkin
1	cup	half and half
½	teaspoon	salt
¼	teaspoon	pepper

In large saucepan combine broth, onion and 2 tablespoons jalapeño pepper. Bring to a boil. Reduce heat; cover and simmer 20-25 minutes or until onion and pepper is tender. Stir in pumpkin, blend well. Cover, simmer 5-10 minutes or until thoroughly heated. Add half and half, salt and pepper; cook and stir until heated. DO NOT BOIL.
To serve pour soup in bowl and spoon 1 tablespoon of pesto on top.

Note: This is a delicious fall soup that was very popular at the restaurant. It also holds up well in the crock pot on low heat.

Quick Vegetarian Chili

Makes: 4-6 servings   Prep Time: 45 minutes

1	can	garbanzo beans (chick peas)
1	can	black beans
1	can	dark red kidney beans
16	ounces	vegetable or tomato juice
1	can	tomatoes, diced
1	package	chili mix
1	can	corn
1	tablespoon	brown sugar
1	tablespoon	molasses
1	12-16 ounce package	veggie crumbles (optional)
1	whole	diced jalapeño pepper (or drop a whole pepper in the sauce and simmer)

Mix all ingredients and bring to a slow boil. Turn down the heat and simmer for about 30 minutes until flavors marry.

Quick Vegetable Soup

Makes: 4 servings   Prep Time: 45 minutes

1	can	tomatoes, diced, or fresh, peeled and seeded
2	cups	water
1	tablespoon	vegetable base
1	whole	onion, diced
½	cup	carrots, diced
1	clove	garlic, chopped
1	cup	potatoes, diced
¼	cup	parsley, fresh, chopped
1	15 ounce can	chick peas
2	cups	spinach, fresh, chopped

Bring tomatoes, water and vegetable base to a boil; add onion, carrots, garlic, parsley and potatoes and simmer until veggies are tender. Add chick peas and spinach; simmer until spinach is wilted.

Roasted Red Pepper Soup

Makes: 6 servings   Prep Time: 30 minutes

1	can	roasted red peppers, drained
¼	cup	onion, diced
2	teaspoons	chicken base
2	cups	half and half
1	teaspoon	garlic, minced
1	tablespoon	basil, fresh, chopped

Put all ingredients in a blender or food processor and puree. Heat and serve.

Note: this is also very good topped with a teaspoon of fresh basil pesto.

Tomato Bisque

Makes: 8 servings   Prep Time: 15-25 minutes

2	15-ounce cans	tomatoes, diced or 4 cups fresh, skinned, seeded, cut into chunks
2	tablespoons	chicken base
1 ½	cups	half and half
½	cup	basil, fresh, chopped
½	cup	sweet onion, diced

Puree together in blender. Heat to serve. You can sprinkle with parmesan cheese or serve with croutons on top. This is a wonderful fresh tasting soup especially when using fresh garden tomatoes and basil. This soup can be canned and put through a hot water bath. See the recipe in the *Canning and Preserving* Chapter.

Vegetarian Lentil Soup

Makes: 4 servings   Prep Time: 1 hour

1	16 ounce package	lentils
6	cups	water
1	cup	tomatoes, diced
½	cup	onion, diced
3	tablespoons	vegetable base
1	teaspoon	parsley
½	teaspoon	salt
1	dash	pepper

Put lentils and water together in a large pot. Bring to boil and add the remaining ingredients. At this point you can add whatever vegetables you would like; then simmer for 30-45 minutes. Following are a few suggested vegetables to add: diced sweet potatoes or butternut squash, carrots, zucchini, broccoli, green beans, corn etc. Fresh chopped kale, spinach or cabbage can be added the last 5 minutes.

White Cheddar Cheese Soup

Makes: 6 cups   Prep Time: 45 minutes

¼	cup	butter, unsalted
1	cup	onion, diced
½	cup	celery, diced small
1	teaspoon	garlic, fresh, minced
¼	cup	flour
2	teaspoons	dry mustard, ground
1	teaspoon	salt
1	teaspoon	white pepper
½	cup	dry white wine
1 ½	cups	chicken broth
1 ½	cups	whole milk
1 ½	cups	half and half
4	cups	white cheddar cheese, grated
1	whole	tomato, diced

Sauté onion and celery in butter in a large pot over medium-low heat. Cook for 10 minutes; add the garlic and sauté another 2 minutes. Stir in the flour to coat the vegetables. Add dry mustard, salt and pepper. Stir constantly 2-3 minutes. Whisk in wine, then broth, milk and half and half, scraping the bottom of the pot. Bring soup to a boil, reduce heat and simmer 15 minutes. Stir in cheese and remove from heat. Continue stirring until cheese is melted. Garnish soup with tomatoes. Serve with crusty bread.

Note: You can use beer instead of wine.

Wild Rice and Mushroom Soup

Makes: 4 servings   Prep Time: 1 hour

3	cups	chicken broth
1/3	cup	wild rice
1/2	cup	green onion, sliced
1	cup	half and half
2	tablespoons	flour
1	teaspoon	thyme, fresh
1	dash	pepper
1/2	cup	mushrooms, fresh, sliced
1	tablespoon	cooking sherry

In a medium saucepan, combine chicken broth and uncooked wild rice and bring to a boil. Reduce heat and simmer, covered, for 40 minutes. Stir in green onion and cook 5-10 minutes more or until rice is tender. Combine half and half, flour, thyme and pepper. Stir into rice mixture along with mushrooms. Cook and stir until thickened and bubbly. Cook and stir one minute more. Stir in sherry and heat through out. You can use any kind of mushrooms, portobello, button, etc. You can also add chicken.

Vegetables and Sides

Brussels Sprouts with Apple and Onion
Brussels Sprouts with Bacon and Onion
Creamed Spinach
Green Beans with Feta
Herb Roasted Potatoes
Herb Stuffing
Hot Potato Salad
Macaroni and Cheese
Crab Macaroni and Cheese
Margy's Mashed Potatoes
Parmesan Roasted New Potatoes
Parmesan Zucchini Sticks
Pesto Mashed Potatoes
Potato Casserole
Roasted Mushrooms
Roasted Vegetables
Scalloped Potatoes
Sweet Potato Casserole
Summer Squash Casserole
Vegetable Gratin
Zucchini Pancakes

Brussels Sprouts with Bacon and Onion

Makes: 6-8 servings   Prep Time: 1 hour

3	packages (6 cups)	Brussels Sprouts, cleaned, trimmed.
1-2	tablespoons	canola oil
1	pound	bacon chopped
½	cup	apple cider vinegar
2	teaspoons	sugar
¾	cup	onions, diced

To prepare Brussels Sprouts- Cut off ends. Blanch in boiling water for 5-10 minutes. Cut in half and coat with canola oil then season with salt and pepper. Roast in a preheated 375 degree oven for 20-30 minutes until tender.

Cook bacon until almost done; add onions. Cook until tender; add sugar and vinegar, cook until thickens 10-15 minutes on medium heat. (The sauce can be made the day before). Toss warm Brussels sprouts with the sauce and serve.

Brussels Sprouts with Apples and Onions- Prepare Brussels sprouts as directed above. Toss Brussels Sprouts with oil and 1/8 cup apple cider vinegar with ½ cup chopped onions and 1 diced apple, instead of the bacon. Bake 30 minutes in 350 degree preheated oven.

Creamed Spinach

Makes: 4 servings   Prep Time: 15 minutes

1	10 ounce bag	spinach, fresh, stemmed, chopped
1	tablespoon	butter
5	ounces	Boursin cheese
		Salt and pepper to taste

Cook spinach in 1 tablespoon water for about 2 minutes. Drain water from spinach, add butter and melt with spinach. Add cheese and stir until melted with spinach. Add salt and pepper to taste.

Green Beans with Feta

Makes: 6-8 servings   Prep Time: 2 hours 15 minutes

1 ½	pounds	green beans, trimmed
1	small	red onion, chopped (about ½ cup)
½	cup	Lemon Basil Dressing (see recipe)
2	ounces	feta cheese, crumbled
½	cup	walnuts, toasted and chopped

Cook green beans in boiling salted water to cover, 8 minutes or until crisp-tender. Drain and plunge into ice water to stop the cooking process; drain and pat dry. Place in serving bowl; cover and chill at least 2 hours. Add chopped onion and lemon dressing to beans, tossing to coat. Sprinkle with feta and walnuts.

Herb Roasted Potatoes

Makes: 6-8 servings   Prep Time: 1 hour

2 ½	pounds	red new potatoes, sliced thin
¼	cup	olive oil
1	tablespoon	seasoned salt
1	tablespoon	garlic powder
⅛	cup	rosemary, fresh, chopped

Put potatoes in a large pot covered with water. Boil until potatoes are soft, not mushy. Drain water and put in a large bowl. Drizzle olive oil over potatoes and add salt, garlic and rosemary. Toss gently. If potatoes seem dry, add a little more oil. Place potatoes in a shallow baking dish and roast in the oven at 350 degrees until browned, for about 20-30 minutes.

These were our signature potatoes at the restaurant and the potatoes used in the breakfast casserole. (See recipe).

Herb Stuffing

8	cups	bread, fresh, cubed or stuffing mix
1	tablespoon	chicken or turkey base
¼	pound	butter
1 ½	cups	water
1	cup	celery, chopped
1	cup	onion, chopped
1	teaspoon	garlic, minced
¼	cup	parsley, fresh, chopped
¼	cup	sage, fresh, chopped
1	teaspoon	thyme, fresh, chopped

Sauté celery, onion, garlic, parsley, sage and thyme in 1 tablespoon butter for about 3-4 minutes. Then add water and chicken base. Mix and bring to a boil on medium heat. Pour over bread cubes. Stuff the turkey. You can use poultry seasoning instead of the fresh herbs if you like. You can add chopped oysters, cooked chopped giblets, cranberries, golden raisins, apple pieces, walnuts, or whatever you like. You can also bake the stuffing in a baking pan if you prefer not to stuff the turkey or have extra stuffing. Refrigerate until ready to bake.

Hot Potato Salad

4	cups	potatoes, cooked, peeled, cubed
½	cup	onion, diced fine
1	pound	bacon, cooked, crumbled
1	pound	sharp cheddar cheese , shredded
1	cup	Miracle Whip

Cook potatoes as if making potato salad. Put all ingredients in a baking pan and mix well. Bake at 350 degrees for 30-45 minutes. Stir about every 15 minutes.

Macaroni and Cheese

Makes: 4-6 servings

Prep Time: 45 minutes

8	ounces	macaroni pasta
¼	cup	butter
¼	cup	flour
2	cups	milk (use at least 2%)
8	ounces	American cheese, cubed
4	ounces	sharp cheddar, shredded or cubed
1	tablespoon	minced onion
½	teaspoon	salt
½	teaspoon	Worcestershire sauce
¼	teaspoon	pepper
¼	teaspoon	dry mustard
6	tablespoons	bread crumbs
4	tablespoons	butter

Cook macaroni and place in a greased, 2 quart baking dish; set aside. Melt ¼ cup butter in a large sauce pan over low heat; whisk in flour until smooth. Cook 1 minute, whisking constantly. Gradually whisk in milk. Cook over medium heat whisking constantly, until mixture is thickened and bubbly. Reduce heat, and add onion, cheese, salt, Worcestershire sauce, pepper, and mustard; stir until cheese melts. Pour cheese mixture over macaroni, and mix well. Melt 4 tablespoons butter and stir in bread crumbs. Sprinkle on top of macaroni. Bake uncovered at 350 degrees for 30-40 minutes until browned on top and hot throughout.

Crab Macaroni and Cheese- Sauté 1 pound lump crab meat with 2 tablespoons of prepared butter (recipe below). Pour over the baked macaroni and cheese. Serve. You can also stir just the crab meat into the macaroni and cheese before baking. I have done it both ways and they are both really good.

Prepared butter- 4 tablespoons unsalted butter, softened, 1 dash pepper, 1 dash salt, ¼ teaspoon garlic powder, ¼ teaspoon parsley. Mix together.

Note: When making macaroni and cheese the key is the sauce. If the cheese sauce gets too hot it will break/curdle. For additional flavor and color try stirring in tomatoes, green onions, roasted bell peppers, sautéed squash, grilled eggplant or your favorite vegetables.

Margy's Mashed Potatoes

Makes: 6 servings   Prep Time: 1 hour

2 ½	pounds	new potatoes, whole with skins
¼	cup	butter, softened
½-¾	cup	milk, ½ and ½, or cream
½	cup	sour cream
1	teaspoon	garlic powder
½	cup	spinach leaves, whole, chopped, fresh
1	teaspoon	salt
1	teaspoon	pepper

Boil whole new potatoes until soft. Drain and mash immediately. Add butter, milk, sour cream, spices and fresh spinach. Mix just until smooth. Do not over beat or they will turn to glue. You may need a little more milk but finish with other ingredients first, to see if needed. Consistency should be smooth, creamy and somewhat thick. I always use new potatoes because they have a sweet taste to them. Left over mashed potatoes make a great cream of potato soup. (See recipe.)

Parmesan Roasted New Potatoes

Makes: 4 servings   Prep Time: 30 minutes

4	medium	red new potatoes, slice thin
¼	cup	olive or canola oil
½	teaspoon	seasoned salt
½	teaspoon	seasoned pepper
½	teaspoon	garlic powder
½	cup	Parmesan cheese

Put ½ of the olive oil in the bottom of a 9" x 13" baking sheet. Lay potatoes individually on the olive oil. Top the potatoes with salt, pepper, garlic and Parmesan cheese. Put the remaining olive oil on top of the seasoned potatoes. Bake at 350 degrees for 30 minutes or until browned and crispy. Can add fresh chopped basil on top of Parmesan.

Parmesan Zucchini Sticks

Makes: 6 servings

Prep Time: 30 minutes

3	whole	zucchini, medium size
¼	cup	parmesan cheese
¼	stick	butter

Cut zucchini into sticks, the size of carrot sticks. Put them on a sheet pan, dot with butter and sprinkle with parmesan. Bake in a preheated 375 degree oven for approximately 25-30 minutes or until crunchy and brown. You can also cook these on the grill.

Pesto Mashed Potatoes

Makes: 5-6 cups

Prep Time: 30 minutes

2 ½	pounds	potatoes, peeled and chopped
¾	cup	Basil Pesto (see recipe)
½	stick	butter
¾	cup	milk, warm

Mash potatoes with the butter and milk. Stir in the pesto by hand.

Potato Casserole

Makes: 12 servings

Prep Time: 1 hour 15 minutes

1	can	cream of chicken soup
2	cups	sour cream
1 ½	pounds	cheddar cheese, shredded
¼	pound	butter, melted
2	pounds	hash brown potatoes, frozen
¾	cup	onion, diced
4	cups	corn flake crumbs
1	teaspoon each	salt and pepper
8	ounces	cheddar cheese, shredded

In large mixing bowl combine soup, sour cream, butter and onion. Stir in cheese and potato. Put in large buttered baking dish and cover top with finely crushed corn flake crumbs. Bake uncovered at 350 degrees for 1 hour. You can also shred or slice fresh potatoes. For variations add diced ham, chicken, turkey, asparagus, broccoli or green beans to make a full meal. You can use a mixture of cheeses.

Roasted Mushrooms

Makes: 12 servings

¼	cup	soy sauce
½	teaspoon	ginger
2	teaspoons	garlic, minced
¾	cup	olive or canola oil
1	pound	mushrooms, button whole or a variety

Mix together soy, ginger, garlic, and oil. Toss the mushrooms in the mixture trying to get all the mushrooms coated with the marinate. Roast in a preheated 375 degree oven on a baking sheet for about 30 minutes. You can use a variety of cremini, button or shitaki.

Roasted Vegetables

Makes: 6 servings

1	medium	zucchini, sliced
1	medium	yellow squash, sliced
1	medium	red onion, sliced
1	cup	snow peas, fresh
1	medium	red and green bell peppers, sliced
2	teaspoons	minced garlic, fresh
¼	cup	basil, fresh, chopped
¼	cup	olive or canola oil
½	teaspoon	pepper
½	teaspoon	seasoned salt

Put all ingredients in a bowl and mix well. Place on a baking sheet and bake at 350 degrees for 30 minutes or until desired firmness. You can use different vegetables, add mushrooms, eggplant, etc. These vegetables are great served on a toasted bun with cheese melted on the top of the vegetables.

Scalloped Potatoes

Makes: 6-8 servings   Prep Time: 1 hour 30 minutes

1		recipe Alfredo Sauce
2 ½	pounds	Idaho baker potatoes, sliced ¼ inch thick

Spray 9" x 13" pan and shingle (layer potatoes like shingles; overlapping) potatoes in pan then push them down. Pour sauce over potatoes. Bake 1 hour and 15 minutes in a 375 degree preheated oven. Check doneness of potatoes by inserting a knife. When they are tender the knife will go through easily. Add parmesan on top and bake the last 15 minutes or until browned. Let sit 15 minutes before serving.

Note: this is also great with chopped prosciutto ham added.
This recipe is from my chef friend, Bun Lim.

Sweet Potato Casserole

Makes: 6-8 servings   Prep Time: 1 hour

3	cups	sweet potatoes, boiled, smashed
¾	cup	butter, divided
1	teaspoon	vanilla
1	teaspoon	cinnamon
½	cup	white sugar
2	large	eggs
⅔	cup	brown sugar
½	cup	flour
½	cup	pecans, chopped

In large bowl, mix well sweet potatoes, half cup butter, vanilla, cinnamon, sugar and eggs; spoon into a 9" x 13" casserole dish. In a separate bowl, combine brown sugar, flour, remaining butter and pecans. Sprinkle mixture over top of potatoes. Bake 30 minutes in a preheated 400 degree oven. This recipe is delicious and from my mother. Thanks Mom!

Summer Squash Casserole

Makes: 4-6 servings   Prep Time: 1 hour

4	pounds	yellow or zucchini squash sliced (or use half and half)
4	tablespoons	butter, divided
1	whole	sweet onion, chopped
2	cloves	garlic, minced
2 ½	cups	plain bread crumbs, divided
1 ¼	cups	parmesan cheese, shredded, divided
1	cup	sharp cheddar cheese, shredded
½	cup	chives, fresh, chopped
8	ounces	sour cream
½	teaspoon	cayenne pepper
1	teaspoon	salt
2	whole	eggs, beaten

Cook squash in enough boiling water to just cover the squash. Boil for 8-10 minutes until squash is tender. Drain well.

Melt 2 tablespoons butter in skillet over medium heat; add onion and garlic; sauté 5-6 minutes until tender. Remove skillet from heat; stir in squash, 1 cup breadcrumbs, ¾ cup parmesan and cheddar cheeses, chives, sour cream, salt, pepper and eggs.

Spoon into greased 9" x 13" baking dish. Melt remaining 2 tablespoons butter. Stir butter with the remaining 1 ½ cups bread crumbs, ½ cup parmesan cheese and salt.

Sprinkle mixture over top of the casserole. Bake 35-40 minutes or until set.

Vegetable Gratin

Makes: 6 servings

Prep Time: 1 hour

2	cloves	garlic, chopped
2	small	shallots, chopped
1	tablespoon	basil, fresh, chopped
½	teaspoon	salt
¼	teaspoon	pepper
2	medium	yellow squash, thinly sliced
2	medium	zucchini, thinly sliced
3	medium	tomatoes, sliced
3	tablespoons	parmesan, grated
¼	cup	bread crumbs

Preheat oven to 400. Lightly oil an 8" square baking dish. Evenly spread the garlic, shallots and basil in the bottom of the pan; season with salt and pepper. Layer the yellow squash, zucchini and tomatoes until all vegetables are used up; alternating each ingredient. Sprinkle the top with the cheese, then the bread crumbs. Bake 40-45 minutes, until the vegetables are tender. Let set 5 minutes before slicing to serve.

Zucchini Pancakes

Makes: 4-6 pancakes

Prep Time: 25 minutes

2	cups	shredded zucchini, water squeezed out
¼	cup	onion, chopped fine
2	tablespoons	basil, fresh, chopped
1	teaspoon	parsley, fresh, chopped
¼	cup	flour
¼	cup	cornmeal
1	large	egg
¼	teaspoon	salt
¼	cup	oil

Beat egg; add all ingredients adding flour last. Mix well. Heat oil in skillet, when hot drop pancakes by tablespoon into oil. Brown on both sides. Serve with fresh diced tomatoes.

Cooking Terminology

Al Dente- An Italian phrase meaning "to the tooth" used to describe pasta or other food that is cooked only until it offers a slight resistance when bitten into.

Baste- To brush or spoon pan drippings or other fat or liquid over food as it cooks to keep the surface moist and to add flavor.

Beat- To stir rapidly in a circular motion. Usually 100 strokes by hand equals about 1 minute by an electric mixer.

Blackened- To cook meat or fish (usually rubbed with a Cajun spice mixture) in an extra hot, cast-iron skillet. The high heat combined with the seasoning rub gives food an extra crispy crust.

Blanch- To immerse food (usually vegetables and fruits) briefly into boiling water, then into cold water to stop the cooking process. Blanching is used to loosen skins (as with peaches and tomatoes) and to set color and flavor. Blanch is a synonym for Parboil.

Boil- To cook food in a boiling liquid. "Bring to a boil" refers to heating a liquid until bubbles break the surface. A full rolling boil is one that cannot be stirred down.

Braising- A combination of cooking methods that includes browning, deglazing and simmering. Searing and deglazing is done at the beginning. Then once it's in the oven you might forget about it (except for the great aroma. So set a timer.) This is a great technique for a tough cut of meat such as a brisket or chuck roast. Besides the meat, the one essential in a braise is the liquid. As it simmers it let's off steam which melts fat and breaks down the tough fibers and muscle tissue. You can use stock (broth), beer, wine, water or a combination. Be sure the pot is covered with a tight fitting lid. This builds up the penetrating steam heat and keeps it in the pot. It also helps capture the juices from the meat, concentrating them into the sauce.

Bread- To coat.

Broil- To cook food directly under or above the heat source. Food can be broiled in an oven or on a barbecue grill.

Browning- The flavor and color foundation for this technique lies in browning. First, the browner the meat the better. To brown well use a large, heavy Dutch oven or stock pot. It will distribute heat evenly and will be less likely to have hot spots that scorch. Second, be sure the meat is blotted dry. A moist surface creates steam, and that prevents good browning. Finally, use medium-high heat to sear, and don't be afraid to use a fair amount of oil to prevent burning.

Butterfly- To split a food (such as shrimp or steak) down the center, cutting almost but not completely through. The two halves are then opened flat to resemble a butterfly shape.

Caramelize- To melt sugar without scorching it until it turns golden brown. To cook onions and other vegetables until sweet and golden.

Cheesecloth- A lightweight natural cotton cloth used for straining liquids, lining molds or forming a packet for herbs and spices that can be dropped into a soup or stock pot.

Chop- To cut into bite size or smaller pieces. Chopped food is more coarsely cut than diced or minced.

Citrus Zest- The colored outer layer of the peel, that is zested or chopped into very fine pieces.

Cream- To beat an ingredient until the mixture is soft, smooth and fluffy.

Cube- To cut food into 1/2 inch cubes. Cubes of food are larger than diced

Curdle- To coagulate or to separate into liquid containing small solid particles (caused by over cooking or by too much heat). Acids such as lemon juice can also cause curdling.

Cut in- To mix a solid, cold fat, (such as butter or shortening) with dry ingredients (such as a flour mixture) until the combination is in the form of small pea size particles. This technique can be achieved with a pastry blender, food processor or fork.

Dash- A very small amount of seasoning. (Also a pinch)

Deglazing- Browning the meat creates a caramelized layer of sugars and proteins stuck on the bottom of the pan. To loosen it the pan has to be "deglazed". Liquids are usually used for this. You can also use chopped vegetables to loosen it. The vegetables release enough moisture as they cook to deglaze the pan. Scrape the pot well-as that stuck- on layer is loosened and dissolves it establishes the deep color and flavor for the sauce. Using vegetables to deglaze the pan also flavors the broth and keeps the meat from resting on the bottom of the pan. After deglazing most of the work is done. The oven finishes the job.

De-grease- To skim fat from the surface of a liquid, such as soup, stock or gravy. Another way to de-grease is to chill the mixture until the fat becomes solid and can be easily lifted off the surface.

Dice- To cut food into tiny (1/8 to l/4 inch cubes).

Dollop- A small glob (about 1 heaping tablespoon) of soft food such as whipped or sour cream.

Dredge- To lightly coat food to be fried with flour, cornmeal or bread crumbs.

Drippings- The melted fat and juices that gather in the bottom of a pan in which meat or other food is cooked. Drippings are used as a base for gravies and sauces.

Egg Wash- Egg and milk (1 egg to a half cup of milk) beaten together.

Fillet- A boneless piece of meat or fish. To cut the bones from a piece of meat or fish, is to fillet.

Finishing- To finish, remove the meat from the pot, strain the broth and return it to a clean pan.

Fold- To gently combine a light, delicate, aerated substance, such as whipped cream or beaten egg whites, into a heavier mixture by lifting the mixtures up and over with each stroke.

Fry- To cook food in hot fat over moderate to high heat.

Garnish- To decorate a completed dish, making it more attractive.

Knead- To work dough with hands in a fold-and-press motion. Well kneaded dough is smooth and elastic.

Marinate- To soak a food such as meat, fish or vegetables in a seasoned liquid mixture called a marinade. The purpose of marinating is for the food to absorb the flavor or as a tenderizer.

Mirepoix -(mihr-PWAH)-A fancy French name for a combination of vegetables -onions, carrots, and celery. Classic Mirepoix is 50% onion, 25% celery and 25% carrots. Mirepoix is usually sautéed in butter or oil to establish a dishes flavor base. But it can also deglaze a pan. If roasting meat or chicken, scatter the Mirepoix in the pan to create a bed for the roast or bird. When preparing the Mirepoix, keep in mind the type of dish it's for. Big chunks are ok for slow cooked dishes and stocks. Dice vegetables for soups and sauces uniformly so they cook evenly and quickly.

Mince- To cut food into very small pieces. Minced food is smaller than chopped or diced

Pastry Blender- A kitchen tool with 5 or 6 parallel unshaped, sturdy steel wires, which are attached to a handle. It's used in making pastry dough to cut in cold fat or butter with flour.

Poach- To gently cook in simmering liquid so that food retains its shape.

Prick- To make small holes in the surface of the food. As in unfilled pie crust to keep from baking without blistering or rising.

Proof- To dissolve yeast in a warm liquid and set it aside in a warm place until it swells.

Punch down- To excel air from a risen yeast dough by pushing it down with fist.

Puree- To grind or mash food until it is completely smooth.

Reduce- To boil a liquid (usually stock, wine or a sauce mixture) rapidly until the volume is reduced by evaporation, thickening the consistency and intensifying the flavor.

Roast- To oven cook food in a uncovered pan, a method that usually produces a well-browned exterior and moist interior.

Roux- Mixture of melted fat and flour, cooked until bubbly to remove the raw, starchy taste of flour. Used to thicken soups and stews and to make gravy.

Scald- To heat milk just below the boiling point (when tiny bubbles appear).

Sear- To brown meat on all sides over high heat. The object is to seal in the meats juices.

Sautéing- A form of dry heat cooking that uses a very hot pan and a small amount of fat to cook the food very quickly. It's important to heat the pan for a minute, then add a small amount of fat and let the fat get hot as well, before adding the food to the pan. This hot fat helps to brown the surface of the food. It's important to avoid overloading or overcrowding the pan.

Sift- To pass dry ingredients through a sifter to remove any large pieces and to incorporate air.

Simmer- To cook food gently in liquid at a temperature low enough that tiny bubbles just begin to break the surface.

Skim- To remove fat or scum from the surface of a liquid with a spoon or bulb baster.

Steam- To cook food on a rack or in a steamer basket over boiling or simmering water in a covered pan.

Stew- To cook food gently in simmering water.

Stock- The strained liquid that is the result of cooking vegetables, meat or fish and seasonings in water. Most soups and many sauces are based on stocks.

Temper- To heat gently and gradually or the process of slowly adding a hot liquid to eggs or other foods to raise their temperature without causing them to curdle. To add the hot liquid to the eggs, whisk constantly, while trickling the heated mixture into the eggs.

Test with a Toothpick- To insert a toothpick, cake tester or knife into the center of baked goods. If the toothpick comes out clean, the dish is done.

Truss- To secure poultry or other food (usually meat) with string, pins, or skewers so the food maintains a compact shape.

Water Bath- To place a container of food in a large, shallow pan of warm water, which surrounds the food with low heat.

Whip- To beat rapidly with a whisk or electric mixer, incorporating air to lighten a mixture and increase its volume.

Whisk- To beat with a whisk. A kitchen utensil with multiple looped wires.

Family Meal

The Family Meal is something that is very important to me and my husband. We want our kids and grandkids to grow up together knowing and feeling they are part of a family and how important that is. We like to have dinner with our kids and grandkids as often as possible. So we started a family tradition about 10 years ago which we call Sunday Dinner. We get together Sunday nights at our house for dinner, drinks, games and laughs and we have a blast. It is casual, laid back and relaxing. The adult kids hang out and talk about their week and what's going on with them, the little kids catch up on their play time, the aunts and uncles play catch up with their nieces and nephews. There is never any pressure on the kids- all they have to do is show up. When weather permits, before and after dinner, the kids may play with the animals, play baseball, football, kickball, badminton, or explore in the woods.

I read a recent study Barilla (the pasta company) did for their family dinner project, "Share the Table", on the importance of the family meal. Their latest study included the children's view of the family meal. I thought that was a great idea. So I did my own study with our family (our kids and grandkids) to see what their thoughts were on the family meal and here is what they had to say when asked what they like about our Sunday Dinners:

Mason DeHoff, our 9 year old grandson said:
"I love them. I love all of it about Sunday dinners; the family, the food, spending time with my cousins, everything!"

Candas and Jeff DeHoff (Mason's parents) both said:
"Good times, good family and good food"

Sophie St. John, our 7 year old granddaughter said:
"The thing I like best about family dinner is playing and eating. I like Grandma's food and her cookies too!"

Halle St. John, our 5 year old Granddaughter said:
"The thing I like best about family dinner is playing. My favorite foods that Grandma makes are mashed potatoes and macaroni cheese. Family Dinners are fun!"

Ian St. John, our 2 year old grandson said:
"Baby Chicks"

Myah St. John, (mother to Sophie, Halle and Ian) said:
"I love the time of family connection, Margy's food, lots of laughs and (shhh... I don't have to cook!)"

Josh St. John, (father to Sophie, Halle and Ian) said:
"What's not to like....its quality family time...an "organic" environment - few expectations with good food and drink...perfect way to start the week."

Camille Cupa
"I would say that the best part is spending time with the family while enjoying great food. It's a time to keep in touch and watch how my nieces and nephews have grown, as well as us adults. Many things change through the years, and changing with each other as a family is priceless."

The results of the "Share the Table" study showed sharing dinner with your family makes people happier and healthier. Family Dinners strengthen family connections and help kids develop. The study also reviewed family dinner's matter as much to kids as they do to adults. There are benefits for both parents and children (no matter what the ages) when families share dinner together: kids and parents feel closer to each other; kids appreciate their parents more; and they feel that their parents are more relaxed and fun to be around. Laughter is the top attribute that defines a quality family dinner. It's the simple things that bring the most joy in family life.

To help you start a Family Meal tradition of your own or to make your current Family Meal tradition easier, I have put together a list of menu ideas and holiday traditions for the Family Meal. These are all menus and traditions I have used for our family and the recipes are included in this cookbook. I have the menu items broken down by categories. You can select how ever many items from each category that you like. Having a list like this helps me at times when I am too tired or too busy making it difficult to be creative and decisive. I keep track of the family favorites and rotate them seasonally. We eat seasonally so these items are what are either in season or on are family favorite list. Feel free to create your own menu idea list.

Easter- We fill plastic Easter eggs with coins and hide them in the woods for our Easter egg hunt. Instead of candy I buy the kids things like books, kites, bug catchers and balloons. For the kids I place a small Easter basket or decorative Easter box at each place setting, tie them with ribbon or raffia, and place a name card on it which also serves as their place cards. I fill the basket or box with a little candy, but mostly balloons, mini pads of paper, things like that. For the adults I get little Easter boxes and fill them with candy, or candles, little gift type things then tie them with ribbon or raffia, with a name card and use them for the adult place cards. They all (adults and kids) look forward to seeing what Grandma has put in their boxes this time. I do this for every holiday, just different boxes stuffed with different things. I always decorate the dinner table for holidays. The kids run in the house to see the decorations every holiday.

Halloween- My husband takes the kids on hay rides with our tractor and wagon. I set up bails of straw as a prop to take pictures of the kids in their costumes. I hang ghosts in trees by the hay props (old white sheets over balloons). I use a large tree branch from outside and hang mini pumpkins with flameless candles from it. I put Halloween bags along the drive way with sand and candles in them to create a walk way. I play Halloween music inside and out. I buy glow in the dark necklaces and bracelets for the kids to wear outside. We have a big bon fire, to cook hot dogs and roast marshmallows. We set up a hot chocolate station by the bon fire. We cook Chicken Corn Rival Soup in a kettle outside over a fire.

Thanksgiving and Christmas- I decorate the dinner table and use all china, crystal and linen. I buy a small, decorative, holiday themed box or create a gift for each person and use the gift as their place card at the table. Sometimes the gift may be a candle and I tie raffia and a card to the candle or I wrap a box with a gift inside and tie a ribbon and card to the box. I usually find these items at a craft store. I do the same for the kids but I usually get them items that will keep them busy at the table for a few minutes. Like crayons, paper, puzzles, small toys etc.

I hope this information will motivate you to preserve the ritual of sharing quality family dinners together. Someday I will pass the torch along to the girls to preserve the Family Meal, our Sunday Dinners, but for now I am thoroughly enjoying every minute of our Family Meal time together. The study is correct, it does make people happier. I am glad I did a study with our family because now I know what is important to my kids and grandkids about our Family Meal, and as you can see food is a big part of it.

Menu Ideas for Spring and Summer

Appetizers
Asparagus Spears in Puff Pastry
Caprese Kebabs
Carrots with Ranch
Celery w/Peanut Butter
Cheddar Cheese Ball
Chips w/Homemade Salsa
Garden Eggplant Sauce
Guacamole w/Chips Salsa
Pickles, Homemade
Roasted Garlic Bruschetta
Sun-dried Tomato Cheesecake
Tomato and Basil Bruschetta
Zucchini Dip

Salads
Arugula Vegetable Topping
Black Bean Salad
Broccoli salad
Carrot Salad
Chow Mein Chicken Salad
Cole Slaw
Corn and Tomato Salad
Cucumbers in Dilled Sauce
Easy Bean Salad
Fresh Tomato Salad
Garden Bean and Potato Salad
Garden Vegetable Salad
Greek Cucumber Salad
House Salad
Ice Box Slaw
Margy's Potato Salad
Margy's Spinach Salad
Spring Pea salad
Seven layer salad
Tomato, Feta and Cucumber
Zucchini Tomato Salad

Sides
Apple Blackberry Sauce
Apple Pear Sauce
Applesauce
Black Bean Salad
Corn Bread

Corn Fritters
Corn on the Cob
Deviled eggs
Fresh Green Beans
Macaroni and Cheese
Macaroni Salad
Parmesan Zucchini Sticks
Peas, Sautéed with Butter
Pickled Beets
Pickled Eggs
Roasted or Grilled Asparagus
Roasted Parmesan Potatoes
Roasted Mushrooms
Roasted or Grilled Squash
Roasted or Grilled Veggies
Rolls
Vegetable Gratin
Zucchini Fritters
Zucchini Pancakes

Sandwiches
Brats on the grill
Eggplant and Goat Cheese
Grilled Garden Sandwich
Hamburgers on the Grill
Hotdogs Grilled w/Coney Sauce
Italian Sausage on the Grill
Roasted Portobello Mushroom

Entrées
BBQ Baby Back Ribs
Beef Brisket
Shredded Beef Fajitas
Garden Shrimp Creole
Grilled Fish with
 Tomato Basil Sauce
Grilled Tenderloin Tips
Herbed Beef Tenderloin
Italian Garden Vegetable Stew
Oven Roasted Chicken Breasts
Roasted Pork Tenderloin with
 Apricot Glaze
Summer Lasagna
Summer Stuffed Chicken

Vegetable Stuffed Portobello
Taco Bar
Veggie Fajitas

Desserts
Berry Cobbler
Blackberry Cake
Blackberry Cobbler
Berry Crisp
Blackberry or Raspberry Sorbet
Cherry Cobbler
Cherry Pie
Chocolate Sundae Brownie Triffle
Chocolate Chip Cookies
Coconut Cream Pie
Fresh Berries
Fruit Salad
Frozen Key Lime Pie
Mango Sorbet
Mini Blackberry Turnovers
Mixed Berry Cobbler
Oatmeal Carmelita's
Peach Crisp
Peanut Butter Rice Krispies
Raspberry Bars
Raspberry Cake
Rhubarb Crunch
Strawberry Cake
Strawberry Shortcake Cups
Strawberry Pizza
Sugar Cookies
Zucchini Brownies

Beverages
Berry Smoothies
Blackberry Lemonade
Raspberry Iced Tea
Watermelon Lemonade
Sweet Tea
Summer Sangria

Menu Ideas for Fall and Winter

Appetizers
Apple Slices
Broccoli, Cheddar Dip
Carrot Sticks with Ranch
Cheese and Crackers
Chips and Homemade Salsa
Corned Beef Cheese Ball
Fresh Veggies with Ranch
Grapes
Raspberries
Spinach Artichoke Dip
Sweet Pickles, Homemade

Salads
Broccoli Salad
Caesar Salad
Garden Bean and Potato
German Potato Salad
House Salad
Ice Box Slaw
Lettuce with Tomato, Cucumber,
  Croutons and Italian dressing
Spicy Sweet Potato Salad
Zucchini Tomato Salad

Sides
Applesauce
Apple Fritters
Broccoli, Steamed
Brussels Sprout w/Bacon or Apples
Corn
Creamed Spinach
Garlic Bread
Green and Red Peppers Roasted
Green beans
Herb Roasted Potatoes
Macaroni and Cheese
Margy's Mashed Potatoes
Mashed Cauliflower
Mashed Sweet Potatoes
Peas, Steamed or Sautéed
Pesto Mashed Potatoes
Roasted Eggplant
Potato Casserole
Roasted Mushrooms

Roasted Asparagus
Roasted Portobello
Roasted Assorted Veggies
Scalloped Potatoes
Summer Squash Casserole
Sweet Potato Rolls

Entrées
Beef and Noodles
Beef Stew
Cheese and Chicken Enchiladas
Cheese Tortellini Bake
Chicken and Dumplings
Chicken and Noodles
Chicken Hash
Chicken Lasagna
Chicken Perisenne
Chicken with Blackberries
Crock Pot, Pot Roast
Dad's Spaghetti Sauce
Eggplant Casserole
Garden Vegetable Spaghetti Sauce
Lasagna
Meat loaf
Oven Roasted Chicken Breasts
Parmesan Chicken
Pasta Bar
Potato Bar
Roasted Chicken
Stuffed Acorn Squash
Swiss Steak
Vegetable Garden Pasta

Desserts
Apple Dumplings
Apple Pie
Berries
Brownies
Butter Pecan Cake
Caramel Apple Cheesecake
Chocolate Chip Cookies
Cupcakes, Red Velvet
Fresh Fruit
Pumpkin Bars
Pumpkin Cheesecake

Raisin Spice Cake
Raspberry Bars
Sugar Cookies

Beverages
Apple Cider
Apple Juice
Mulled Wine
Pear Raspberry Smoothie

New Years Day

Appetizers
Baked Brie in Puff Pastry
Cheese Ball and Crackers
Crab Stuffed Mushrooms
Cranberry, Jalapeño Meatballs
Fruit, Nuts and Veggies
Ham Balls with Pineapple Sauce
Relish Tray

Salads
Mixed Green Salad
Waldorf Salad

Sides
Greek Spinach Pie
Green Beans
Macaroni and Cheese
Mashed Potatoes
Potato Casserole

Entrées
Beef Bourguignon with Noodles
Chicken and Dumplings
Chicken and Noodles
Chili bar- *Chili, macaroni noodles,
 green onions, shredded cheddar,
 sour cream, hot dogs*
Lasagna
Pork Roast and Sauerkraut
Pulled Pork Sandwiches
Spaghetti and Meatballs

Desserts
Baklava
Left over Christmas Cookies and
 Candies
New York Cheesecake with
 Cherries

Beverages
Cranberry Punch

Play games after dinner

Valentines Day

Appetizers
Crab Martini
Fresh Veggies with Ranch
Pickles
Shrimp Cocktail

Salads
Caesar Salad
Margy's Spinach Salad

Sides
Fresh Green Beans
Garlic Bread
Roasted Mushrooms
Sautéed Onions
Twice Baked Potatoes

Entrées
Herbed Beef Tenderloin
Raspberry Chicken
Roasted Pork Tenderloin with
 Apricot Glaze
Shrimp Scampi

Desserts
Chocolate Heart Shaped
 Brownies
Mini Heart Shaped, Frosted
 Sugar Cookies
Turtle Cheesecake

Beverages
Strawberry, Orange, Banana
 Smoothie
Wine

St. Patty's Day

Appetizers
Cabbage Soup
Corned Beef Cheese Ball
Green Grapes
Rueben Soup

Salads
Cole Slaw
House Salad

Entrées
Corned Beef and Cabbage
Corned Beef with Jalapeño
Pepper
 Jelly
Rueben Bake

Desserts
Shamrock Cut Out Sugar
Cookies,
 Frosted

Beverages
Green Apple Smoothie

Easter

Appetizers
Carrot Sticks and Ranch
Cheddar Cheese Ball

Salads
Margy's Spinach Salad
Spring Pea Salad

Sides
Baked Beans
Brussels Sprout with Apples and
  Onions
Corn
Deviled Eggs
Mashed Sweet Potatoes with
  Cinnamon Butter
Potato Casserole
Roasted Asparagus
Roasted Mushrooms
Sautéed Peas
Scalloped Potatoes

Entrées
Baked Ham with Pineapple,
  Mustard Sauce
And Cherry Sauce

Desserts
Coconut Cream Pie
Frosted Sugar Cookie Cut Outs
Mini Easter Egg Shaped Cakes,
  Frosted and Decorated

Beverages
Bing Cherry Smoothie
Sangria with Berries

Mother's Day

Appetizers
Baked Brie with Raspberry
Baked Crab Dip
Chips and Salsa
Salsa- Regular, Mango and
Watermelon
Guacamole

Sides
Black Bean Salad
Corn Tomato Salad
Green Beans with Feta
Roasted Vegetables

Salads
Broccoli, Chicken Pasta Salad
Cheese Tortellini Pasta Salad
Chicken Pasta Salad
Southwestern Chicken Pasta
Tropical Chicken Salad

Entrées
Chicken Enchiladas
Chicken Perisenne
Eggplant Pesto Crepes
Orange Pecan Chicken
Taco Bar-*Shredded beef fajita
  meat, ground beef, roasted sliced
  Portobello's, roasted vegetables,
  shredded lettuce, shredded jack,
  Mexican white cheese crumbled,
  green onions diced, tomatoes
  diced, sour cream, fresh chopped
  cilantro, black olives sliced,
  sliced avocado, tortillas*

Desserts
Chocolate Sundae Brownie Trifle
Key Lime Frozen Pie
Mango Sorbet
Strawberry Cake

Beverages
May Wine
Strawberry Lemonade

Memorial Day

Appetizers
Fresh Fruit
Pickles
Roasted Red Pepper Hummus
Veggie Tray

Salads
Broccoli Salad
Cucumbers in Dilled Sour
  Cream
Margy's Potato Salad
Shrimp and Crab Salad

Sides
Baked Beans
Corn on the Cob
Deviled Eggs

Entrées
Hotdogs, Hamburgers, Italian
  Sausages, and Portobello
  Mushrooms on the Grill

Desserts
Chocolate Chip Cookies
Homemade Ice Cream
(Make Ice cream sandwiches)
Strawberry Pizza
Mini Strawberry Shortcakes

Beverages
Sangria with Berries
Strawberry Lemonade
Strawberry Swirl Smoothie

Father's Day

Appetizers
Fresh Fruit
Olives and Pickles
Veggie Tray

Salads
Cucumber in Dilled Sour Cream
Easy Bean Salad
Garden Fresh Vegetable Salad
Spicy Sweet Potato Salad

Sides
Herb Roasted Potatoes
Roasted Mushrooms
Roasted Vegetables
Watermelon

Entrées
Beef Brisket with Homemade
  BBQ
Burgers on the Grill
Garden Shrimp Creole
Grilled Tenderloin Tips
Oven Roasted Chicken Breasts

Desserts
Mixed Berry Cobbler
Strawberry Shortcake

Beverages
Strawberry Lemonade
Watermelon-Strawberry
  Smoothie

Fourth of July

Appetizers
Veggie Tray
Zucchini Dip

Salads
Broccoli Salad
Caesar Potato Salad
Crab, Corn, Tomato Salad
Garden Bean and Potato
Macaroni Salad
Seven Layer Salad
Shrimp Salad

Sides
Baked beans
Corn on the Cob
Watermelon

Entrées
BBQ Baby Back Ribs
Brats and Burgers on the Grill

Desserts
Berry Cobbler
Mini Blackberry Turnovers
Peanut Butter Rice Krispies
Raspberry Cake
Zucchini Brownies

Beverages
Berry Blast Smoothie
Blackberry Lemonade
Watermelon lemonade

Labor Day

Appetizers
Caprese Kebabs
Zucchini Dip

Salads
Carrot Salad
Creamy Dilled Potato Salad
Tomato, Feta, Cucumber Salad

Sides
Apple Fritters
Raspberry Applesauce
Summer Squash Casserole
Zucchini and Tomato Au Gratin

Entrées
Hotdogs and Hamburgers on
  the Grill

Desserts
Apple Dumplings
Blackberry Pie
Ice Cream
Peach Crisp

Beverages
Raspberry Lemonade
Pear Raspberry Smoothie
Summer Sangria

Halloween

Appetizers
Carrots with Ranch
Chicken, Corn Rival Soup
Grapes
Raspberries

Salads
Italian Tossed Salad
Spinach Salad with Berries and
  Nuts

Sides
Applesauce
Corn and Peas
Corn Bread
Garlic Toast
Hot Dogs
Macaroni and Cheese

Entrées
Lasagna, Vegetable and Regular

Desserts
Brownies with Spiders
Caramel Apples
Chocolate Cupcakes with Spiders
  and Gummy Worms
Mini Pumpkin Sugar Cookies,
  Frosted

Beverages
Apple Cider, Cold and Hot
Hot Chocolate
Pear Raspberry Smoothie

Thanksgiving

Appetizers
Carrots
Baked Brie
Cheese and Crackers
Corned Beef Cheese Ball
Relish Tray

Salads
Waldorf Salad
Frozen Cranberry Salad

Sides
Brussels Sprout with Bacon and
  Onion
Corn
Cranberry Chutney
Gravy
Green Beans with Buttered
  Crumbs
Herb Stuffing
Mashed Potatoes
Sweet Potato Casserole
Sweet Potato Rolls with
  Orange Honey Butter

Entrées
Turkey

Desserts
Baklava
Caramel Apple Cheesecake
Pumpkin Pie with Ginger Streusel
New York Cheesecake with
  Cherries
Pumpkin Cheesecake with
  Ginger crust
Mini Pumpkin Sugar Cookies;
  Frosted

Beverages
Cranberry Punch
Wine-Pinot Noir

Christmas

Appetizers
Cheese and Crackers
Relish Tray
Vegetable Tray

Salads
Fresh Fruit
Lettuce Salad with Veggies

Sides
Brussels Sprout
Corn
Potato Cheese Casserole
Sautéed Green Beans
Scalloped Potatoes

Entrées
Baked Ham with Pineapple,
  Mustard Sauce
Beef Bourguignon over Noodles

Desserts
Baklava
Buckeyes
Decorated Gingerbread Cookies
Decorated Sugar Cookies
New York Cheesecake with
  Cherries
Pinwheel cookies

Beverages
Cranberry Punch
Mulled Wine

Halloween with Iron Man (AKA Mason), Halle, Sophie, Ian and Myah

Candas

Preparing for the family Christmas Dinner

Fresh Fruit Equivalents

Apples	1 pound (3 medium) = 2-3/4 cups sliced
Apricot	1 pound (8 to 12 medium) = 2-1/2 cups sliced
Bananas	1 pound (3 medium) = 1-1/3 cups mashed; 2 cups sliced
Berries	1 pint = 1-1/2 to 2 cups
Cherries	1 pound = 3 cups whole; 3-1/2 cups halved
Cranberries	12 ounces = 3 cups whole; 2-1/2 cups finely chopped
Grapefruit	1 medium = 1 cup juice; 1-1/2 cups segments
Grapes	1 pound = 3 cups
Lemons	1 medium = 3 tablespoons juice; 2 teaspoons grated peel
Limes	1 medium = 2 tablespoons juice; 1-1/2 teaspoons grated peel
Nectarines	1 pound (3 medium) = 3 cups sliced
Oranges	1 medium = 1/3 to 1/2 cup juice; 4 teaspoons grated peel
Peaches	1 pound (4 medium) = 2-3/4 cups sliced
Pears	1 pound (3 medium) = 3 cups sliced
Pineapple	1 medium = 3 cups chunks
Raspberries	1 pound = 3 half pints
Rhubarb	1 pound = 3 cups chopped (raw); 2 cups (cooked)
Strawberries	1 pint = 2 cups hulled and sliced

Helpful Kitchen Hints by Margy

I use canola oil for most of my recipes because it is the healthiest of the oils and the most versatile. It is considered an inflammation fighter and a good fat. (Of course it needs to be used sparingly.) I use it for salad dressings, baking and frying.

Eat by color to get a balance of vitamins and nutrients. Eat red, orange, blue and green.

I use seasoned salt in many of my recipes because it has 1/3 less sodium than regular salt.

To use less dressing on your salad put the salad in a bowl and toss it with a small amount of dressing. You get more coverage and use less dressing.

Do not bake with fat free cheeses; they don't melt very well. Low fat works fine.

Toast almonds and keep in an airtight container. Sprinkle on salads or casseroles instead of croutons or bread crumbs. This will save you a lot of calories and carbs. Bake the almonds at 325 degrees for 10-25 minutes until lightly browned. Don't spray the pan.

I freeze banana peppers and jalapeño peppers whole and then drop them in chili soup as it cooks. This is also great for roasting fajita meats.

I use extra garden vegetables to stuff in meatloaf and/or to make Shepard's pie.

I add homemade salsa to my chili and my Garden Shrimp Creole recipes.

I buy plastic, disposable chefs gloves and use them for handling raw meat and hot peppers. You can get them at any restaurant supply store. They are under $10 for a large quantity and great to have in any kitchen.

To keep cheesecakes from cracking place a pan of water on the lower oven rack.

Convection ovens tend to dry out baked goods like cookies, scones, muffins and cakes. I put a pan of water on the lowest rack in the oven which keeps them from drying out. Remember to lower the oven temperature by 25 degrees when baking in a convection oven.

I designate a few hours one day a week, usually Saturday or Sunday, to cook and or prepare food for the week. It sure makes Monday and Tuesday a lot easier. I make things like soups, chicken or vegetable broth, cream of mushroom soup to cook with, casseroles etc., to jump start the week.

At the end of the week, and before my weekly grocery trip I clean out the refrigerator and use leftover meats and vegetables in a soup, quiche, fajita or I sauté them with pasta.

When sautéing, heat the pan first before adding the fat. This will reduce sticking.

Add a little oil to the water when cooking pasta to keep the water from boiling over and the pasta from sticking together.

Plastic wine corks are perfect to make thumbprint cookies.

When making fresh fruit pies, brush the bottom of the unbaked pie crust with beaten egg whites to keep the crust from becoming soggy.

I keep a shaker filled with flour in my kitchen to use for dusting meat, making sauces and rolling out cookies or pie crusts.

Helpful Cleaning Hints by Margy

I make a multipurpose cleaning solution by mixing 50/50 white vinegar and water and put it in a spray bottle. The vinegar smell does not linger and disappears as soon as the liquid dries, so not to worry. You can add Tee Tree oil, which is a natural antiseptic, or for a natural scent you can add an essential oil if you like. You can find these oils at a vitamin store or on line. A small bottle will last a long time. The nice thing about using these is they are all natural, with no harmful chemicals and the kids can eat off the floor (which we all know they do at times). I have allergies and am allergic to most chemical cleaning supplies and perfumes so this solution works perfect for me. White vinegar is quite inexpensive and has many uses so you don't have a cupboard full of 50 different cleaning supplies.

I mop all my floors, including my hardwood floors, tile and linoleum with a mixture of 50/50 warm water and white vinegar. It is a safe solution for hard wood floors and cleans them without damaging the wood or the shine.

When your auto drip coffee maker slows down it is most likely due to a mineral deposit build up. You can remove the mineral deposits by filling the water reservoir in your coffee maker with 1 cup of white distilled vinegar and running it through a whole cycle. Run it once or twice more with plain water to rinse clean.

Window and mirror cleaner-again mix 50/50 white vinegar and water, but do not add oil it will steak the windows.

Toilet Bowl Cleaner-mix 1 cup white vinegar and ¼ cup baking soda and let it set a few minutes in your toilet bowl. Then scrub.

Add 1/3 cup of white vinegar to the rinse cycle of your washing machine in stead of fabric softener (which I am also allergic to). No, it will not fade your clothes and they do not come out smelling like vinegar.

Add white vinegar to the rinse aid compartment of your dishwasher instead of commercial rinse aids like Jet Dry. It works just as well but again, it's inexpensive with out the harsh chemicals.

Homemade hand sanitizer-fill a small spray bottle with water and add several drops of Tea Tree Oil. Shake it to mix. Spray on hands as needed. Again no chemicals or alcohol.

How to use Common Herbs

Keep dried herbs stored in tightly closed containers in a cool, dark, dry place. Keep them away from heat. Dried herbs start to loose flavor after a year of storage. When fresh herbs are available, substitute them by using three times the amount of the dried herb called for in the recipe. Example: If recipe calls for 1 teaspoon of dried basil, substitute 1 tablespoon minced fresh basil.

Basil– licorice flavor basil leaves are used fresh or dried. Most frequently used in tomato or pasta dishes and pesto. Basil also adds flavor to dips, soups, salads, salad dressings, vegetables, stews, fish, beef, poultry, cheese dishes, eggs and potatoes.

Bay leaves– most often used as a whole dried leaf. It can be crushed. Bay leaf is most effective when allowed to simmer or marinate in a recipe for several hours. Try 1-2 bay leaves in soups, stews, pot roasts, poultry dishes, gravies, sauces and pickle brines. Whole leaves are always discarded before serving. I put bay leaves and whole peppercorns in a tea strainer and hang on the side of the pot.

Chives– have long spiky leaves that are used fresh, frozen or dried. To add a mild onion flavor. Chives are great in egg dishes, poultry and fish dishes, as garnish to soups, salads, salad dressings and vegetables. You can preserve chives by snipping with scissors and freezing in airtight containers. I only use the frozen in dishes I will be cooking, not for garnish or in fresh salads. For garnish and fresh salads I only use the fresh.

Cilantro– also known as coriander or chinese parsley, has zesty flavored green leaves mostly used in mexican style foods. Cilantro leaves add a distinctive flavor to salsa, dips, sauces, soups, chili, pesto and eggs. Cilantro is best used fresh just before serving to retain its flavor.

Dill– has a distinctive caraway flavor. Dill is used fresh or dried to season pickles, sauces, salad dressings, dips, fish, shell fish, eggs, muffins and breads.

Garlic– is a strong-flavored herb and is available fresh, dried, minced and in powder form. Garlic can be used in a large variety of foods, including dips, salad dressings, soups, flavored butters, casseroles, stews, grilled meats and vegetables, sauces, marinades, meats, vegetable dishes, potatoes, the list is endless. Garlic is a natural antibiotic and most effective if used fresh.

Italian– is a combination of basil, oregano, marjoram and sometimes rosemary. Italian seasoning can be used in soups, salads, entrees, red sauces and salad dressings.

Marjoram– used fresh or dried, marjoram's green leaves have a strong sweet aroma much like oregano. Add to meat, poultry, fish, eggs, homemade sausage, vegetable dishes and as a garnish.

Mint– available fresh and dried, mint has a spicy flavor and aroma. Use in stews, sauces, salads, and mint jellies. Great used in spaghetti sauce. Mint is often used as a garnish for fruits, desserts and beverages such as ice tea and lemonade.

Oregano– the dark green leaves are used fresh or dried in Italian, Mexican, and Greek dishes. Oregano flavors soups, stews, chili, poultry, ground beef, seafood, marinades, salad dressings, sauces, hot or cold pasta dishes and pizza. Also can be used as a garnish.

Parsley– available in curly and flat-leaf varieties, fresh parsley adds a refreshing flavor and a spark of green garnish to soups, salads, salad dressings, sauces, fish, poultry stuffings, to any entree as a garnish; potato, grain, bean and pasta dishes. Flat -leaf or Italian parsley has a stronger flavor than the traditional curly variety. Dried parsley is mild in flavor and color. Great used to garnish large food trays.

Poultry– Is a combination of thyme, sage and rosemary. Poultry seasoning is great used in chicken soups, stews, casseroles, dumplings and stuffing.

Rosemary– known for its needle like leaves, rosemary has a distinctive fragrant evergreen scent and bold flavor. Fresh or dried complements lamb, pork, poultry, marinades, potato dishes, herb butters and flavored mayonnaise, homemade savory breads and soups. Also makes a great garnish used whole. Can be used tied with a ribbon at each place setting for a dinner party.

Sage– the pale green leaves of sage can be enjoyed fresh or dried and rubbed into a fluffy powder. Sage is well known for adding a distinctive flavor to poultry stuffings, poultry, roasted red meats, soups, stews, and Italian dishes. Use whole leaves as a garnish.

Tarragon– has a mild licorice like flavor and can be used fresh or dried. Tarragon flavors chicken, chicken salads, poultry marinades, pasta salads, potato salads, vegetables, sauces, salad dressings, fish and egg dishes. Use whole as a garnish.

Thyme– has a bold, earthy taste and strong aroma. There are many varieties, including the popular lemon thyme. Use fresh or dried to season fish, potatoes, soups, stuffings, stews, rice, poultry and meat marinades. Also whole makes a great garnish.

Drying Herbs– Wash and pat dry your herbs. You can either hang them to dry in a cool, dry place or lay flat on a baking sheet or tray lined with paper towels. They can take anywhere from 2 weeks to a few months to dry, depending on the herb and how dry they were to begin with. I usually let them dry at least a few months. Grind once they are dried and store in air tight containers. You can find herb grinders at kitchen stores in season and small herb jars at craft stores.

Miscellaneous Food Equivalents

Bread	1 loaf = 16 to 20 slices
Bread Crumbs	1 slice = 1/2 cup soft crumbs; 1/4 cup dry crumbs
Butter or margarine	1 pound = 2 cups; 4 sticks
Corn, fresh	1 pound = 5-6 ears = 3 cups kernels
Cottage cheese	1 pound = 2 cups
Shredded cheese	4 ounces = 1 cup
Chocolate chips	6 ounces = 1 cup
Cocoa, baking	1 pound = 4 cups
Cream Cheese	8 ounces = 16 tablespoons
Cream, Whipping	1 cup = 2 cups whipped
Egg Whites	1 cup = 8 to 10 whites
All-Purpose flour	1 pound = about 3-1/2 cups
Whole wheat flour	1 pound = about 3-3/4 cups
Frozen whipped topping	8 ounces = 3-1/2 cups
Gelatin, unflavored	1 envelope = 1 tablespoon
Nuts-Almond	1 pound = 3 cups halved; 4 cups slivered
Ground	3-3/4 ounce = 1 cup
Pecans	1 pound = 4-1/2 cups chopped
Walnuts	1 pound = 3-3/4 cups chopped
Popcorn	1/3 to 1/2 cup un-popped = 8 cups popped
Sugar-Brown	1 pound = 2 1/4 cups
Confectioners	1 pound = 4 cups
Granulated	1 pound = 2 1/4 to 2 1/2 cups

Seasonal Fruits and Vegetables

Summer Produce in the Midwest

June-Arugula, asparagus, cabbage, carrots, cherries, garlic, leeks, onions, peas, potatoes, snap beans, radishes, rhubarb, spinach, strawberries

July-Arugula, beans, blackberries, blueberries, broccoli, cabbage, cantaloupe, cauliflower, cucumbers, garlic, eggplant, herbs, honey dew, onions, peaches, peppers, potatoes, radishes, raspberries, squash, strawberries, sweet corn, tomatoes, watermelon, yellow squash, zucchini

August-Arugula, blueberries, broccoli, cabbage, collards, eggplant, herbs, kale, beans, okra, peaches, pears, peppers, potatoes, raspberries, spinach, squash, sweet corn, tomatoes

Selecting and Storing your Farmer's Market Produce

Apples- You want to select apples that are firm and free of bruising and blemishes. Store in a paper bag in the refrigerator for up to one month. Prepare your apples as required for your recipes. See the Canning and Preserving chapter for apple recipes.

Arugula- Look for long, slender, young leaves with a bright green color. Avoid any wet or bruised leaves. Store arugula in a plastic bag in the refrigerator up to 4 days. Handle with care to avoid bruising; its leaves are delicate. Arugula bunches trap soil and grit. Immerse the leaves in cold water, letting them soak a few minutes then lift them out, letting the grit settle at the bottom. Dry well in a salad spinner or shake them gently in a clean kitchen towel.

Asparagus- Look for firm stalks with tight, dry tips. I always push on the tips to check for firmness. Store in an open plastic bag for up to 5 days in the back of the refrigerator. Bend a few spears to find the natural breaking point and cut the others to the same length.

Beets- Look for firm, rounded beets with out bruising. Avoid buying beets with wilted greens as that is an indicator of freshness. Beet tops/ greens are really good for you and delicious tossed in with other greens in a salad. Beets are best when cooked whole. See the Canning and Preserving chapter for instructions on working with beets.

Blackberries and Raspberries- Look for berries that are bright colored. Check the bottom of the container for bruised, wet or moldy fruit. Plan to use them as soon after picking or purchasing as possible. Store in the refrigerator in their original containers until ready to use and avoid washing them until right before eating.

Blueberries- Select firm, dry, smooth, powdery blueberries. They can be refrigerated in an airtight container for up to one week or easily frozen (see the Canning and Preserving chapter) to enjoy all year. Handle with care as they are delicate. Remove stems, rinse under cool water just before serving.

Broccoli- heads should have tight florets and a dark green color with no signs of yellowing. Avoid dry stems. Broccoli will keep stored in a plastic bag in the refrigerator for up to a week. Trim off the bottoms of the stalks and cut into the desired size.

Cabbage, Green- Heads of cabbage should be firm with tight leaves, depending on the variety. Color is an indication of freshness. If the stem-end has not cracked around the base it is fresh. Pull off and discard the outer, wilted leaves. Remove the core by cutting out a cone at the base of the core.

Cabbage, Red- Handle and select red cabbage the same as you would with green but look for a vibrant purple color. To keep red cabbage from turning pale when cooking, add a small amount of vinegar or lemon juice, or cook the cabbage with acidic ingredients like apples or wine.

Cantaloupe and Honeydew- Select melons that when pressed on the end will have a slight give, are sweet smelling and feel heavy for their size. Make sure they are free of deep blemishes, mold, and a soft or shriveled peel. Cut the melons in half either direction and scoop out the seeds with a large spoon. Melons taste sweeter if served at room temperature.

Carrots- Look for bright carrots without cracks. Leave about an inch of greens on them to keep moisture and freshness. Store in a plastic bag in the refrigerator for up to two weeks. I like to scrub them and leave the skins on.

Cauliflower- Look for firm tight heads with cream florets that is free of brown spots. Cauliflower can be kept in the refrigerator for up to a week stored in a plastic bag. Trim the bottom to separate the florets.

Chard and Kale- Look for dark green color and crisp, large leaves. Leaf shape and size will vary. Avoid bunches with brown or yellow leaves, or ribs that are wilted enough to bend. Store in a plastic bag in the refrigerator for 4-5 days. Immerse the leaves in cold water, letting them soak a few minutes then lift them out, letting the grit settle at the bottom. Dry well in a salad spinner or shake them gently in a clean kitchen towel. Cut out the tough center vein that runs along the center of each leaf and discard.

Cherries- Look for large, plump, smooth cherries with stems and leaves that is green. Avoid, sticky, wet, soft, shriveled or bruised, Cherries should be used as soon as possible, need refrigerated and freeze well. They will keep refrigerated for up to 5 days. Keep the stems on until ready to use. Wash them under cold water right before using them to keep them from molding. To use cherries in recipes, pit them with a cherry pitter, a small sharp knife or my favorite; a bobby pin.

Corn- Choose ears with green husks and no browning or drying. The silk tassels should be pale yellow and moist. Choose ears with plump, juicy kernels. Fresh corn does not keep well. As soon as the corn is picked the natural sugars begin converting to starch. That is why it is important to cook corn as soon as possible. Store un-shucked ears in a plastic bag in the refrigerator for 3-4 days. Cooking times: boil 3-7 minutes, steam 5-10 minutes, blanch 3-5 minutes, and roast in husk 25 minutes or in foil 15 minutes. Soak your corn in water before roasting in husk to prevent scorching. Corn can also be cut from the cob and eaten raw in salads or salsas. Don't salt fresh corn while cooking; salt will toughen it. Instead cook corn with ½ teaspoon of sugar. It will sweeten the corn plus keep it tender.

Cucumbers- Look for slender, firm, dark green cucumbers without yellowed areas. Young, tender cucumbers do not need seeding or peeling before use. Larger ones can be seeded by cutting in half lengthwise and then scraping out the seeds with the tip of a spoon. To rid cucumbers of bitterness remove the ends, peel and slice then sprinkle with salt. Let drain in a colander for about 30 minutes then rinse. The salt will draw out the bitterness. Cucumbers won't water down salad dressings if salted first. Store cucumbers in frig 3-5 days in a plastic bag.

Green Beans- Choose beans that are bright in color are free from brown spots and snap easily when broken. Green beans can be stored in an open plastic bag for up to 5 days in the refrigerator.

Lettuces- Delicate-Choose heads of lettuce that is heavy for their size. Avoid wilted, torn or brown leaves. Let the leaves soak 10 minutes in cold water to refresh and crisp them. This will also let the grit and dirt float to the bottom. Dry lettuces well in a salad spinner or shake them gently in a clean kitchen towel. This will avoid diluting their flavor and allow dressing to coat the leaves. Tear large leaves individually instead of cutting the heads to avoid discoloring or crushing their leaves.

Lettuces- Sturdy-Choose heads or loose leaves that is free of wilting or browning. Avoid any with large, thick stems which can be bitter. Sturdy lettuces can be stored unwashed in a plastic bag in the refrigerator for 3-5 days. Wash lettuces just before using; immerse them in a large bowl filled with cold water, letting dirt and grit settle to the bottom. Dry lettuces well in a salad spinner or shake them gently in a clean kitchen towel. Remove wilted or yellow leaves and thick stalks.

Potatoes- Choose firm potatoes that are not wrinkled, tinged with green, blemished or cracked. If potatoes do have buds they should not be sprouting. Potatoes keep well in a cool, dark place for up to 2 weeks. Make sure it is a well-ventilated place such as a pantry or drawer. I cover my potatoes with loose newspaper. Do not store potatoes in the refrigerator to preserve their flavor and texture. Scrub potatoes under cool water. You can cook with them peeled or unpeeled. Green spots on potatoes are known to be mildly toxic so make sure to cut away any green before cooking.

Rhubarb- Select crisp, firm, brightly colored stalks free of blemishes. The younger stalks with darker red or pink are usually sweeter and tenderer. Trim away the leaves and limp stalks. Cut to the size required for your recipe. To retain the color while cooking par boil them first.

Spinach- Select spinach with crisp, dark leaves free of bruises, tears and wetness. Look for smaller leaves for fresh salads. Look for larger leaves for cooking. If you are buying spinach in bundles, look for firm stems and avoid wet leaves. Refrigerate the spinach unwashed in a plastic bag for 3-5 days. Fill a large bowl with cold water, immerse the leaves, and let them soak to remove the grit and soil. Dry lettuces in a salad spinner or shake them gently in a clean kitchen towel. I like to remove the stems for a more delicate texture.

Squashes- Squashes are divided into two categories: Summer and winter. Acorn and other winter squashes have thick flesh and their shells are hard. They have a long shelf life. Zucchini and yellow squash, among other summer varieties have soft, thin skin and moist flesh. The seeds of many winter varieties and the flowers of summer squash are also edible. Summer squashes are best when young and small early in the summer.

Yellow Squash- Select yellow squash when small for tender, seedless flesh. As they grow, they become firmer and seedier. They should have bright color and feel heavy and firm for their size. Look for smooth skins with no blemishes. Store in the refrigerator up to 5 days. There is no need to peel zucchini or yellow squash; simply rinse, trim the ends, and then slice, chop or shred as called for in the recipe. They are both great for sautéing, roasting or grilling.

Zucchini- Select zucchini that is dark, firm and heavy for their size. Small ones will have crisp texture and a sweet flavor; they become softer and bitterer as they grow bigger. Store zucchini for up to 5 days in the refrigerator.

Acorn and Butternut Squashes- Acorn and Butternut Squashes should be firm and feel heavy for their size. These hard-shelled winter squashes keep well and can be stored for several months in a cool, dark place if free of cuts and bruises. Once cut, winter squashes should be stored in a plastic bag in the refrigerator up to 5 days. Cut long shaped squash in half lengthwise using a large, sharp chef's knife. With a large metal spoon, scoop out the seeds and strings and discard. If the skin needs to be removed before cooking, use a sharp vegetable peeler or paring knife to peel it away carefully.

Cutting Squashes- Raw winter squash can be scary to cut. Its round shape and hard flesh make dealing with it a real kitchen danger. But it can be done without drawing blood-par bake it first. To start, preheat the oven to 350 degrees, and then prick the squash with a fork. Bake it just until tongues leave an indentation on the skin. A small squash about the size of a pop can takes about 30 minutes, larger ones the size of a 2 liter can take an hour or more. Let the squash cool until easy to handle, and then trim off the skin. The flesh won't be cooked through at this point, so finish cooking it according to the recipes instructions.

Onion Varieties- Onions fall into two main categories: dried and fresh (green). Cleaning-Green fresh onions, (leeks, green onions and scallions).These fresh onions grow in layers trapping grit and sand between layers. Rinse under cool, running water separating the layers until there is no dirt remaining.

Garlic- Bulb with white or red papery skin, encasing individual cloves, also covered with papery skin. Can be used fresh, cooked, roasted etc. Garlic can be used in a large variety of foods. Choose plump garlic heads with smooth, firm cloves. Whole garlic heads keep well when stored in an open container in a cool, dark well- ventilated place for up to 2 months.

Leeks- Long, fresh onion with a white root end and large green tops. Used in stews, soups, sauces, as a main ingredient or flavoring. Select the smallest leeks with dark green tops that are firm and free of blemishes. Use the root as well as the stalk trimming the stringy roots and cutting away the dark green leaves. The leek is then slit along its length leaving the root end still in tact.

Mild Onions- Pearl Onions- Small oval onions may be white or red. Can be boiled, picked or brined. Often used in stews or creamed. Choose onions with tight, smooth peels that are dry. Store onions in a cool, dark, well- ventilated place. Do not keep them in plastic bags, as it causes moisture and they will spoil.

Cipollini- Mini onions- These fill the gap between the last of the winter-stored onions and the early new onions. Mild and sweet, these early spring onions are ready with the peas. Great baked, grilled or in casseroles. Select and handle them the same as the mild onions.

Red Onions- Small, round, flattened onions with red, papery skin. Flesh is red and white. Eaten raw on salads and sandwiches, grilled, in compotes or marinades with a mild, sweet flavor. Select and handle them the same as the mild onions.

Green Onions- Fresh young onion pulled before the bulb is enlarged. Use the white and the tender green tops. Mild sweet flavor, eaten raw in salads, cooked in casseroles and uncooked sauces. Select green onions that are vibrant green, look fresh, not wilted and with white bulb ends. Avoid dry or wet roots. Store in a plastic bag in the refrigerator for up to 1 week.

Scallions- Fresh green onion forming a thick basal portion (white root end) without a bulb. Mild, sweet flavor used especially in salads, and uncooked sauces. Use the white and the green. Handle and select as you would for the green onion.

Spanish Onion- Large onions with yellow to yellow-brown skin. The flesh is milder than a yellow onion. Used in soups, stews and sauces. Select and handle them the same as the mild onions.

Sweet Onion- Walla Walla, Vidalia and Maui. Generally has a flattened shape. Flesh is sweet. Eaten raw in salads, grilled, sautéed, roasted. Select and handle them the same as the mild onions.

Yellow or White Onions- Moderate size with either yellow brown or white papery skin. Pungent flesh. Used in soups, stews and sauces. Select and handle them the same as the mild onions.

Peppers and Chiles- Look for firm, bruise free, brightly colored peppers and chilies. Refrigerate up to one week. Peppers and chilies should be trimmed, seeds and white membrane removed. Some peppers and chilies can burn your skin so wear gloves when working with the hot ones.

Pumpkin- Choose pumpkins that feel solid and heavy. Pumpkins dry out and become pale as they age. The skin should be hard, without cracks or soft spots. Their hard shells prevent them from spoiling quickly; whole ones with out blemishes will keep up to 1 month when stored in a cool, dry place. Once cut, winter squashes should be stored in a plastic bag in the refrigerator up to 5 days. To cut a pumpkin, steady it on a thick towel, insert a large heavy knife near the stem and cut down through the curved side. Always cut away from you. Turn the pumpkin and repeat on the other side. Follow the instructions for acorn and butternut squash for seeding and peeling.

Strawberries- Choose fragrant strawberries with a bright red color and fresh green caps. Avoid berries with white or green shoulders, shriveled caps, bruising or wetness. Gently rinse berries in cold water just before eating as moisture will cause them to mold. Also avoid slicing strawberries until ready to eat as they start to lose their nutritional value once sliced.

Tomatoes- Tomatoes are the best looking and tasting at the height of the season. For the best flavor, choose those that are bright in color. Tomatoes can be stored at room temp for up to 3 days. If they are slightly unripe put them in a sunny place where they can ripen further. Rinse, dry and remove the stem ends just before using. To remove seeds for sauces, halve the tomatoes and squeeze and shake out the seeds gently over a bowl.

Watermelon- Look for a large, pale yellow patch on one side of the watermelon. This means it was vine ripened. Check for soft spots and bruising. A whole watermelon can be stored at room temperature for up to 3 days and once cut stored in the refrigerator in an airtight container up to a week.

Substitutions

Baking powder	1 teaspoon	1/2 teaspoon cream of tartar plus 1/4 teaspoon baking soda
Broth	1 cup	1 cup hot water plus 1 teaspoon bouillon granules or 1 bouillon cube or 1 teaspoon chicken, beef or vegetable base
Brown Sugar	1 cup	1 cup granulated sugar + 1 tablespoon molasses. Mix together.
Buttermilk	1 cup	1 tablespoon lemon juice or vinegar plus enough milk to measure 1 cup; let stand 5 minutes. Or 1 cup plain yogurt
Cajun seasoning	1 teaspoon	1/2 to 1 teaspoon hot pepper sauce, 1/2 teaspoon dried thyme, 1/4 teaspoon dried basil and 1 minced garlic clove
Chocolate semisweet	1 square (1 ounce)	1 square (1 ounce) unsweetened chocolate plus 1 tablespoon sugar or 3 tablespoons semisweet chocolate chips
Chocolate, unsweetened	1 square (1 ounce)	3 tablespoons baking cocoa plus 1 tablespoon shortening or vegetable oil
Cornstarch (for thickening)	1 tablespoon	2 tablespoons all-purpose flour
Corn syrup, dark	1 cup	3/4 cup light corn syrup plus 1/4 cup molasses
Corn syrup, light	1 cup	1 cup sugar plus 1/4 cup water
Cracker crumbs	1 cup	1 cup dry bread crumbs
Cream half and half	1 cup	1 tablespoon melted butter plus enough whole milk to measure 1 cup
Egg	1 whole	2 tbsp corn oil and 1 tbsp water
Flour, cake	1 cup	1 cup minus 2 tablespoons (7/8 cup) all-purpose flour
Flour, self-rising	1 cup	1 cup all-purpose flour plus 1 teaspoon baking powder, 1/2 teaspoon salt and 1/4 teaspoon baking soda
Garlic, fresh	1 clove	1/8 teaspoon garlic powder
Ginger root, fresh	1 teaspoon	1/4 teaspoon ground ginger
Honey	1 cup	1 1/4 cups sugar plus 1/4 cup water
Lemon juice	1 teaspoon	1/4 teaspoon cider vinegar
Lemon peel	1 teaspoon	1/2 teaspoon lemon extract
Milk, whole	1 cup	1/2 cup evaporated milk plus 1/2 cup water or 1 cup plus 1/3 cup nonfat dry milk powder
Molasses	1 cup	1 cup honey
Mustard, prepared	1 tablespoon	1/2 teaspoon ground mustard plus 2 teaspoons vinegar
Onion	1 small (1/3 cup chopped)	1 teaspoon onion powder or 1 tablespoon dried minced onion
Poultry seasoning	1 teaspoon	3/4 teaspoon rubbed sage plus 1/4 teaspoon dried thyme
Sour cream	1 cup	1 cup plain yogurt
Wine	equal amounts	broth

Healthy Recipe Makeover Substitutions

Instead of	Use	Calories Saved	Fat Saved(g)
Dairy			
1 cup whole milk	1 cup fat-free milk	64	8
	1 cup buttermilk (for baking)	51	6
	1 cup 1% milk	48	6
	1 cup 2% milk	29	4
1 can sweetened Condensed milk (14 ounces)	1 can fat-free sweetened condensed milk (14 ounces)	155	35
1 can evaporated milk (12 ounces)	1 can fat-free evaporated milk (12 ounces)	191	25
1 cup heavy cream	1 cup 1% milk + 1tablespoon cornstarch	688	86
	1 cup fat-free evaporated milk	622	88
1 cup whipped cream	1 cup frozen light whipped topping, thawed	250	36
	1 cup frozen whipped topping, thawed	171	25
1 cup sour cream	1 cup fat-free plain yogurt	355	48
	1 cup fat-free sour cream	244	48
1 cup shredded cheddar cheese (4 ounces)	1 cup shredded fat-free cheddar cheese	279	37
	1 cup shredded reduced-fat cheddar cheese (2%)	185	16
4 ounces blue cheese	2 ounces blue cheese + 2 ounces fat-free cream cheese	149	16
4 ounces feta cheese	2 ounces feta + 2 ounces cream cheese	110	12
4 ounces goat cheese	2 ounces goat cheese + 2 ounces fat-free cream cheese	153	17
8 ounces cream cheese	8 ounces fat-free ricotta cheese	630	79
	8 ounces fat-free cream cheese	586	79
	4 ounces fat-free cream cheese + 4 ounces light cream cheese	394	62
	8 ounces light cream cheese (tub style)	296	44
	8 ounces light cream cheese (block style)	200	25
8 ounces mascarpone cheese	4 ounces mascarpone + 4 ounces fat-free cream cheese	502	52

Instead of	Use	Calories Saved	Fat Saved(g)
Fat			
½ cup oil	½ cup fat free chicken broth (for salad dressings and marinades)	952	109
	¼ cup unsweetened applesauce + ¼ cup buttermilk (for baking)	913	108
	½ cup unsweetened applesauce (for baking)	911	109
	½ cup baby food prunes (for baking)	799	109
	1/3 cup vinegar+ ¼ cup fat-free Chicken broth + ¼ cup pineapple juice+ 2 tablespoons strong flavored oil (for salad dressings and marinades)	681	82
½ cup (1 stick) butter or margerine	½ cup unsweetened applesauce (for baking)	788	92
	¼ cup unsweetened applesauce + ¼ buttermilk (for baking)	763	91
½ cup (1stick) butter or margerine; continued	½ cup baby food prunes (for baking)	699	92
	½ cup marshmallow crème (for frostings and fillings)	436	92
	½ cup light butter	414	48
2 Tbsp oil	2 tbsp fat-free broth (for sautéing)	238	27
	2 tbsp wine (for sautéing)	221	27
1 cup chopped walnuts	½ cup chopped walnuts, toasted	385	35
1 cup chopped pecans	½ cup chopped pecans, toasted	397	40
1 cup slivered almonds	½ cup sliced almonds, toasted	518	46
	½ cup slivered almonds, toasted	398	35

Protein

Instead of	Use	Calories Saved	Fat Saved(g)
6 ounces pork sirloin, cooked	6 ounces pork tenderloin, roasted	167	19
6 ounces flank steak, cooked	6 ounces round steak, roasted	46	9
6 ounces chicken thigh, no skin, cooked	6 ounces chicken breast, no skin, roasted	76	12
6 ounces dark turkey no skin, cooked	6 ounces turkey breast ,roasted	16	2
1 whole egg	2 egg whites	41	5
6 ounces tuna in oil	6 ounces tuna in water, drained	140	13
1 pound ground beef	1 pound ground turkey breast	839	83
	1 pound chopped pork tenderloin	581	67

Instead of	Use	Calories Saved	Fat Saved(g)
	1 pound chopped chicken breast	576	67
	1 pound ground turkey	257	29
	1 pound extra-lean ground beef	123	17
6 ounces pork sausage, cooked	6 ounces turkey sausage cooked	258	29

Miscellaneous

Instead of	Use	Calories Saved	Fat Saved(g)
1 cup frozen whipped topping	1 cup light whipped topping	79	11
1 cup chocolate chips	½ cup mini chocolate chips	405	25
	½ cup chocolate chips	300	29
	⅔ cup chocolate chips	276	17
	¾ cup chocolate chips	203	13
1 cup flaked coconut	1 teaspoon coconut extract	337	24
	½ cup flaked coconut	176	12
1 cup sliced olives	½ cup sliced olives	78	7
1 ounce baking chocolate	3 tablespoons unsweetened cocoa powder	111	14
Single pie crust	3 sheets phyllo dough (6 half- sheets)	779	59
1 can condensed cream of mushroom soup (10.7 ounce)	1 can condensed reduced-fat cream of mushroom soup	141	16
1 cup sugar	¾ cup sugar	194	0
1 small package flavored gelatin mix (4 servings)	1 small package sugar-free gelatin mix (4 servings)	292	0
1 cup basic white sauce (1 cup whole milk, 2 tbsp flour, and 2 tbsp butter)	1 cup basic white sauce (1 cup 1% milk and 1 tbsp cornstarch)	111	15

These are very reliable fat-saving swaps that can lower the fat and calories in your favorite dishes.

The Benefits of Menu Planning

Menu Planning is a way to save significant time and money while adding peace to your life. Whether you are extremely organized or more spontaneous, Menu Planning benefits all. Through Menu Planning, you will eat healthier foods, make fewer trips to the store, save money and prevent headaches created from the 5 o'clock stare into the fridge and pantry!

Menu Planning can be easy and efficient. Most likely, your family consistently eats the same 15-20 meals. Sit down with your family members and have them all share a few favorite meals. Make a list of "Favorite Meals" and then create your monthly rotation. Create a master grocery list from those meals. You will realize what items to always have in your pantry and fridge - and you can stock up on them at their lowest prices and plan your weekly menu based on stores' sales. If you are intentional with stocking up on your favorite, healthy items when they're at their lowest prices, possibly grow a garden, buy locally and in abundance while fruits and vegetables are in season, can and preserve - you will save significant money while eating healthy.

I plan a week at a time using monthly calendars that I print from the computer and pencil in my menus for the month - one week at a time - shifting meals around when needed - based on sales, items I need to use up and family schedules. I save these calendars for my next month's planning. It gets easier and easier each month, and I'm able to consistently stay in our grocery budget. If I'm over budget, it's a leftover buffet the rest of the week!

I plan a couple new recipes each month - sometimes those end up on our list of "Favorite Meals" and sometime they don't! We usually take a vote.

I also plan a couple soups each month, and try to cook a double batch and freeze half.

Crockpot recipes are very helpful, so give those a try and add a few to your list of "Favorite Meals".

Many recipes found in this cookbook are easy, healthy and family friendly while keeping budgets in mind - making them perfect to add to your Monthly Menu Plan.

The Benefits of Menu Planning was provided by Myah St John. Thanks Myah

The Farm to Fork Phenomenon

Farm to Fork

The food chain from agricultural production to consumption. This is an increasingly popular topic world wide. The term is related to organic farming initiatives, sustainable agriculture, and community supported agriculture; a "Farm to Fork Experience".

The Farmers' Market

1. *Why farmers markets have become so popular.*
They are the best place to find great local produce. The produce is fresher, more flavorful, keeps longer, and in many cases is organically grown. Farmers' Markets can be a wonderful learning experience for children and great places to socialize. You can taste test new fresh ingredients before you buy and in many cases there is entertainment and recipes provided. Buying fruits and vegetables at the peak of their season make it easy to prepare healthy, flavorful meals.

2. *Why it is important to support your local farmers.*
Farms are good for the environment because they contribute oxygen and remove carbon dioxide from the air. They provide local jobs and money stays in the local economy. When you purchase your produce at the farmers' market, the price you pay goes directly to the farmers and their local operations. Your supermarket dollar goes to transportation, packaging, advertising, and other costs that have little to do with the fruit you are buying. Although the price you pay at your local farmers' market is sometimes higher-family farms are expensive to run especially if organic-you know that every dollar stays in your community, and that benefits you. Farmers' markets are an important income source for many of the farmers who sell at them. Without market patronage, some would be unable to maintain their farm business.

3. *The increased health benefits of fresh, locally grown produce.*
The fresher the product the more vitamins and nutrients provided. The majority of imported foods in the US have been altered to prolong shelf life as most travel 1300 miles over a 1-2 week period to get to the family table. At the farmers' market, the locally grown produce was most likely picked the day before or that morning. Canning, drying, and freezing fresh fruits and vegetables are excellent ways to cash in on seasonal foods that are lower in cost but higher in taste and nutrition. See the Canning and Preserving chapter in this book.

4. *Where to find locations and information about local farmers markets.*
They are usually posted on the internet and in your local newspaper late March or early April. Most Markets start in May–June in the Midwest, and continue into the fall.

5. *What to look for at a farmers' market.*
Make sure they are either the grower or manager and not someone who buys the produce from another state and ships it in. Ask if the produce is organic, natural or conventional. Conventional farming uses the most chemicals. Natural may use small amounts of chemicals or no chemicals but are not certified organic. Organic uses no chemicals at all and requires third-party USDA certification to claim and promote organic. The brighter the color of the produce, the fresher it is. See the Seasonal Fruits and Vegetables Chapter in this book on how to Select and Store your Farmers' Market produce.

6. The benefits of restaurants buying from local farmers' markets.
It allows them to buy smaller quantities, a fresher, longer lasting, better tasting and more nutritious product for their customers. It also supports the community and keeps jobs and money in the local economy, which also benefits them.

7. What is a CSA program (Community Supported Agriculture) and how does it work?
These programs allow you to regularly enjoy a share of a local farm's harvest by receiving weekly boxes of fresh fruits and vegetables. You're getting it straight from the farm, sometimes picked that morning. It's usually organic and it's much more delicious because it's so fresh. And you're supporting local farms.

8. What is a Food Co-Op?
A food cooperative or food co-op is a collectively owned grocery store with an emphasis on making whole, natural foods more affordable for co-op members. There are a number of different styles of food co-ops, but all of them share common values of group management and decision making, social responsibility, and equality. Some co-ops are member only while others are open to the public. To become a member there is usually a small initiation fee. Most co-ops support the local farms.

9. What is the Slow Food Movement?

Slow Food is an idea, a way of living, and a way of eating that links the pleasure of food with a commitment to community and the environment. Food without all the harmful additives that are present in processed foods and food made in a clean environment that does not pose any harm to the earth or the inhabitants within.

"Slow food aims to be everything fast food is not"-USA Today.

Why Organic?
The main reason is organic foods are produced free of hormones, chemical pesticides and other non-natural ingredients. Organic farming practices are designed to encourage soil and water preservation and reduce pollution. The chemicals and additives used in conventional farming are what do the most damage to your body. Organic foods have up to 75% more vitamins and nutrients than non-organic. Eating organic lessens the toxic burden in our bodies, on the environment, and farm workers. Eating organic has been accounted for rising energy levels, less health problems, and overall just feeling better.

The USDA has established an Organic Certification Program that requires all organic foods to meet strict government standards. These standards regulate how such foods are grown, handled and processed. Any farmer who labels and sells a product as organic must be USDA certified as meeting these standards. There are costs involved with growing organic and receiving certification so many times organic foods cost more.

Conventional Farming vs. Organic Farming

Conventional	Organic
Apply chemical fertilizers to promote plant growth.	*Apply natural fertilizers, such as manure or compost, to feed soil and plants. Also green cover crops like rye and clover which builds organic matter in the soil which fixes nutrients like nitrogen.*
Spray synthetic, chemical based insecticides to reduce pests and disease.	*Use beneficial insects and organic based pesticides.*
Use synthetic, chemical herbicides to manage weeds.	*Rotate crops, till, hand weed or mulch to manage weeds. There are also natural plant based herbicides like cinnamon and clove oil.*
Give animals antibiotics, growth hormones and medications to prevent disease and spur growth.	*Give animals organic feed and allow them access to the outdoors. Use preventative measures-such as rotational grazing, a balanced diet and clean housing-to help minimize disease.*
Food will keep much longer as they are treated with waxes and preservatives. They may have perfect appearances, but may also lack in flavor.	*Some organic foods may spoil faster because they are not treated with waxes and preservatives. With the new organic farming methods the appearances are the same or better than the treated conventional produce. Organic fruits and vegetables burst with flavor.*

June 2010, a report from the Environmental Working Group (a nonprofit group focused on public health) hit the news big with its reference to a list of foods called 'The Dirty Dozen" . Their research concluded that these 12 fruits and vegetables still contained 47-67 pesticides per serving after the produce was washed with USDA high-power pressure water system. These foods are believed to be most susceptible because they have soft skin that tends to absorb more pesticides. The report suggests limiting consumption of pesticides by purchasing organic for these 12 fruits and vegetables.

Dirty Dozen:
Apples
Bell peppers
Blueberries
Celery
Cherries
Imported Grapes
Lettuce
Nectarines
Peaches
Potatoes
Spinach /Kale /Collard Greens
Strawberries

Clean Fifteen:
Asparagus
Avocados
Cabbage
Cantaloupe
Eggplant
Grapefruit
Honeydew melon
Kiwi
Mango
Onions
Pineapple
Sweet corn
Sweet peas
Sweet potato
Watermelon

Not all non-organic fruits and vegetables have as high a level of pesticides. The Clean Fifteen list has a stronger outer layer that provides a defense against pesticide contamination. But even the Clean Fifteen need to be washed well. Because pesticides are created to be water-resistant (they have to stay on even when it rains), just water is not enough to get the chemicals off. I clean them with equal parts water and white vinegar.

For 31 years, I have studied the relationship between chemicals on our food and our health. I have not in all these years read about or found a positive coorelation between the two. What I do know is there's a domino effect with chemical farming that effects us in ways I am sure we don't even know about yet. For these reasons, I have always had an organic garden and one of the reasons we now have Tanglewood Berry Farm; an organic fruit and vegetable farm.

Weight and Measure Equivalents

Dash or Pinch	=	less than 1/8 teaspoon
3 teaspoons	=	1 tablespoon; 1/2 fluid ounce
2 tablespoons	=	1/8 cup; 1 fluid ounce
4 tablespoons	=	1/4 cup; 2 fluid ounces
5 1/3 tablespoons	=	1/3 cup
8 tablespoons	=	1/2 cup
10 2/3 tablespoons	=	2/3 cup
12 tablespoons	=	3/4 cup
14 tablespoons	=	7/8 cup
16 tablespoons	=	1 cup; 8 fluid ounces, 1/2 pint
7/8 cup	=	3/4 cup plus 2 tablespoons
2 cups	=	2 pints; 16 fluid ounces
4 cups	=	2 pints; 1 quart; 32 fluid ounces
4 quarts	=	1 gallon; 128 ounces
8 quarts	=	1 peck
4 pecks	=	1 bushel
16 ounces	=	1 pound

Common Abbreviations

tsp.	teaspoon
tbsp.	tablespoon
pt.	pint
qt.	quart
pk.	peck
bu.	bushel
oz.	ounce
lb.	pound
sq.	square
min.	minutes
hr.	hour
mod.	moderate
doz.	dozen

Wine Basics

Wine Tasting Etiquette

White wines are generally tasted first, followed by reds, and then dessert wines. Within these categories, lighter-bodied wines precede fuller-bodied ones. Water and crackers are usually offered to cleanse the palate between each wine. Correct wine etiquette does not require that you must finish every glass. Most wine tasting's provide containers to dispose of excess wine. Do not feel you have to sample every wine offered-taste what appeals to you. If you are tasting at a winery and ask for a second tasting of a particular wine, it is in good taste to buy a bottle. Many wineries charge tasting fees which are generally applied to any purchase. It is not mandatory that you buy wine; purchase only what you desire. That being said, if you have made an appointment at a small winery, it is in good taste to make a purchase.

General Restaurant Wine Etiquette

When choosing a wine from a restaurant's wine list for a party you are hosting at a restaurant, the main goal is to accomplish a suitable wine pairing with the entrees of your guests. If the food orders are too different to generalize with one wine, consider ordering a bottle of red and a bottle of white wine. Waiters and sommeliers are there to answer your questions.

After ordering, the waiter/sommelier will retrieve your selection, and then present it, label forward, to the host of the party. This is merely to verify it is the correct wine and vintage (year) that you ordered. The cork is removed and placed on the table. Unless it is clearly tainted, (the waiter/sommelier should notice if it is) do not touch or smell it, as it means nothing. A dry cork can indicate it was not stored properly and mold will indicate the wine may be too old.

A small amount will then be poured for the host. Swirl the wine in the glass, smell, and then taste. This is to make sure the wine is not spoiled and it is not an opportunity to send back a sound wine that you are not crazy about. After approval, the wine will be poured clockwise to the right, ladies first. The host's glass will be topped last. Remember though, that red wines will need to "open up", (be exposed to air for awhile) to taste their best. Make sure your wine is served at the proper temperature. The biggest mistake restaurants make is they automatically put all white wine into an ice bucket. All wine should be chilled to the correct temperature before arriving at your table. Keeping white wine in an ice bucket will make it too cold. If a sommelier has assisted you, it's good etiquette to tip them 10-20% of the wine price.

Corkage Etiquette

It is customary in many parts of the country for restaurants to extend corkage policies for patrons whom wish to bring their own wine. However, this is not the case everywhere (and is illegal in Indiana), and proper wine etiquette dictates that several things be kept in mind.

Always call the restaurant in advance to verify that corkage is allowed. Ask what the fee is to avoid any surprises. Very few restaurants charge over $20 as a corkage fee. Some restaurants will waive this fee if an additional bottle is purchased from the wine list, but do not assume that this is the case.

Wine brought to a restaurant should be relatively unique or rare, and definitely should not appear on the restaurant's wine list. After the waiter/sommelier opens and pours the contents, proper wine etiquette requires that you offer them a taste. Following these guidelines will ensure an enjoyable corkage experience.

Wine at Home-The Duty of the Host

If you're serving wine at home during your own dinner party, basic wine etiquette tells us that you serve a wine that pairs well with food. Also remember before serving; always allow wine time to breathe at room temperature.

If your guests would like to enjoy a glass of wine before dinner, a lighter white wine or sparkling wine is most appropriate. This doesn't mean you can't serve a glass of Pinot Noir if you know your guests well and this is their favorite.

When you serve your guests, it's nice to use the appropriate wine glasses. You should not serve wine in plastic or paper. Always serve wine to your guests in clean, spotless wine glasses. This may seem obvious, but it is a very common mistake. Additionally, if more than one wine is served, make sure that they are poured in a logical progression.

Never fill a glass to the top with wine. You should leave at least 1/2 the glass empty.

When you are a guest at someone else's home, its good wine etiquette to allow the host/hostess to serve your wine for you, unless he or she suggests you help yourself.

When planning the amount of wine to purchase for your party you should plan on 2-3 glasses of wine per guest if you pour 4 glasses per bottle.

Re-corked wine can be stored for 3-5 days.

Bringing Wine to Dinner

When you are invited to someone's home for dinner, it's always appropriate to bring a bottle of wine. It's not good wine etiquette to expect your wine to be opened that evening. Do not bring a bottle of white wine already chilled. This assumes you expect the host/hostess to open it. Most hosts/hostesses will have their wine planned out ahead of time to pair with their meal.

Wine as a Gift

Many people ask what kind of wine to give as a gift. If you're buying the wine for someone you know, the obvious answer would be to choose a bottle you know they'll enjoy. Another suggestion would be to get them a bottle they may not be familiar with, but you know they'd be open to trying. If you're buying wine for someone you don't know well, stay neutral. Buy a medium priced wine of medium body. I suggest a $15-$20 bottle of Sauvignon Blanc if it's warm outside or a $15-$20 bottle of Merlot or Zinfandel if it's cool outside. Shop at a wine shop and ask for recommendations. Don't go to a grocery store and choose blindly.

Toasting Etiquette

Have some thoughts memorized-keep it brief. Speak slowly and loud enough for all to hear. Make eye contact with the honoree along with other guests. Stand to do the toast if in a crowd or a party, but stay seated at a small dinner party. Smile, laugh, and be positive. Start, stay, and end on an up beat note. Clearly raise your glass at the appropriate time to alert others when to join in. Everyone should touch glasses just after the spoken toast and before any sipping. All should join in, even with an empty glass and or a non-alcoholic beverage.

The 6 Major Types of White Wines

Chardonnay- (Shari-dun-NAY) The most important and expensive white grape, now grown all over the world. Nearly all French white Burgundy wines are made from 100 percent Chardonnay. Food pairings: shellfish, sole, halibut, salmon, tuna, poultry, mild cheese, cream based dips.

Sauvignon Blanc- (SO-vin-yon Blahnk) A white grape grown in France, Washington State, and California. Food pairings: Dishes with cream sauce, shellfish, sole, halibut, poultry, pasta, mild cheese, cream based dips.

Pinot Gris/Pinot Grigio- (PEA-no GREE-jzhee-o/PEA-no GREE) The most popular white wine from Italy made from the grape variety Pinot Grigio, or Pinot Gris. Food Pairings: shellfish, sole, halibut, salmon, tuna, spicy food (whether beef, poultry, or fish), poultry, pork, veal, mild cheese, pasta, cream based dips.

Riesling- (REES-ling) A white grape grown primarily in Alsace, Germany, and California. Food pairings; fruit, creamy desserts, dishes with cream sauce, shellfish, sole, halibut, spicy food (whether beef, poultry or fish), poultry, mild cheese, cream based dips.

Chenin Blanc- (Shen'n BLANKH) A white grape native to the Loire valley; also grown in California and Texas. Food pairings: fruit, creamy desserts, dishes with cream sauce, pasta, shellfish, sole, halibut, spicy food (whether beef, poultry, or fish), poultry, mild cheese, cream based dips.

Champagne- (Sham-pane) The region in northern France that produces the only sparkling wine authentically called Champagne. Elsewhere it is usually referred to as Sparkling wine even if the same process is used to make the wine/Champagne. Food pairings: Extra Dry: medium dry - dishes with cream sauce, shellfish, and sole, halibut, and mild cheese, cream based dips. Brut: dry - dishes with cream sauce, shellfish, sole, halibut, mild cheese, and cream based dips. Demi Sec: slightly sweet – Fruit, creamy desserts. Rose (typically Brut style) - dishes with cream sauce, shellfish, sole, halibut, salmon, tuna, mild cheese, cream based dips.

The 8 Major Types of Red Wine

Shiraz- (Sah-ra or Shi-raz) Shiraz or syrah are two names for the same variety. Europe vintners only use the name syrah. Food pairings: meat (steak, beef, wild game, stews, etc.) Syrah excels in California, Australia, and in France's Rhone Valley. Aromas and flavors of wild black fruit (such as black currant), with overtones of black pepper spice and roasting meat are usually present.

Merlot- (Mare-lo) The softness of Merlot has made it an "introducing" wine for new Red-wine drinkers. Food pairings: any will do. A key player in the Bordeaux blend, merlot is now also grown in Italy, Romania, California, Washington State, Chile, Australia, etc. Typical taste and scents include black cherry, plums and herbal flavors.

Cabernet Sauvignon- (Ca-burr-nay so-veen-yaw) Widely accepted as one of the world's best varieties. Cabernet sauvignon is often blended with cabernet franc and merlot. It usually undergoes oak treatment. Food pairings: best with simply prepared red meat. Cabernet sauvignon is planted wherever red wine grapes grow except in the Northern fringes such as Germany.

Malbec- (Mal-bek) Food pairings: all types of meat-based meals. Malbec has its origins in the French Bordeaux region. Malbec is widely grown in Argentina, where it is the most popular red grape variety. It is also available in Chile, Australia, and in the cooler regions of California. Malbec generally tastes of plums, berries, and spice. Malbec is often blended with other varieties such as cabernet franc, cabernet sauvignon, merlot, and petit verdot to make Bordeaux style wines.

Pinot Noir- (Pee-know na-wahr) One of the noblest red wine grapes. Pinot noir is difficult to grow, rarely blended, with any roughness. Food pairings: excellent with grilled salmon, chicken, and lamb. Very unlike Cabernet Sauvignon, the structure is delicate and fresh. The aromatics are very fruity (cherry, strawberry, plum), often with notes of tea-leaf, damp earth, or worn leather.

Zinfandel- (Zin-fan-dell) Perhaps the world's most versatile wine grape, making everything from blush wine (White Zinfandel), to rich, heavy reds. Food pairings: very much depends on the freshness/heaviness of the wine; tomato-sauce pastas, pizza, and grilled and barbecued meats. Only found in California. Often a zesty flavor with berry and pepper.

Sangiovese- (San-gee-oh-ve-zee) Food pairings: a good choice for Italian and other Mediterranean-style cuisines. Sangiovese produces the Chiantis of Italy's Tuscany region and, of late, good wines from California. The primary style is medium-bodied with fresh berry and plum flavors.

Chianti- (key-AHN-tee) A red wine from the Tuscany region of Italy.

Chianti Classico- (Key-AHN-tee Class-ee-ko) One step above Chianti, in terms of quality, this wine is from an inner district of Chianti.

The Health Benefits of Red Wine

Wine can prevent heart disease, stroke and control intestinal Bacteria. Used in moderation, wine, especially red wine, can help lower cholesterol and fight hardening of the arteries and heart disease. What evidence has suggested here is that moderately drinking wine can be a helpful addition to a diet. The daily limit for women is (1) 5 ounce glass a day and for men (2) 5 ounce glasses a day. Go for the full bodied robust varieties. For years researchers have tried to figure out why the French can indulge in buttery croissants, fatty pates, and creamy sauces and were still 2 ½ times less likely to develop heart disease than Americans. Well it appears that the French have healthier hearts because they drink red wine regularly. Red wines are rich in compounds that lower cholesterol and keep blood platelets from sticking together and forming dangerous clots. Three of the most heart healthy wines are Cabernet Sauvignon, Syrah and Merlot. White wine does not have the healing powers that red wine has.

The Ten Rules-of-Thumb for Wine Pairing

1. If you are taking wine as a gift to a dinner party, don't worry about matching the wine to the food, unless you have been requested to do so. Just bring a good wine. Match quality of food and wine. A nice dinner party with multiple courses deserves a better wine than hamburgers on the grill with chips in a bag.

2. When you're serving more than one wine at a meal, it's customary to serve lighter wines before full-bodied ones. Dry wines should be served before sweet wines unless a sweet flavored dish is served early in the meal. In that case match the sweet dish with a similarly sweet wine. Lower alcohol wines should be served before higher alcohol wines.

3. Balance flavor intensity. Pair light-bodied wines with lighter food and fuller-bodied wines with heartier, more flavorful, richer and fattier dishes.

4. Consider how the food is prepared. Delicately flavored foods — poached or steamed — pair best with delicate wines. It's easier to pair wines with more flavorfully prepared food, braised, grilled, roasted or sautéed. Pair the wine with the sauce, seasoning or dominant flavor of the dish.

5. Match flavors. An earthy Pinot Noir goes well with mushroom soup and the grapefruit/citrus taste of Sauvignon Blanc goes with fish for the same reasons that lemon does.

6. Pair wine and cheese. Wine and cheese are natural food partners. Choosing a wine that goes best with cheese is very much a question of personal taste. Some say red wines go best with mild to sharp, hard cheeses, and soft cheese like Camembert and Brie, while others say white wine is better with soft cheeses and intensely flavored cheese goes better with a sweeter wine and Goat cheeses pair best with dry white wine. Which ever combinations you choose make sure to always serve the cheese at room temperature and remember, you cannot go wrong serving friends wine and cheese, or eating a light meal of cheese, crusty bread, and wine.

7. Adjust food flavor to better pair with the wine. Sweetness in a dish will increase the awareness of bitterness and astringency in wine, making it appear drier, stronger and less fruity. High amounts of acidity in food will decrease awareness of sourness in wine and making it taste richer and mellower –sweet wine will taste sweeter.

8. Balance sweetness. But, beware of pairing a wine with food that is sweeter than the wine, although I find chocolate and Cabernet Sauvignon are a perfect pair.

9. Consider pairing opposites. Very hot or spicy foods — some Thai dishes, or hot curries for example — often work best with sweet desert wines. Opposing flavors can play off each other, creating new flavor sensations and cleansing the palate.

10. Match by geographic location. Consider serving nice Chianti to go with your Italian dish or a French wine to go with your French dish.

Cooking with Wine

How Much Wine?

Be careful not to use too much wine, as the flavor could overpower your dish. The first step is to try a small amount of wine so the flavors will blend and not become too overpowering. As you are cooking try sampling your dish and add as needed.

What Kinds of Wine to Use for Cooking

The type of wine you use is very important. Cook only with wine that you would drink. A well made medium grade for under $10 is just fine. I prefer Sauvignon Blanc as a white wine for sautéing, marinating, and in sauces for seafood, and chicken. I like using Cabernet Sauvignon or Chianti for meats and meat based sauces. It is best to stay away from wines that are heavily flavored with oak. These wines tend to give off a bitter taste. The more you cook with wine, the better you will become at predicting how a specific wine will enhance your menu.

Good Places to Put Wine in Your Food

1. When a recipe calls for water, replace the water with a favorite wine.

2. Stir in 1 to 2 tablespoons of a full-bodied red into brown gravy. Let simmer to create rich brown gravy for red meat.

3. Mix wine with your favorite oil to baste meat and poultry.

4. For meat dishes calling for wine, first heat the wine. Do not boil the wine, this will loose the flavor.

5. Adding cold wine tends to make meat tough, while warm wine helps tenderize it.

6. Dry red wines have better chemistry with heavier red meats.

7. Serve the same wine with dinner that you cooked with, as they will balance each other. If you prefer to use a fine wine during dinner, try to stay within the same wine family. Just be sure that you don't cook with what you would not drink!

Index

A

Alfredo Sauce 251
American Chowder 257
Apple Butter 84
Apple Carrot Cucumber Smoothie 197
Apple Dumplings 132
Apple Fritters 36
Apple, Ham and Cheddar Quiche 75
Apple Pancakes 71
Apple Pear Blackberry Applesauce 84
Apple, Pecan French Toast Casserole 68
Apple Pie 132
Apple Scones 41
Apple Walnut Turkey Sandwich 240
Applesauce 84
Apricot Dressing 146
Apricot Horseradish Sauce 251
Arugula Vegetable Topping 202
Asparagus Spears Baked in Puff Pastry 8

B

Baked Brie 8
Baked Cheese Grits 52
Baked Crab Dip 9
Baked Halibut with Avocado Salsa 180
Baked Ham 184
Baked Oatmeal 53
Baked Salmon 180
Baklava 112
Balsamic Vinaigrette 146
Banana Chocolate Chip Bread 43
Banana Pancakes 71
Basic Quiche Recipe 75
Basics of Canning 80
Basil Dressing 146
Basil Pesto 248
BBQ Baby Back Ribs 185
BBQ Sauce 252
Beef and Noodles 154
Beef Bourguignon 156
Beef Brisket 155
Beef Stew 157
Berry Baked French Toast 68
Berry Blast Smoothie 29
Berry Crisp 135
Bing Cherry Bash Smoothie 29
Black and Blue Smoothie 30
Black Bean Mango Salsa 15
Black Bean Salad 212
Black Bean Soup 270
Black Belt Smoothie 30
Black Raspberry Sorbet 126
Blackberry Applesauce 84
Blackberry Bars 122
Blackberry Bread 43

Blackberry Buckle 44
Blackberry Cobbler 134
Blackberry Dressing 147
Blackberry Iced Tea 25
Blackberry Jam 86
Blackberry Lemonade 26
Blackberry Muffins 37
Blackberry Pie 134
Blackberry Smoothie 30
Blackberry Sorbet 127
Blackberry Spice Cake 96
Blackberry Syrup 64, 85
Blackened Seasoning 244
Blueberry Banana Smoothie 31
Blueberry Bars 122
Blueberry Bread 45
Blueberry Compote 64
Blueberry Filling 140
Blueberry Muffins 37
Blueberry Pancakes 71
BLT Chicken Salad 213
Brazilian Black Bean Soup 264
Bread and Butter Pickles 87
Breakfast Casserole 58
Breakfast Sandwich 60
Broccoli, Cauliflower, Cheddar Salad 230
Broccoli Cheese Soup 271
Broccoli Chicken Pasta Salad 222
Broccoli Salad 229
Brussels Sprouts 282
Buckeyes 128
Butter Pecan Cake 97
Buttermilk Pancake Mix 71
Buttermilk Ranch Dressing 147
Butternut Squash Soup with Toasted Pumpkin
  Seeds 271

C

Cabbage Soup 264
Caesar Potato Salad 226
Caesar Salad 216
Caesar Salad Dressing 148
Cafe Benedict 53
Canning and Preserving 79
Caprese Kebabs 196
Caramel Apple Cheesecake 106
Caramel Sauce 252
Carrot Cake Bread 45
Carrot Cake Pancakes-Buttermilk 71
Carrot Cake Pancakes-Multigrain 73
Carrot Salad 230
Cheddar Cheese Ball 16
Cheese and Chicken Enchiladas 164
Cheese Tortellini Bake 185
Cheese Tortellini Pasta Salad 222

Cheeseburger Soup 257
Cheesecake, Plain 107
Cheesesteak Benedict with Smoked Cheddar
  Hollandaise 54
Cherry Bars 122
Cherry Filling 140
Cherry Pinwheel Cookies 114
Cherry Sauce 184
Chicken Alfredo Spinach Pizza 165
Chicken and Dumplings 166
Chicken and Noodles 167
Chicken and Pasta with Tomato Mushroom
  Pesto 168
Chicken Broth 261
Chicken Club Pasta Salad 222
Chicken Corn Rival 261
Chicken Crepes 66
Chicken Enchilada Casserole 168
Chicken Hash 169
Chicken Lasagna 169
Chicken Pasta Salad 223
Chicken Perisenne 170
Chicken Pesto Focaccia Sandwich 234
Chicken Salad Panini 234
Chicken, Tomato Rice Florentine 262
Chicken with Blackberries 170
Chili 258
Chili Cheese Stuffed Chicken 171
Chocolate Bread Pudding 129
Chocolate Chip Cheesecake 108
Chocolate Chip Crunch Bars 115
Chocolate Chip Pancakes 71
Chocolate Chip Pecan Pie 136
Chocolate Dipped Strawberries 129
Chocolate Mousse Cake 98
Chocolate Sundae Brownie Trifle 130
Chow Mein Chicken Salad 216
Cinnamon Honey Butter 244
Cinnamon Rolls 63
Cinnamon Streusel Coffee Cake 61
Cinnamon Syrup 65
Cioppino Soup 269
Clam Chowder 269
Classic Chicken Salad 213
Cobb Chicken Salad 214
Cocktail Sauce 252
Coconut Cream Pie 136
Coconut Shrimp 9
Cole Slaw with Apples and Raisins 204
Cole Slaw with Bacon and Tomato 205
Common Abbreviations 325
Coney Sauce 253
Corn and Tomato Salad 205
Corned Beef and Cabbage 157
Corned Beef Cheese Ball 16
Corned Beef Hash 63
Corned Beef with Jalapeño Pepper Jelly Glaze 158
Corn Chowder 272

Corn Fritters 36
Cornbread 36
Crab and Vegetable Pasta 181
Crab Cake Benedict 55
Crab Cake on Croissant 234
Crab Cakes 10
Crab, Corn and Tomato Salad 219
Crab Macaroni and Cheese 285
Crab Martini 17
Crab Stuffed Mushrooms 11
Cranberry Chutney 245
Cranberry Jalapeño Meatballs 11
Cranberry Punch 24
Cranberry Relish 245
Creamed Spinach 282
Creamy Broccoli Chicken Soup 262
Creamy Dill Dressing 148
Creamy Dilled Potato Salad 226
Cream of Artichoke Soup 273
Cream of Mushroom Soup 273
Cream of Potato Soup made with left over
  Mashed Potatoes 265
Cream of Potato Soup with Sausage and
  Cheese 265
Cream of Sausage Soup 266
Crock Pot, Pot Roast 158
Cucumbers in Dilled Sour Cream Sauce 231
Curry Chicken Salad 214

D
Dad's Spaghetti Sauce 159
Deviled Eggs 17
Dill Pickles 87
Double Chocolate Chip Cookies 115

E
Easy Bean Salad 212
Easy Broccoli Enchiladas 189
Easy Chicken Enchiladas 172
Easy Chicken Tortilla Soup 263
Easy Chocolate Fudge 130
Egg Salad BLT Sandwich 241
Egg Salad with Veggies 205
Egg, Tomato and Bacon Benedict with Basil
  Hollandaise 56
Eggplant and Goat Cheese Sandwich 235
Eggplant Casserole 186
Eggplant Parmesan 190
Eggplant Pesto Crepes 191
Eggs Benedict with Hollandaise 55
Equivalents 305, 310
Espresso Brownies 116

F
Family Meal 297
Farm to Fork Phenomenon 321
Filet of Beef Japanese 160
Florentine Benedict 57

French Toast 69
Fresh Fish Marinade 246
Fresh Garden Eggplant Sauce 196
Fresh Garden Green Beans 206
Fresh Tomato Salad 206
Fresh Vegetable Broth 209, 274
Frosty Key Lime Pie 137
Frosty Orange Pie 137
Frozen Cranberry Salad 130
Fruit Fillings 140
Fruitarian 69
Fudge Brownies 116

G
Garden Bean and Potato Salad 227
Garden Fresh Vegetable Salad 207
Garden Shrimp Creole 198
Garden Vegetable Relish 202
Garden Vegetable Spaghetti Sauce 88
Gazpacho Soup 209
German Potato Salad 227
Ginger Mayonnaise 246
Gingerbread Cake 98
Gingerbread Cookies 117
Granola 70
Granola Pancakes 71
Gravy-Turkey 178
Greek Cucumber Salad 231
Greek Pasta Salad 223
Greek Spinach Pie 12
Green Beans with Feta 283
Grilled Fish with Tomato Basil Sauce 199
Grilled Garden Sandwich 210
Grilled Tenderloin Tips 160
Guacamole 18

H
Ham and Bean Soup 266
Ham and Broccoli Strata 58
Ham and Egg Crepes with Mushroom Sauce 67
Ham Balls with Pineapple Sauce 12
Ham Salad 220
Hawaiian Chicken Sandwich 235
Helpful Hints 306
Herbed Beef Tenderloin with Tomato Relish 161
Herb Roasted Potatoes 283
Herb Stuffing 284
Herbs 308
Hershey's Chocolate Frosting 100
Hershey's Double Chocolate Cake 99
Hollandaise Sauce 55
Honey Mustard Chicken Sandwich 236
Hot Apple Cider 25
Hot Bacon Cheese Dip 13
Hot Bacon Dressing 149
Hot Broccoli Cheddar Dip 13
Hot Potato Salad 284

House Salad 217
Hummus 18

I
Ice Box Slaw 207
Italian Cream Cake 100
Italian Crock Pot Pasta 187
Italian Dressing 149
Italian Garden Vegetable Soup 274
Italian Garden Vegetable Stew 199
Italian Grilled Cheese Flat Bread Sandwich 236
Italian Seasoning Mix 203
Italian Turkey Salad 220
Italian Vegetable Meatball Soup 259
Italian Vegetable Sausage Soup 267

J
Jalapeño Mayonnaise 247
Jalapeño Pepper Jelly 86
John Wayne Breakfast Casserole 59

L
Lasagna 161
Lasagna Soup 268
Lemon Basil Dressing 150
Lemon Bread 46
Lemon Curd Tarts 90
Lemon Meringue Pie 137
Lemon or Lime Sorbet 127
Lemon or Orange Curd 89
Lemon Raspberry Cheesecake 108
Lemon Sour Cream Muffins 38
Lemon Thyme Pesto 248

M
Macaroni and Cheese 285
Macaroni Salad 224
Malibu Chicken Sandwich 237
Mango Sorbet 127
Margy's Mashed Potatoes 286
Margy's Potato Salad 228
Margy's Signature Spinach Salad 217
Marinated Tomato, Mozzarella & Cucumber
  Salad 208
Meatloaf 162
Mediterranean Flat Bread Pizza 14
Menu Planning 320
Mini Blackberry Turnovers 138
Mixed Berry Cobbler 139
Mixed Berry Compote 65
Monkey Bread 47
Mulled Wine 28
Mushroom Marinade 246

N
New York Style Cheesecake 109
No Bake Chocolate Cookies 119

O
Oatmeal Carmelitas 118
Oatmeal Cookies 119
Orange Cranberry Bread 47
Orange Dreamsicle Milkshake 27
Orange Honey Butter 244
Orange Pecan Chicken 172
Orange Pecan Pound 101
Orange Poppy Seed Dressing 150
Orange Rosemary Mayonnaise 247
Orange Sour Cream Muffins 39
Oreo Cheesecake 111
Oven Roasted Chicken Breasts 173

P
Pancakes-Carrot Cake Multigrain 73
Pancakes-Multigrain 72
Pancakes-Pumpkin Multigrain 74
Parmesan Chicken 173
Parmesan Roasted New Potatoes 286
Parmesan Zucchini Sticks 287
Peach Coffee Cake 62
Peach Compote 65
Peach Crisp 141
Peach Dumplings 132
Peach Popsicle 28
Peanut Butter Banana Smoothie 31
Peanut Butter Cookies 120
Peanut Butter Rice Krispies 120
Pear Raspberry Smoothie 31
Pecan Haddock 181
Pesto Mashed Potatoes 287
Philadelphia Pepper Relish 91
Pickled Beets 91
Pickled Eggs 92
Pickles, Zucchini 88
Poached Eggs 74
Pork Roast with Sauerkraut 187
Portobello Fajitas 192
Portobello Mushroom with Leek Soup 275
Potato Casserole 287
Potato Salad with Bacon Dressing 228
Preserving by Freezing 82
Pulled Pork Sandwich 237
Pumpkin Bars 120
Pumpkin Bread 48
Pumpkin Cheesecake 110
Pumpkin Muffins 39
Pumpkin Pie 142
Pumpkin Scones 41
Pumpkin with Jalapeño Pesto Soup 276

Q
Quiche-Sausage and Cheddar 76
        Southwestern Chicken 77
        Spinach, Feta Sun-dried Tomato 77
        Three Cheese 78
Quick Cookies 122

Quick Vegetable Soup 277
Quick Vegetarian Chili 277

R
Raisin Spice Cake 102
Raspberry Applesauce 84
Raspberry Bars 122
Raspberry Bread 43
Raspberry Cake 103
Raspberry Chicken 173
Raspberry Daiquiri 24
Raspberry Dressing 151
Raspberry Fruit Filling 141
Raspberry Ice Tea 26
Raspberry Pie 135
Raspberry Sauce 253
Raspberry Sorbet 127
Raspberry Streusel Muffins 40
Red Pepper Pesto 249
Red Raspberry Jam 85
Red Velvet Cake 104
Reeces Peanut Butter Cheesecake 111
Rhubarb Crunch 123
Roasted Chicken 173
Roasted Mushrooms 288
Roasted Pork Tenderloin with Apricot Glaze 188
Roasted Red Pepper Hummus 19
Roasted Red Pepper Soup 278
Roasted Tomato Bruschetta 19
Roasted Vegetable Pizza 192
Roasted Vegetables 288
Rueben Bake 237
Rueben Soup 260
Russian Dressing 151

S
Salmon Cucumber Salad 218
Salmon with Orange Glaze 182
Salsa 92
Sausage and Cheddar Quiche 76
Sausage Cheese Casserole 60
Scalloped Potatoes 289
Seasonal Fruits and Vegetables 311
Seven Layer Salad 218
Shredded Beef Fajitas 163
Shrimp and Crab Bisque 270
Shrimp and Crab Melt 238
Shrimp and Crab Salad 220
Shrimp and Pasta Salad 224
Shrimp Cocktail 20
Shrimp Cocktail Sauce 20
Shrimp Salad 221
Shrimp Scampi 182
Shrimp Wrap 241
Simple Syrup 33
Smoked Sausage Soup 267
Southern Fried Chicken 174
Southwest Pasta 193

Southwestern Chicken and Pasta 175
Southwestern Chicken Pasta Salad 225
Southwestern Chicken Quiche 77
Spicy Mustard Sauce 218
Spicy Sweet Potato Salad 229
Spinach Artichoke Cheese Dip 14
Spinach, Feta, Sun-dried Tomato Quiche 77
Spinach Pesto 249
Split Pea with Ham Soup 268
Spring Pea Salad 232
Strawberry Bread 49
Strawberry Butter 245
Strawberry Cake 105
Strawberry Daiquiri 24
Strawberry Ice Cream 128
Strawberry Jam 86
Strawberry Lemonade 27
Strawberry Orange Banana Smoothie 32
Strawberry Pancakes 71
Strawberry Pizza 143
Strawberry Popsicle 29
Strawberry Scones 42
Strawberry Shortcake Cups 131
St mer Squash Casserole 290
Summer Stuffed Chicken Breasts 176
Sun-dried Tomato Basil Cheesecake 21
Sun-dried Tomato Basil Pesto 250
Sweet Potato Casserole 289
Sweet Potato Rolls 50
Sweetened Brewed Ice Tea 26
Swiss Steak 164

T
Taco Salad 219
Tarragon Chicken Salad 214
Tarragon Mayonnaise 247
Teriyka Glazed SalmoThanksgiving Turkey 176
Terminology 293
Thanksgiving Turkey Stuffing 179
The Ultimate Brownie 124
Three Cheese Quiche 78
Tomato and Basil Topped Bruschetta 196
Tomato and Goat Cheese Bruschetta 197
Tomato and Mushroom Pesto 250
Tomato Basil Pasta with Shrimp 183
Tomato Basil Viniagrette 151
Tomato Bisque Soup 93, 278
Tomato, Feta & Cucumber Salad 232
Tomato Vegetable Juice 93
Tropical Chicken Salad 215
Tuna Noodle Casserole 183
Tuna Melt 239
Tuna Salad 221
Turkey Club Wrap 241
Turkey Rueben Sandwich 239
Turtle Cheesecake 112

U
Ultimate Grilled Cheese Sandwich 240

V
Vanilla Ice Cream 128
Vegetable Beef Soup 260
Vegetable Cocktail 198
Vegetable Frittata 200
Vegetable Garden Pasta 201
Vegetable Gratin 291
Vegetable Stuffed Portobello Mushrooms 201
Vegetable Tart 15
Vegetarian Lentil Soup 279

W
Waldorf Chicken Salad 215
Watermelon Basil Viniagrette 152
Watermelon Bellini's 33
Watermelon Daiquiri 24
Watermelon Lemonade 27
Watermelon Salsa 204
Watermelon-Strawberry Smoothie 32
Weight and Measures 325
White Cheddar Cheese Soup 279
White Chicken Chili 263
White Chocolate Bread Pudding 129
White Chocolate Cherry Cookies 125
White Sauce 254
Wild Rice and Mushroom Soup 280
Wine Basics 326

Z
Zucchini and Tomatoes Au Gratin 208
Zucchini Bread 49
Zucchini Brownies 125
Zucchini Dip 197
Zucchini Fritters 36
Zucchini Pancakes 291
Zucchini Pickles 88
Zucchini Relish 91
Zucchini Sausage Casserole 189
Zucchini Tomato Salad 208